IDEAS, THEIR ORIGINS, AND THEIR CONSEQUENCES

The G. Warren Nutter Lectures in Political Economy

The G. Warren Nutter Lectures in Political Economy were instituted to honor the memory of the late Professor Nutter, to encourage scholarly interest in the range of topics to which he devoted his career, and to provide his students and associates an additional contact with each other and with the rising generation of scholars.

At the time of his death in January 1979, G. Warren Nutter was director of the Thomas Jefferson Center Foundation, adjunct scholar of the American Enterprise Institute, director of AEI's James Madison Center, a member of advisory groups at both the Hoover Institution and The Citadel, and Paul Goodloe McIntire Professor of Economics at the University of Virginia.

Professor Nutter made notable contributions to price theory, the assessment of monopoly and competition, the study of the Soviet economy, and the economics of defense and foreign policy. He earned his Ph.D. degree at the University of Chicago. In 1957 he joined with James M. Buchanan to establish the Thomas Jefferson Center for Studies in Political Economy at the University of Virginia. In 1967 he established the Thomas Jefferson Center Foundation as a separate entity but with similar objectives of supporting scholarly work and graduate study in political economy and holding conferences of economists from the United States and both Western and Eastern Europe. He served during the 1960s as director of the Thomas Jefferson Center and chairman of the Department of Economics at the University of Virginia and, from 1969 to 1973, as assistant secretary of defense for international security affairs.

The American Enterprise Institute
1150 17th Street, N.W.
Washington, D.C. 20036

IDEAS, THEIR ORIGINS, AND THEIR CONSEQUENCES

Lectures to Commemorate
the Life and Work of
G. Warren Nutter

The Thomas Jefferson Center Foundation

American Enterprise Institute for Public Policy Research
Washington, D.C.

Distributed by arrangement with
UPA, Inc.
4720 Boston Way
Lanham, MD 20706

3 Henrietta Street
London, WC2E 8LU England

ISBN 0-8447-1386-4

Printed in the United States of America

American Enterprise Institute for Public Policy Research
1150 Seventeenth Street, N.W., Washington, D.C. 20036

Contents

Foreword

The Thomas Jefferson Center Foundation was organized in 1967 by the late Professor G. Warren Nutter. Under his leadership until his death in 1979, the foundation conducted research and published its results, emphasizing political economy as it was conceived and practiced by Nutter.

Professor Nutter's distinguished contributions as a scholar, as a senior official in the Department of Defense, and as a student of public affairs attracted both intellectual and financial support. It is regretted that his death brought the program to an end, leaving unspent funds he had secured from those who admired his talents and his attention to values.

The surviving directors of the foundation, all colleagues and friends of Professor Nutter, used these assets to further his interests as a political economist. Among the projects they organized was a series of lectures presented in cooperation with the American Enterprise Institute for Public Policy Research, and in one instance with the Hoover Institution. The lecturers were former students or colleagues, or both, who admired and respected the man to whom they did honor. Each lecturer chose a subject that Professor Nutter would have enjoyed or one related to a facet of his career. After each lecture, a dinner was held at which Professor Nutter's friends could talk about him and his ideas in a setting of conviviality. Perhaps these events could be described as a very special kind of wake.

The series extended over seven years and ended May 5, 1987, in accord with one of Nutter's "laws"—namely, that endowed activities are to be avoided to prevent the inevitable corruption of the original purpose to which the resources were dedicated.

The Board of Directors of the Thomas Jefferson Center Foundation has published the fifteen lectures as a set to memorialize the life and work of G. Warren Nutter. It commends the series to those who are serious students of the discipline Adam Smith, a favorite of Nutter's, did so much to establish.

FRANK S. KAULBACK, JR.
President
Thomas Jefferson Center Foundation

A Biographical Note

Gilbert Warren Nutter was born on March 10, 1923, in Topeka, Kansas. After earning his bachelor's, master's, and doctoral degrees at the University of Chicago, he served in the U.S. Army from 1943 to 1946 and won the bronze star and the combat infantryman's badge.

He taught at Lawrence College and at Yale University before moving in 1956 to the University of Virginia, where he became chairman of the Department of Economics and Paul Goodloe McIntire Professor of Economics. From 1969 to 1973, he took leave to serve as assistant secretary of defense for international security affairs. As an adjunct scholar and a member of the Council of Academic Advisers of the American Enterprise Institute, he published three monographs—*Kissinger's Grand Design* (1975), *Central Economic Planning: The Visible Hand* (1976), and *Growth of Government in the West* (1978)—and "Freedom in a Revolutionary Economy," a bicentennial lecture. His other books include *The Extent of Enterprise Monopoly in the United States 1899-1939* (1951), *Growth of Industrial Production in the Soviet Union* (1962), and *The Strange World of Ivan Ivanov* (1969), a collection of his articles from the *Philadelphia Inquirer*. His essays are collected in *Political Economy and Freedom* (1983).

G. Warren Nutter died on January 15, 1979.

Adam Smith's "Invisible Hand" in a Velvet Glove

S. Herbert Frankel

April 25, 1980

S. HERBERT FRANKEL was professor of economics and chairman of the Department of Economics and Economic History at the University of the Witwatersrand from 1931 to 1946; professor of the economics of underdeveloped countries at Oxford University from 1946 to 1971; and visiting professor of economics at the University of Virginia in 1967 and from 1969 to 1974. Since 1971 he has been professor emeritus at Oxford University.

Introduction

John H. Moore

I FEEL highly privileged tonight. Warren Nutter was my teacher when I was a graduate student at Virginia and my colleague, mentor, and close friend for the eleven years of my tenure on the Virginia faculty. I deeply admired him for his intellect, his courage, his integrity, his loyalty, and his strength of character. He combined the best of scholarly abilities and instincts with a rare dedication to the preservation of the free society. His dedication and his sense of responsibility led him to active involvement in public affairs and to high public office. More than that, he had a warmth and sense of humor known to all of his friends. We all stand in his debt, and it would be a privilege to be included in any program connected with his name.

But the privilege I feel is doubled by having the honor of introducing tonight's speaker, who will present the first of the G. Warren Nutter Lectures in Political Economy. Warren was responsible for many good things that have come my way, and meeting Herbert Frankel was one of the best. Professor Frankel's career, like Warren's, reflects a deep commitment to scholarship and to the free society.

Professor Frankel was born in Johannesburg and educated at St. John's College and the University of the Witwatersrand in Johannesburg. After receiving the Ph.D. from the University of London in 1928, he returned to South Africa and became professor of economics at the University of the Witwatersrand in 1931. His distinguished writing career bore early fruit with the publication in 1930 of his jointly written book *Coming of Age: Studies in South African Citizenship and Politics*. This is not a book in economics, please note. It is a collection of essays on the political and social issues facing South Africa on the twenty-first anniversary of its independence, especially the possibility of creating a free society there. Coming as it did at the dawn of his career, this book exemplifies Professor Frankel's lifelong commitment to the cause of human freedom and dignity, a commitment that animated all his works in economics, politics, and philosophy—indeed his very career.

It is also significant that one of his coauthors was Jan Hofmeyr. The collaboration on the book was an early phase of a long association with Hofmeyr that included Professor Frankel's serving as his financial adviser while Hofmeyr was minister of finance in the Smuts government in South Africa.

Professor Frankel remained at Witwatersrand until 1946. During those fifteen years, he was head of the Department of Economics and Economic History there and joint editor of the *South African Journal of Economics*. He wrote and published extensively on matters related to the social and economic development of South Africa, including racial problems and their relation to economic policy. Had his views on these matters been adopted and promoted, South Africa would have been spared much of the trouble that has led to its present precarious situation.

He was asked in the early 1930s to prepare a memorandum on capital investment in Africa for the African Research Survey. Characteristically, Professor Frankel was not satisfied with meeting the bare requirements of the assignment. Instead he produced a classic book, published in 1938, entitled *Capital Investment in Africa: Its Course and Effects*. As Lord Hailey put it in his foreword, "The scope of the work is not limited to the assembling of statistical data regarding the program of capital investment; Professor Frankel has endeavored at the same time to interpret the effect of modern economic forces on the structure of African society."

In 1946 Professor Frankel accepted an invitation to take up the chair in the economics of underdeveloped countries at Oxford University and, with that, left his native land. He was professor in Oxford and professorial fellow of Nuffield College from 1946 until his retirement in 1971. During his quarter century at Oxford, he continued the fusion of outstanding scholarship and involvement in public affairs that characterized his entire career. His expertise on African affairs led to his being called to serve on a number of special commissions and as adviser to several governments. He was, among other things, chairman of the Commission of Enquiry into the Mining Industry of Southern Rhodesia, a member and author of the report of the Official Working Party investigating the Tanganyika groundnuts project, and a member of the East Africa Royal Commission from 1953 to 1955. In 1946 he was economic adviser to the governor of Kenya and in 1957 and 1958 was consultant adviser to the Urban African Commission of the government of Southern Rhodesia.

In addition to meeting the demands put on him by these activities and his responsibilities as professorial fellow of Nuffield College, Professor Frankel made contributions to the understanding of economics and economic development that will illuminate policy discussion as long as his books exist. Besides writing numerous articles and reports connected with the government commissions on which he served, he published several major books, among them *The Economic Impact on Underdeveloped Societies.* This remarkable collection of essays on economic development is distinguished, as always, by deep concern for liberty and the individual—a concern conspicuously absent from most writing on economic development. Another of his books was *Investment and the Return to Equity Capital in the South African Gold Mining Industry,* a study combining analysis of the gold mining industry with statistical measurement of the rate of return in gold mining. It demolished the myth that investment in the mines produced above-normal rates of return.

Professor Frankel retired from active duty at Oxford in 1971 and is now professor emeritus of that university. But that is not to say that he has retired from intellectual work—that would be impossible for him. For two years after his formal retirement, he was visiting professor at the University of Virginia, and he continued an informal but very active visiting arrangement with the Thomas Jefferson Center Foundation after that. His very important book *Two Philosophies of Money,* in which he explores the nature of money and the crucial importance for social stability of trust in the monetary order, was published in 1978. Professor Frankel shows in this book how Keynesian economic policy erodes and eventually destroys that trust. His latest work, *Money and Liberty,* will be published by the American Enterprise Institute later this year.

Introductions are supposed to focus on objective matters, but I would be remiss if I did not add a more personal note. Herbert has been one of my closest friends since his first visit to Virginia in 1967. He and Ilse have made my family's visits to England among the most enjoyable of our lives. More than that, Herbert's wisdom and understanding of the powers and limits of economics have influenced me more deeply than I can describe—perhaps even than I know. So

I take personal, as well as professional, pride in having the honor to introduce him.

This lecture series is entitled the G. Warren Nutter Lectures in Political Economy. Its purpose is twofold. It is intended, of course, to honor the memory of a man whose untimely death deprived us of a loyal friend, outstanding scholar, and dedicated champion of liberty. The second purpose flows from the first. The high value that Warren placed on the individual and on liberty animated his scholarly work and his lifelong interest in political economy. A series of scholarly lectures in political economy, prepared by scholars who shared his outlook, seems a fitting memorial. Herbert Frankel's professional qualifications, as I hope these remarks have shown, ideally suit him to inaugurate this series.

Adam Smith's "Invisible Hand" in a Velvet Glove

S. Herbert Frankel

I

I DID not expect to be called upon by fate to address you on this occasion, on which we have come together to pay respect to the memory of Warren Nutter. It is an ennobling occasion, and I have accepted the honor of giving this first of a series of memorial lectures in the spirit best described by the Latin word *pietas*. *Pietas* had a deeper meaning than our word "piety." It conveyed a sense of awe and respect for one's ancestors, one's country, one's elders, and one's gods.

Warren was my friend, the best friend I had in this great land of liberty and the achievements of liberty. He was younger than I by many years; but in the thirty years that my wife and I knew him, I always felt that I was looking up to him as if he were the older one. It was an instinctive feeling based on the recognition that I was in the presence of one who deserved to be treated as an exceptional person. Warren was a very modest man. He would have rejected any attempt to single him out in this way.

Yet he was exceptional—as a scholar, as a teacher, as an economist, above all as a citizen who served his country with courage. He served it painstakingly in peace through his fearless search for truth, and he served it in one war as a combatant and in another in high office, as assistant secretary of defense for international security affairs.

But Warren Nutter was more than this. He was a man of great humanity and humanity's friend, as he was a personal friend to so many in this room tonight. Above all he was a friend of liberty. To him one can without hesitation apply the words used to describe Dr. Hutcheson, the teacher of Adam Smith: .

> As he had occasion every year in the course of his lectures to explain the origin of government and compare the different forms of it, he took peculiar care, while on that subject, to inculcate the importance of civil and religious liberty to the happiness of mankind: as a warm love of liberty and manly zeal for promoting it were ruling principles in his own breast, he always insisted upon it at great length and with the greatest strength of argument and earnestness of persuasion: and he had such success on this important point, that few, if any, of his pupils, whatever contrary prejudices they might bring along with them, ever left him without favourable notions of that side of the question which he espoused and defended.[1]

There are many who can testify likewise concerning Warren Nutter's influence. That influence was exerted because of his incisive powers of logic, applied not only to economic analysis and historical interpretation but to the gravest issues of foreign policy.

In Warren Nutter's vocabulary, freedom was an issue that no man or woman could dare leave to be determined by others. Every citizen had to consult his own conscience and evaluate his own experience. He wrote: "Good judgment comes from experience, and experience comes from bad judgment."[2]

It was Warren Nutter's thirst for freedom that caused him to examine many popular misconceptions with that perspicacity and integrity that characterized all he undertook. It was this also that led him to unravel the effects of monopoly in the United States and to expose the false claims for the achievements of the economy of the Soviet Union. It was this same concern with truth as the indispensable bulwark of freedom that caused him to contrast the real life of the ordinary citizen in the Soviet Union with that of those fortunate enough to be citizens of the United States.

II

The subject of my lecture this evening is also concerned with the maintenance of freedom. I have chosen it because it may prove

---

[1] Adam Smith, *The Wealth of Nations*, ed. Edwin Cannan (New York: Random House, Modern Library, 1937), p. xlix.

[2] G. Warren Nutter, "Freedom in a Revolutionary Economy," in *The American Revolution: Three Views* (New York: American Brands, 1975), p. 119.

helpful at this time to recall some of Adam Smith's observations on both domestic and foreign policies.

In the continuing cacophony of class and party strife and propaganda, we are apt to forget that Smith was primarily concerned with individuals, with the formation of their character, and with what impelled them to improve themselves. It was this concern for individuals that characterized the work of all the great economic teachers who followed him.

My excuse for taking up an old problem is the same as that of my teacher Edwin Cannan on a similar occasion: I hope that what I shall say is true. As for its being new, however, I can only aspire to be like the candidate for the Ph.D. degree who, when his supervisor said "I cannot see that you are discovering any new facts," pleaded anxiously, "But don't you think I might be held to have exercised independent critical power?"

It is fashionable nowadays always to ask, What of the future? I propose instead to ask, What of the past? That is a more trustworthy guide to what terrors the future may hold in store.

It is not my intention to follow established fashion by analyzing all the personal motives, predilections, prejudices, or other sources of Adam Smith's every turn of phrase or opinion. This has been rightly described as "like standing on some beach and discussing whether this or that particular wave had most to do with the rising tide."[3]

Such discussion is at any rate of little consequence. The same cannot be said of attempts to explain Adam Smith's views as merely the expression of historical forces: as if he were helplessly in their grip and what he wrote was, as Max Lerner argued:

> the expression of forces which were working, at the very time he wrote it, to fashion that strange and terrible new species—*homo oeconomicus*, or the economic man of the modern world. . . .
> I use that term not in the sense of the lifeless abstraction which economic theorists have invented to slay any proposals for social change, and which has in turn slain them. I use it rather for the very living and human *business man, in defense of whom the economists have written and in whose interests they have invented their lifeless abstractions.* All the forces which were at work in Europe creating the business man, and the society he was to dominate, were

---

[3] Cannan, Introduction to Smith, *Wealth of Nations*, p. lv.

> at work also creating the framework of ideas and institutions within which Adam Smith wrote his book. And that book, as though conscious that one good turn deserved another, became in its own way a powerful influence to further the work of those forces [emphasis added].[4]

This historical interpretation has become commonplace. It has had far-reaching consequences, which are still very much in evidence today. It was already in vogue when my benevolent teacher Harold Laski contended that with Adam Smith the practical maxims of business enterprise achieved the status of theology. Far from idealizing the businessman, Adam Smith was frequently uncomplimentary to him and his tendency to join his fellow men in monopolistic conspiracies against the public interest.

III

The Wealth of Nations is not only an epic analytical work: it is also a tract against misplaced pride, prejudice, and privilege.

Anybody who reads *The Wealth of Nations* can discover for himself that it is ridiculous to suggest that it dignified either greed or the predatory impulses. Smith's personal sympathies were with the poor and the oppressed, with laborers, with farmers and against ecclesiastical, corporate, or aristocratic interests.

Equally untenable is the view that Adam Smith was simply reacting, in the interests of a particular class, against the elaborate apparatus of controls that the surviving feudal and mercantilist institutions still imposed on the individual. Of course, the need for removing those controls was one of his basic themes, but let no one make the mistake of thinking that he was merely concerned with market forces in the abstract.

Smith was no academic dogmatist. He attacked the mercantilists because their objective was to increase not the power of the nation but the power of government. In his view, to increase the power of the state was to weaken the power of society, dependent as it is on the activities of all the free individuals of whom it is composed. In our neomercantilist century, it is well to recognize that Adam Smith was the philosopher of liberty in the economic sphere as John Locke was in the political sphere.

The mercantilist system, as it has been loosely called, was the reverse of the laissez-faire liberalism that succeeded it and far more

---

[4] Max Lerner, Introduction in Smith, *Wealth of Nations*, p. v.

akin to the authoritarian century in which we live. The mercantilists aimed primarily at enlarging the isolating power of the nation-state, not at promoting the economic freedom of the individual across national boundaries, which characterized the dominant outlook of the nineteenth century. The mercantilist powers looked on the regions or countries that they dominated as their economic preserve—much as the Soviet Union does the satellite countries behind the Iron Curtain.

One turns to *The Wealth of Nations*, as Warren Nutter did in his *Adam Smith and the American Revolution*, because it challenged both a system of institutional controls and a system of ideas—particularly the idea that the power of the state rests merely on power. Adam Smith argued that power, like patriotism, is not enough, that the real well-being and strength of a nation depend on the activities of individuals and their freedom to pursue them at home and abroad. Above all he criticized the bureaucracy of absolutism represented by the court nobility in England and France. The monarchies of all the new nation-states had built up large companies of personal retainers paid for by royal patronage at the expense of the people. These bureaucrats were the real controllers of these absolutist regimes, as their counterparts are in today's authoritarian states and as they are fast becoming in many countries still supposedly part of the free world.

The mercantilists, we would do well to remember, sought the benefits of commerce to increase the external power of the state, to which all economic activity was subordinated. They thought that military power could capture and exploit the commercial activities of those countries in which they flourished, by what we today call "Finlandizing" them—or worse. Commerce, if it could not be captured, might even have to be destroyed to weaken the power of the enemy or potential enemy.

"Trade," wrote Colbert in 1666, "is the source of (public) finance and (public) finance is the vital nerve of war."[5] In 1664, in a memorandum of advice to Louis XIV, he explained that it was essential to the lofty ambitions that the king set himself "to limit all the industrial activity of Your subjects, as far as possible, to such professions as may be of use in furthering these great aims,"[6] that is, to agriculture, to trade and manufacture, and to war on sea and land.

---

[5] Eli F. Hechscher, *Mercantilism*, trans. Mendel Shapiro, vol. 2 (London: Allen & Unwin, 1935), p. 17.

[6] Ibid.

Colbert was convinced that the commercially successful Dutch had political motives in their eagerness to gather the trade of the whole world into their own hands. "It is certain," he wrote to the French ambassador at The Hague in 1666, "that their whole power has hitherto consisted in trade; if we could manage their trade, they might find it more difficult in the future to carry out their preparations for war than they have hitherto done."[7] In 1670 Colbert, in a memorandum on the finances of France prepared for the king, wrote in terms that have a very modern ring:

> It seems as if Your Majesty, having taken in hand the administration of your finances, has undertaken a monetary war against all European states. Your Majesty has already conquered Spain, Italy, Germany, England, and several other countries, and has forced them into great misery and poverty. At their expense Your Majesty has waxed rich. . . . There remains only Holland, which still struggles with all its great power. . . . Your Majesty has founded companies which attack them (the Dutch) everywhere like armies. . . . This war, which must be waged with might and main, . . . in which the most powerful republic since the Roman Empire is the price of victory, cannot cease so soon, or rather it must engage Your Majesty's chief attention during the whole of Your life.[8]

The Wealth of Nations criticized this warped conception of what determined the economic well-being and power of a nation. Its message, in simple terms, was that what is based on freedom cannot be captured by imprisoning it—any more than the song of a bird, which sings only when it is free, can be captured in a cage.

When Adam Smith in the opening lines of *The Wealth of Nations* announced that

> the greatest improvement in the productive powers of labour, and the greater part of the skill, dexterity, and judgment with which it is any where directed, or applied, seem to have been the effects of the division of labour[9]

he was referring to the division of labor not only at home but also across national frontiers:

> This division of labour, from which so many advantages are derived, is not originally the effect of any human wisdom,

---

[7] Ibid., p. 18.
[8] Ibid.
[9] Smith, *Wealth of Nations*, bk. I, p. 1.

which foresees and intends that general opulence to which it gives occasion. It is the necessary, though very slow and gradual, consequence of a certain propensity in human nature which has in view no such extensive utility; the propensity to truck, barter, and exchange one thing for another.[10]

Moreover, as in every society, every individual

endeavours as much as he can both to employ his capital in the support of domestic industry, and so to direct that industry that its produce may be of the greatest value; every individual necessarily labours to render the annual revenue of the society as great as he can. He generally, indeed, neither intends to promote the public interest, nor knows how much he is promoting it. By preferring the support of domestic to that of foreign industry he intends only his own security; and by directing that industry in such a manner as its produce may be of the greatest value, he intends only his own gain, and he is in this, as in many other cases, led by an invisible hand to promote an end which was no part of his intention. Nor is it always the worse for the society that it was no part of it. By pursuing his own interest he frequently promotes that of the society more effectually than when he really intends to promote it. I have never known much good done by those who affected to trade for the public good.[11]

Adam Smith saw clearly what we still so frequently overlook: that society and the individuals of whom it is composed are not two things, but two aspects of the same thing. He did not confuse the abstract representation of a thing with the thing itself, as if one were dealing with two different logical categories when in fact one is dealing with only one. He was fully aware that the national wealth was not something additional to or apart from the wealth and well-being of individuals, as if the well-being of the society or nation were one thing and the well-being of the individuals in it another. That would have been regarded by him as a contradiction in terms. Why then did he refer to the wealth of nations at all? He referred to it because individuals cannot be thought about apart from society.

Like Locke and many other eighteenth-century thinkers, he believed that individuals had not only rights but also obligations arising

---

[10] Ibid., p. 13.
[11] Ibid., p. 423.

from feelings of sympathy: of charity to their fellow men and women and, not least, of responsibility to their descendants. If, however, society were not defended from its enemies within and without, it would revert to the insecure and barbarous state of nature, from which in civilized countries individuals had but recently escaped through the establishment of security under law and freedom of contract in a stable money economy. This, as John Locke had made so abundantly clear, was the foundation of economic progress.

There were, as is well known, scoffers who misunderstood this scenario and regarded it with contempt. Carlyle was one of them. He called it "chaos plus a policeman." Now, I fear, over large parts of the civilized world, we are witnessing chaos without one.

IV

Adam Smith was a realist. He regarded defense of the nation as paramount at all times. The question has therefore to be faced: If it is true that there is a natural coincidence between self-interest and the general good, why does the coincidence not extend beyond national boundaries?

I once believed, with Edwin Cannan, that there was a contradiction here in Smith's thinking. I no longer do so. I believe the misunderstanding arose through insufficient attention to the relevant system of ideas as a whole because of attention to only a part of it.

Adam Smith was a pragmatist and expressed both short-term and long-term views on defense. He did not seek policy prescriptions simply on the basis that "in the long run we are all dead." When Smith wrote the well-known line that defense "is of much more importance than opulence," he followed it by words of approval for the Act of Navigation, an act that sought to strengthen the naval power of Britain, which Smith regarded as essential, by prohibiting the carriage of goods in foreign ships. What was original was his contention that in the long run defense depended on the economic strength of the world economy of which Britain was a part and on free trade with the like-minded nations.

He warned repeatedly that neither the individual nor society could rely on governmental measures to protect the nation. In the end both would become soft and would be overwhelmed by the forces that governments hoped to keep at bay. He was in effect recommending a state of tension and alertness that stretched the political and economic capacities of individuals within the nation to the full.

One is reminded of Tocqueville's view that there are propensities among people in a democracy toward materialism, mediocrity, compassion, domesticity, and isolation. These propensities make democratic man all too prone to accept or drift into what Tocqueville labels a "soft despotism."

Smith prophetically warned against the urge for imperial expansion by means that would give the empire a monopoly of trade and thus ultimately weaken the nation. The wheels of time grind slowly; our century has witnessed the fulfillment of his fears.

Those who support the free world economy today might well bear in mind that it is still in many ways an unfulfilled project rather than a reality. It is like an empire insufficiently developed and insufficiently defended. I think it is not far-fetched to apply to it the words Smith wrote on the eve of the separation of the American colonies:

> But countries which contribute neither revenue nor military force towards the support of the empire, cannot be considered as provinces. They may perhaps be considered as appendages, as a sort of splendid and showy equipage of the empire. . . . The rulers of Great Britain have, for more than a century past, amused the people with the imagination that they possessed a great empire on the west side of the Atlantic. This empire, however, has hitherto existed in imagination only. It has hitherto been, not an empire, but the project of an empire; not a gold mine, but the project of a gold mine. . . . It is surely now time that our rulers should either realize this golden dream . . . or that they should awake from it themselves, and endeavour to awaken the people. If the project cannot be completed, it ought to be given up. If any of the provinces of the British empire cannot be made to contribute towards the support of the whole empire, it is surely time that Great Britain should free herself from the expence of defending those provinces in time of war, and of supporting any part of their civil or military establishments in time of peace, and endeavour to accommodate her future views and designs to the real mediocrity of her circumstances.[12]

Adam Smith envisaged an empire with a world-wide commerce flowing in natural channels. It was to be capable of insisting, in case of need, on the removal of obstructions from those channels and capable also of placing obstructions in them if demanded by the supreme interest of defense. But the minute supervision and management of

---

[12] Ibid., pp. 899–900.

the multitudinous transactions of foreign commerce was a task not to be entrusted to "any senate whatever."

He went so far as to consider the abolition of the empire altogether and the replacement of it by bonds of friendship between independent nations who were prepared to contribute to its defense. How much more prophetic could he have been? He could not in his wildest dreams have foreseen the extent to which the freedom of commerce of the West would increase the productivity and well-being of its inhabitants in the nineteenth century. He could also not have foreseen how in the twentieth century a philosophy of government based on the very practices he was challenging would threaten it.

It is a well-known paradox that while technology continually diminishes distance in our relations and communications with others, our subjective appreciation of this change lags woefully behind. This was certainly true of the mercantilists. They simply could not grasp that they were laboring under a mythical image of their world that failed to encompass what was happening in time and space.

A similar myth in the United States was reflected in Frederick Jackson Turner's essay "The Significance of the Frontier in American History," read before the American Historical Association at Chicago in 1893. That essay has been described as "by far the most influential piece of writing about the West produced during the nineteenth century."[13] Turner's hypothesis developed out of the myth of the garden. Its central idea was that

> Americans had a safety valve for social danger, a bank account on which they might continually draw to meet losses. This was the vast unoccupied domain that stretched from the border of the settled area to the Pacific Ocean. . . . No grave social problem could exist while the wilderness at the edge of civilizations opened wide its portals to all who were oppressed, to all who with strong arms and stout heart desired to hew out a home and a career for themselves. Here was an opportunity for social development continually to begin over again, wherever society gave signs of breaking into classes. Here was a magic fountain of youth in which America continually bathed and was rejuvenated.[14]

Let me pause here to remind you that such myths did not spring straight from the heads of either the gods or the intellectuals. They

---

[13] Henry Nash Smith, *Virgin Land: The American West as Symbol and Myth* (Cambridge: Harvard University Press, 1950), p. 291.

[14] Ibid., p. 295.

were an expression of deep-seated fears—particularly the fear that there might be repeated in the New World the revolutionary up-heavals that had arisen out of the poverty and discontent of the economically disfranchised masses, always ready to seek plunder from, and revenge upon, the more wealthy and fortunate. These myths were no more born of mere academic musings than are the almost frantic—and sometimes equally mythical—ideas of our time for dealing with the sea of mass poverty of the underdeveloped world lapping the shores of the affluent societies.

Of course, the philosophy of the garden was already out of date when it was first propounded. America's bank account had become the rapidly unfolding cooperant efforts of the economically developed and freely accessible world.

I say accessible advisedly. The remarkable achievement of Adam Smith was to perceive so clearly that economic prosperity and devel-opment arise from overcoming isolation. It is salutary to reflect that the failure to do so has been one of the main causes of the decline of nations. Indeed, I believe that one reason for the decline of the European empires in this century has been an undue preoccupation with safeguarding the "absorptive capacity" provided by land for population growth, rather than understanding the opportunities that commerce and industry could create in lieu of it.

But let me return to my central thesis. Excellence, for Adam Smith, is derived from sympathy: "to feel much for others and little for ourselves . . . to restrain our selfish, and indulge our benevolent affections, constitutes the perfection of human nature."[15]

> The man of the most perfect virtue, the man whom we naturally love and revere the most, is he who joins, to the most perfect command of his own original and selfish feel-ings, the most exquisite sensibility both to the original and sympathetic feeling of others. The man who, to all the soft, the amiable, and the gentle virtues, joins all the great, the awful, and the respectable, must surely be the natural and proper object of our highest love and admiration.[16]

I cannot pursue here Smith's treatment of the active virtues that pro-voke the respect and approbation of others. I must confine myself to emphasizing again that for him civic virtue—indeed civilization itself —will be strengthened through commerce, through the freedom of

---

[15] Adam Smith, *Theory of Moral Sentiments* (Murray & Son, 1869), bk. II, 5, p. 24.
[16] Ibid., bk. III, 3, p. 133.

individuals in pursuit of what they consider their interests in accordance with their feelings and passions and their own proper control of them.

The scenario resulting from much of the ideology of this century has other roots. Let me quote a passage from J. M. Keynes, written over fifty years ago, which was as prophetic as it was revealing:

> Our problem is to work out a social organisation which shall be as efficient as possible without offending our notions of a satisfactory way of life.
>
> The next step forward must come, not from political agitation or premature experiments, but from thought. We need by an effort of the mind to elucidate our own feelings. At present our sympathy and our judgment are liable to be on different sides, which is a painful and paralysing state of mind. In the field of action reformers will not be successful until they can steadily pursue a clear and definite object with their intellects and their feelings in tune. There is no party in the world at present which appears to me to be pursuing right aims by right methods. Material Poverty provides the incentive to change precisely in situations where there is very little margin for experiments. Material Prosperity removes the incentive just when it might be safe to take a chance. Europe lacks the means, America the will, to make a move. We need a new set of convictions which spring naturally from a candid examination of our own inner feelings in relation to the outside facts.[17]

In this appeal to elucidate our feelings, Keynes no doubt also had in mind the social importance of sympathy; but there the parallel with Adam Smith's thought ends. Keynes was not advocating, as Smith did, the control of those feelings by the Impartial Spectator—the individual conscience—of the virtuously active citizen, but their control by the "wisdom of the chosen few," whose task it would be to see to it that capitalism was wisely managed. That this was his view became even clearer in his later writings.[18]

He distrusted the businessman because he was allegedly incapable, by the very nature of the capitalist system, of making the rational calculations society required, and he criticized capitalism also because it was unpleasant. But nowhere did Keynes indicate who will

---

[17] J. M. Keynes, *The End of Laissez-Faire* (London: Hogarth Press, 1926), pp. 53–54.

[18] S. H. Frankel, *Two Philosophies of Money: The Conflict of Trust and Authority* (New York: St. Martin's Press, 1978), p. 63.

control the controllers. What he was attempting was to clothe the "invisible hand" in a velvet glove of benign bureaucracy. We are doing likewise.

Current attitudes would not have astonished Adam Smith. He was fully aware of the assumptions on which they rest, and he rejected them. He wrote:

> the sneaking arts of underling tradesmen are thus erected into political maxims for the conduct of a great Empire. . . . By such maxims as these, however, nations have been taught that their interest consisted in beggaring all their neighbours. Each nation has been made to look with an invidious eye upon the prosperity of all the nations with which it trades, and to consider their gain as its own loss. Commerce, which ought naturally to be, among nations as among individuals, a bond of union and friendship, has become the most fertile source of discord and animosity. The capricious ambition of kings and ministers has not, during the present and the preceding century, been more fatal to the repose of Europe, than the impertinent jealousy of merchants and manufacturers.[19]

He was warning against confusing the language of trade with the language of power. He feared the consequences of the belief that policies intended to promote national advantage could be determined according to the accounting principles and procedures of business.

Yet that is precisely what for over fifty years has been thought to be the essence of modern statecraft. We have come to accept the idea that the prime concern of every country must lie in the pursuit of its domestic economic objectives, even at the expense of the survival of the free world economy of which it is a part. Combined with this idea is a tacit negation of the suitability of the free market as a means of attaining economic goals at home, a negation that is also responsible for the multiplication of official agencies to pursue those goals abroad.

Consequently, the need to foster and expand opportunities for individuals and their economic mobility across national boundaries has been relegated to the background or greatly restricted. A simple illustration of such restriction is that in the countries of the European Economic Community there are over 5 million migrant workers who

---

[19] Adam Smith, *An Inquiry into the Nature and Causes of the Wealth of Nations*, bk. IV, chap. III.

are denied the opportunity to settle permanently with their families where they work.

The productive safety valve that migration between countries provided in the nineteenth century has disappeared. Is this not a clue to the tragic paradox of our plan-ridden world? The century that has so loudly proclaimed the need for freedom from fear is also the century of the refugee, permitted only to vote with his feet—but with nowhere to go.

Moreover, is it really so astonishing that the vast programs of official aid to developing countries have neither borne their expected fruit nor reduced the suspicions that drive the free peoples of the world apart? Adam Smith told us why:

> Princes . . . have frequently engaged in . . . mercantile projects . . . they have scarce ever succeeded. The profusion with which the affairs of princes are always managed, renders it almost impossible that they should. The agents of a prince regard the wealth of their master as inexhaustible; are careless at which price they buy; are careless at what price they sell; are careless at what expense they transport his goods from one place to another. Those agents frequently live with the profusion of princes, and sometimes too, in spite of that profusion, and by a proper method of making up their accounts, acquire the fortunes of princes.[20]

The belief that the growth of bureaucracy can be relied upon to bring about world peace and prosperity reminds me of a book that appeared before World War I, which greatly impressed me at the time—Norman Angell's *The Great Illusion*.[21] It lulled many Europeans into a false sense of security.

Angell argued that it was absurd for European countries, particularly Great Britain, to spend vast sums on rearming when it was obvious to any thinking man that no country could profit from a war because all Europe was economically interdependent. No nation would come out of a war better off. European rulers, the book argued, knew this to be the case and could be trusted to reason and act accordingly.

It is easy, with hindsight, to dismiss the whole argument as utterly ridiculous. That would be to miss the important lesson it

---

[20] Ibid., bk. V, chap. II.
[21] Norman Angell, *The Great Illusion: A Study of the Relation of Military Power in Nations to Their Economic and Social Advantage* (London: William Heinemann, 1910).

provides. The argument was wrong because it assumed that the interests of the people were also the interests of their rulers and that the people could trust their rulers. They were mistaken in doing so.

Unless freedom is defended, the hand in the velvet glove will become the iron fist. As Tocqueville discovered, "in a democracy, under certain conditions, it is easier to be a good man than a good citizen":[22]

> True, democratic societies which are not free may well be prosperous, cultured, pleasing to the eye, and even magnificent, such is the sense of power implicit in their massive uniformity; in them may flourish many private virtues (*qualités*), good fathers, honest merchants, exemplary landowners, and good Christians, too. . . . But, I make bold to say, never shall we find under such conditions a great citizen, still less a great nation.[23]

We should not belittle what good citizenship now involves. It cannot escape battling against the tide of bureaucratization threatening to overwhelm us, to free men and women from the iron cage of officialdom and organized restraint on moral personal choice. We should take note of Tocqueville's prescient words:

> It would seem as if the rulers of our time sought only to *use* men in order to make *things* great; I wish that they would try a little more to make great men; that they would set less value on the work and more upon the workman; that they would never forget that a nation cannot long remain strong when every man belonging to it is individually weak; and that no form or combination of social policy has yet been devised to make an energetic people out of a community of pusillanimous and enfeebled citizens [emphasis added].[24]

We must shoulder the burden of civil virtue in its classical meaning and partake in the decision-making process and in political action for the *common* good. For the citizen of the ancient polis to be barred from these tasks was servitude, and to exercise them at the behest of others was corruption.

Let us, as Warren Nutter wrote, "comprehend, before it is too late, that without freedom all else is nothing."[25]

---

[22] Marvin Zetterbaum, *Tocqueville and the Problem of Democracy* (Stanford: Stanford University Press, 1967), p. 80.

[23] Alexis de Tocqueville, *Old Regime*, quoted in Zetterbaum, *Tocqueville*, p. 80.

[24] Tocqueville, *Democracy* II, quoted in Zetterbaum, *Tocqueville*, p. 80.

[25] Nutter, "Freedom," p. 120.

Market
Mechanisms
and Central
Economic Planning

Milton Friedman

March 4, 1981

MILTON FRIEDMAN is a senior research fellow at the Hoover Institution and a Nobel laureate in economic science. He is also Paul Snowden Russell Distinguished Service Professor of Economics at the University of Chicago and was formerly a member of the American Enterprise Institute's Council of Academic Advisers.

Introduction

Colin D. Campbell

It is a pleasure for me to welcome you to the second of the G. Warren Nutter Lectures in Political Economy. The first Nutter Lecture was delivered in 1980, and the speaker was Professor Herbert Frankel. The third Nutter Lecture is scheduled for the fall of 1981 and will be given by Professor Ronald Coase.

The present lecture is being sponsored jointly by the Thomas Jefferson Center Foundation, the Hoover Institution, and the American Enterprise Institute; and the lecture will be published by the American Enterprise Institute. Warren Nutter was actively associated with all three of these organizations. Together with James M. Buchanan, in 1957 he founded the Thomas Jefferson Center for Studies in Political Economy at the University of Virginia. He was an adviser of the Hoover Institution, and he had a long and very close relationship with the American Enterprise Institute. Our speaker, Milton Friedman, also is associated with both the Hoover Institution and the American Enterprise Institute; and he has frequently participated in the programs of the Thomas Jefferson Center. Professor Friedman was one of Warren Nutter's teachers when Nutter was a graduate student at the University of Chicago.

Professor Friedman is so well known to all of you that I am not going to try to summarize his remarkable career. I do, however, want to mention one of his recent achievements, which Rose Friedman shares with him—the phenomenal success of their book, *Free to Choose*. For fifty-one consecutive weeks starting in early 1980, *Free to Choose* was on the best-seller list for nonfiction in the Sunday *New York Times Book Review*. It topped the list for six weeks during that spring; and during most of that summer it ranked number two, just behind a book entitled *Thy Neighbor's Wife*. During the year, it stayed on the list much longer than any of the other best sellers, even though it was competing with books with such intriguing titles as *All You Need to Know about the IRS, The Brethren, Aunt Erma's Cope Book, How You Can Become Financially Independent by Investing in Real Estate, Ordeal, They Call Me Assassin,* and *On a Clear Day You Can See General Motors.* Early in February 1981, *Free to Choose* was missing from the best-seller list, and I feared that the market for it had dropped. But I was wrong. It had just switched from the regular best-seller list to the best-seller list for paperbacks. It is still on the paperback list, and we hope it will stay there for a long time.

When we discussed with Professor Friedman the topic for this lecture, we agreed that it would be appropriate if he would talk about some aspect of socialist economic planning, one of Warren Nutter's main interests. When Nutter was head of the Thomas Jefferson Center, it held annual conferences in Italy that brought together free-market economists and economists from the Communist countries in Eastern Europe. Although at that time the conferences were considered to be a very bold program for promoting the ideas of the free market, recent events in Poland, China, and other Communist countries appear to justify Nutter's efforts to keep alive among Communist economists an understanding of the free-market system.

In the fall of 1980, Professor Friedman received an invitation from the government of China to give a series of lectures in China. I imagine that in some ways his visit to China provided an opportunity for the same kind of exchange of ideas that occurred at the conferences in Italy that were organized by the Thomas Jefferson Center. The remarkable thing about Professor Friedman's visit to China is that the initiative came from the Chinese rather than from persons in the West. Professor Friedman's Nutter lecture is taken from one of the lectures that he gave in China.

Market Mechanisms and Central Economic Planning

Milton Friedman

THIS is very much a family gathering. All of us who were close personal friends or close professional associates of Warren Nutter mourn deeply his untimely passing. We all have benefited from his work, his friendship, his strength as a human being. That is why this is both a sad occasion and yet an occasion for gaining renewed dedication to the kinds of things in which he was particularly interested.

As Colin Campbell mentioned, Nutter was a student at the University of Chicago when I first went there. Indeed, he was the first student at Chicago on whose doctoral thesis committee I served as chairman. But I do not quite accept Professor Campbell's description of the relationship; it is much less clear than he made out who was the teacher and who was the student.

The subject that I am going to talk about—the possibility of introducing market arrangements in centrally planned economies—is one that was very close to Warren Nutter's interests throughout much of his life. As you know, some of his most important work dealt with the Soviet economy and with an understanding of its performance.

Command versus Market Economies

We should begin by drawing a contrast between two kinds of arrangements for organizing economic activity. They are commonly designated by the terms "command economy" and "market economy." The ideal type of command economy is one in which individuals who act do so not as principals but as agents for someone else. They are carrying out an order, doing what they are told. The ideal type of market economy is one in which individuals act as principals in pursuit of their own interests. If any individual serves as an agent for someone else, he does so on a voluntary, mutually agreed upon basis.

In practice, there can be no pure command economy. Such an economy would be composed of robots who had no separate volition, no separate interests. This approach is reflected in Tennyson's "Theirs not to reason why,/Theirs but to do and die." Even in the most extreme case of a command economy—an army battalion on the march—even, I suspect, in a case such as the charge of the Light Brigade, no human being really acts as a pure robot. How wholeheartedly he carries out commands, the degree of venturesomeness and courage he displays— in these respects he acts as a principal in response to his own interests.

A pure market economy is at least conceivable. The economist's favorite example of a market economy is Robinson Crusoe, but even that is modified somewhat by the presence of the man Friday. A Robinson Crusoe without a man Friday would constitute a market economy in which he is acting as a principal in pursuit of his own interests.

For society, there are no pure command or market economies, either as ideals or in practice. Even in the most extreme version of the anarchist-libertarian ideal of a market economy, families exist; and within a family there are command elements. Children sometimes behave in response to orders and not of their own volition as principals, a fact that is equally true of other members of the family. Similarly, as I have already suggested, the most obvious and extreme case of a command economy is an army in which the general supposedly gives an order to the colonel, the colonel to the major, the major to the captain, the captain to the lieutenant, and so on down to the buck private. At every stage the individuals who are responding to those orders have volitions of their own and interests of their own, and they react in part in accordance with these. At every stage in that process they have some element of discretion: They know things about the immediate local circumstances that the general at the top could not conceivably know. Thus actual societies are always mixtures. Only in very small groups such as families can command be even the principal, much less the exclusive, method of organizing economic activities.

Consider the most extreme command economies currently in existence—the Soviet Union and mainland China. I suspect that in the Soviet Union and even in China, if you could only find some way to quantify it, you would discover that most resources are organized through the principle of the market, of voluntary cooperation by people pursuing their own interests, rather than through the elaborate structure of direct command. An obvious example is the private agricultural plots in Russia, which are said to occupy 3 percent of the arable land and to contribute between a quarter and a third of the country's total agricultural output. But let us go beyond that example.

In the Soviet Union's labor market, people are hired and people are fired. Individuals have some freedom to choose where they are going to work and to accept or reject a job. This freedom is not absolute by any manner or means; some people do not have that choice. My wife and I often recall an instance during the trip we made to the Soviet Union. We were being driven from one airport to another, accompanied by the inevitable tourist guide, a young man who was just about to graduate from Moscow University. He was interested, I may say, in American literature. When we asked him who his favorite American author was, no one in this room would guess that it was Howard Fast. We asked him what he was going to do after he graduated from Moscow University; and he. said, "Well I don't know. They haven't told me yet." That is the essence of a command economy; yet most laborers, most workers, in the Soviet Union are not in our guide's position. They are hired and they are fired, with the result that most labor is ultimately allocated through market arrangements.

In a pure command economy, goods and services would be allocated directly to individuals. Each person would get from the central authority a basket of goods, and he would have no choice concerning the content of that basket of goods. If we look at the way goods and services are distributed in the Soviet Union, we will find that they are sold through stores. True, a person may have to stand in long lines or queues to buy things, but the method of distribution is fundamentally a market mechanism of setting prices on goods and having people buy them. In some cases people need more than one kind of money: ration coupons as well as paper money. Nonetheless, the method is in large measure a market method. Again, gray markets spring up everywhere in such a country. If a Soviet citizen's electricity goes haywire, he is much more likely to try to get a private individual to come and fix it for a cash fee than he is to call the government agency assigned the task of fixing his electricity, because he will have little confidence that anyone would arrive from the government agency within a reasonable period of time.

With respect to intrafamily behavior, one notes that while the family is in some ways the ideal type of command economy, it also has very large elements of voluntary exchange and market reaction. In Warren Nutter's marvelous little book *The Strange World of Ivan Ivanov*,[1] which was developed and compiled from a series of newspaper articles he published, he describes in great detail the daily life of a family in the Soviet Union and contrasts it with the life of an American family. There are enormous differences; and yet as you go through the book you are struck by how large a fraction of the activities can be characterized and described as operating through the market. It is a very distorted market, but it is a market nonetheless.

We were very much impressed with the same phenomena in China. Despite recent easing, command elements are more important in the Chinese economy than in the Russian economy. For example, the allocation of labor is dictated much more by command elements. In all the factories that we visited, we kept inquiring what would happen if they needed to employ five more people. "We'd ask the people downtown, and they would send us five people." "Would you have a choice about hiring the five?" "Oh no, no, they are the people we would have to employ." We tried to find out whether there was any possibility that a worker at one plant could arrange a transfer if he believed that he would be better off at another plant. "Oh yes," they told us. If he believed that he could be more useful in another factory, all he would have to do is tell his supervisor, and his supervisor would tell his superior, and so on up to the top. Then the top man would communicate with his counterpart at the other factory, and he in turn would send the message down the line. In that way it would be possible for the worker to transfer. I kept asking whether they knew of any such cases. No, they had not come across any such cases—with one exception, which had to do not with a factory but with a scientific institute.

Despite the ubiquitous command element in the Chinese economy, there are also pervasive market elements. The Chinese have recently started to introduce private agricultural plots in the communes. We were taken to the most prosperous commune in the most prosperous county in the most prosperous province in China. About a year and a half earlier, they had introduced private plots. According to their figures, private plots accounted for 2½ percent of the arable land of the commune but were already producing 10 percent of the income from crops. Similarly, there are many stores, both specialty

---

[1] G. Warren Nutter, *The Strange World of Ivan Ivanov* (New York and Cleveland: World Publishing Co., 1969).

shops and department stores, not to mention food markets. Goods and services are distributed by purchase and sale rather than by direct allocation. It is limited, but there is still some gray market activity and so on.

A question that is typically asked in connection with central economic planning is how extensively market elements can be introduced in a command economy. I believe that this way of putting it is upside down. The real question is how far one can go in introducing command elements into a market economy. I believe that it would be literally impossible for any large-scale economy to be operated on a strictly command basis. Fundamentally, what enables a country such as China or the Soviet Union to function at all is the market elements that are either deliberately introduced or are inadvertently permitted to operate.

When I speak of market elements being introduced into command economies such as China's and the Soviet Union's, I am not speaking of free markets; they are highly distorted markets. That is why those countries have such low standards of living; that is why they are so inefficient.

We all know the key insight that Adam Smith brought to this subject, which underlies the possibility of markets operating to coordinate economic activity. That key insight is that if exchange is voluntary—if two people engage in any exchange on a voluntary basis—the exchange will occur only if both sides benefit. Economic activity is not a "zero-sum game," to use the term that Lester Thurow recently adopted as the title of a book. It is an activity in which everybody can benefit. That, as I say, was Adam Smith's key insight, and it produced his corollary of the invisible hand; that is, a person who seeks to promote only his own interest is "led by an invisible hand to promote an end which was no part of his intention." We are all familiar with this proposition.

If we are to understand the problems that arise in trying to introduce effective market elements into command economies, it is important that we examine in more detail the functions that prices serve in the operation of the invisible hand and the coordination of economic activity.

The Functions of Prices

Fundamentally prices serve three functions in such a society. First, they transmit information. We find out very quickly that it is necessary to conserve energy because that information is transmitted in the form of higher prices of oil. The crucial importance of this function tended to be neglected until Friedrich Hayek published his great article on "The Use of Knowledge in Society" in the *American Economic Review* in 1945. This function of prices is essential, however, for enabling economic activity to be coordinated. Prices transmit information about tastes, about resource availability, about productive possibilities. They transmit a very wide range of information. They transmit information about the availability of goods today versus tomorrow through futures markets, and so on. A second function that prices perform is to provide an incentive for people to adopt the least costly methods of production and to use available resources for the most highly valued uses. They perform that function because of their third function, which is to determine who gets what and how much—the distribution of income.

The reason it is essential to stress these three functions and to show their interrelation is that, in my opinion, essentially all of the problems in central economic planning arise from trying to separate the functions from one another. As we can readily see, prices give people an incentive only because they are used to distribute income. If what a person gets for his activity does not depend in any way on what he does, if prices do not serve the third function of distributing income, then there is no reason for him to worry about the information that prices are transmitting, and there is no incentive for him to act in accordance with that information. If his income does depend on what he does, on the difference between the prices that he receives for selling his services and the prices he has to pay for items he buys—if it depends on the difference between receipts and costs from the point of view of a business enterprise, or wages and costs for a worker, and so on—then he has a very strong incentive to try to ensure that he sells his services in the best market for the highest price, that he produces products at the least cost, that he produces those products for which other people are willing to pay the most. The real beauty, and I use the word "beauty" advisedly, of a price system is precisely the way in which the incentive to act on information accompanies the information that is transmitted. This is not true in a command economy. Information is transmitted from one level of a command economy to another, but that information does not carry with it any incentive to act in accordance with it. There must be some kind of supplementary means of seeing to it that people act on the information.

In every society the distribution of income is a major source of dissatisfaction. That is true in a command economy, and it is true in a market economy; every person always knows that he deserves more than he is getting and that the other fellow deserves less. That is a natural human instinct. I am reminded of a remark made by Alvin Johnson many years ago when he was conducting a study of incomes in different occupations. He found that physicians complained that lawyers were getting more than physicians, and lawyers complained that physicians were getting more than lawyers; carpenters complained that plumbers were getting more than carpenters, and plumbers complained that carpenters were getting more than plumbers; and so on down the line. Johnson finally concluded that life was an underpaid occupation.

In predominantly market economies, a very large fraction of all government activity, particularly the enormous expansion in government activity over the past fifty years, has been directed toward trying to separate the distribution of income from market determination, trying to separate the third function of prices from the other two functions, trying to make the amount that people get independent of the prices at which they can sell their services. It is impossible to accomplish this goal and still preserve the other functions of prices. You have to compromise. Professor Campbell referred to the seminars in which Warren Nutter was involved with Renato Mieli in bringing together economists from the East and the West. I recall very well one of those sessions at which a Hungarian economist gave an absolutely brilliant performance. He had rediscovered all by himself Adam Smith's principle of mutual benefit from voluntary exchange and the invisible hand. The burden of his whole analysis, however, was an attempt to separate the distribution of income from the function of prices in transmitting information and in providing an incentive to operate on that information. Of course, as always, he failed.

However much we might wish it to be otherwise, it simply is not possible to use prices to transmit information and to provide an incentive to act on that information without also using prices to affect, even if not to determine completely, the distribution of income. If a person's income will be the same whether he works hard or not, why should he work hard? Why should he make the effort to search out the buyer who values most highly what he has to sell if he will not get any benefit from doing so, and so on down the line? I need not spell that out in detail.

If prices are prevented from affecting the distribution of income, even if they do not completely determine it, they cannot be used for other purposes. The only alternative is command. Some authority would have to decide who should produce what and how much. That authority would have to decide who should sweep the streets and who manage the factory, who should be the policeman and who the physician.

It is tempting to think that a desire to render social service to benefit the community can replace the incentive provided by the price system. The result has been repeated attempts by leaders—both in countries that rely primarily on the market and in collectivist countries—to exhort their citizens to work harder or to economize or to hold down prices or wages or to engage in other supposedly desirable activities, all in the name of patriotism or the national interest. Such exhortation has an unbroken record of failing to solve the problems that called them forth. The reason is not because people are unresponsive to appeals to their patriotism or to the national interest or to their sense of social cohesion. Those are very powerful sentiments, and they do lead people to make extraordinary exertions. Just look at the way people react to appeals to their patriotism in times of war and the extent to which they are willing to sacrifice their lives for objectives that have very little or nothing to do with their immediate self-interest.

The reason why exhortation fails is much more fundamental. It is because exhortation can seldom be accompanied by the information that is relevant for the response to achieve the desired objective. That is possible when the exhortation, for example, is to enlist in an army. It is almost never possible when the exhortation is directed at behavior designed to promote social or economic coordination. How can the individual judge what is socially desirable or what actions he can take that will benefit the community? His vision is necessarily limited; he cannot envisage the more distant effects of his action. He is as likely to do harm as good when he acts in ignorance under the incentive to aid the "national interest" or to perform "social service." The great virtue of the incentive transmitted through the price system is not that it is necessarily stronger than other types of incentives or that it is "nobler" but simply that it is automatically accompanied by the information that is relevant to the effective operation of the incentive.

When centrally planned economies have tried to use the market, the major obstacle to their success has been their desire to separate the function of prices in distributing income from the function of prices in transmitting information and providing incentives. The attempt to do so and yet preserve the virtues of the free market has produced an extensive literature on alternative devices.

Lange and Lerner "Playing at Capitalism"

As the economists here know very well, the most famous treatment of this subject in modern times, and certainly in the West, was by Oskar Lange, a Polish economist, first in two articles and then in slightly revised form in a book that also included an earlier essay by Fred M. Taylor;[2] and by Abba P. Lerner in a series of articles and later in a book.[3] Lange and Lerner tried to explain how a socialist society could be organized through the market. A very similar approach was presented around the same time by the English economist James Meade in his book on *Planning and the Price Mechanism*.[4]

Essentially the Lange–Lerner solution requires enterprises owned by the state to play at free-market capitalism. The idea is to formulate the end results of the operation of a free competitive market and to translate those results into instructions to managers of state enterprises about how to run those enterprises. In a free competitive market, for example, price tends to equal marginal cost, that is, the cost of producing an extra unit. Accordingly, Lange and Lerner would have the authorities instruct managers of state-run enterprises to set the price of each of their products equal to marginal cost or, alternatively, if the authorities themselves set the price, to adjust the volume of production so that marginal cost equals price. In calculating marginal cost, they would have the managers of enterprises use the closest possible approximation to the wages, the interest rates, the cost of raw materials, et cetera, that would arise in a free market. This was, however, to be "playing at" capitalism because, in their scheme, the incomes received by individuals would not necessarily be those that

---

[2] Oskar Lange, "On the Economic Theory of Socialism," *Review of Economic Studies*, vol. 4 (October 1936), pp. 53–71, and vol. 4 (February 1937), pp. 123–42. A revised version was subsequently published in Oskar Lange and Fred M. Taylor, *On the Economic Theory of Socialism*, Benjamin E. Lippencott, ed. (Minneapolis: University of Minnesota Press, 1938), pp. 55–142.

[3] Abba P. Lerner, "Economic Theory and Socialist Economy," *Review of Economic Studies*, vol. 2 (October 1934), pp. 51–61; idem, "A Note on Socialist Economics," *Review of Economic Studies*, vol. 4 (October 1936), pp. 72–76; idem, "Statics and Dynamics in Socialist Economics," *Economic Journal*, vol. 47 (June 1937), pp. 253–70; and idem, *The Economics of Control* (New York: Macmillan, 1944).

[4] James E. Meade, *Planning and the Price Mechanism: The Liberal-Socialist Solution* (London: G. Allen & Unwin, 1948).

would result from an actual free market. Managers of state enterprises would receive wages and not the "profits" from the enterprise, although perhaps they might receive payments geared to profits. There might be incentive payments. The managers would not be the owners of the enterprise; the state would own the enterprise. When the managers invested capital, they would not be investing their own funds or the funds of identifiable persons for whom they were operating as agents. They would be investing state funds. The risks they would be taking would not be risks for themselves or for identifiable principals but for the state. Similarly, the incomes of the workers would not necessarily be equal to the notional wages that the entrepreneurs would include in calculating how much to produce.

This is a small sample of the ingenious analysis in the Lange–Lerner book. It is an admirable book that has much to teach about the operation of a free market; indeed, much more, I believe, than about their actual objective, how to run a socialist state. It is unnecessary to go into great detail about their analysis, because what seems to me to be the basic flaw in this analysis has little to do with the sophisticated parts of their discussion. Let me emphasize that their approach has a great deal of merit. It forces planners in a society to try to estimate what the results would have been in a free market and therefore to take into account the truly relevant considerations in achieving efficient production. It specifies the principles that the planners in such a society should follow in the trial-and-error process of adjusting prices to experience; that is, to adjust the quantity demanded to the available supply in the short run, and the available supply to the quantity demanded at a price equal to marginal cost in the long run.

I may say that the principles that Lange and Lerner outline are very much neglected in our own society. Let me digress for a moment to give a current example from the British experience. One of the problems that Mrs. Thatcher's government has faced arose out of a commitment that she made during the campaign to accept the findings of a Royal Commission comparing salaries in government service with those in private industry. The commission concluded that the salaries of government servants should be raised by 28 percent to make them comparable with private salaries. If the planners in England had read —and absorbed—Lange and Lerner, they would have known what the right principle was: a job is overpaid if there are many applicants for few jobs; a job is underpaid if there are few applicants for many jobs. There is no doubt about what the situation in Britain was: there were altogether too many government servants; but at the same time, there were a great many applicants for each new job available in the civil service. Obviously the civil servants were being overpaid and not underpaid. Had the Royal Commission followed Lange and Lerner's book, they could never have reached the conclusion that government salaries were too low.

Various forms of the Lange–Lerner system have been tried on a smaller or a larger scale in many countries—in Lange's native land, Poland, where the success of those ventures is not exactly apparent; in Czechoslovakia; in Hungary; and in Romania. Although the results have often been superior to those achieved earlier, they have also uniformly disappointed the hopes of the sponsors of reform.

In 1968 Warren Nutter pointed out the key difficulty in the system in an important article entitled "Markets without Property: A Grand Illusion," from which I quote:

> If we now come full circle and return to Lange's model of socialism, we see how empty his theoretical apparatus is. Markets without divisible and transferable property rights are a sheer illusion. There can be no competitive behavior, real or simulated, without dispersed power and responsibility. And it will not do to disperse the one without the other. If all property is to be literally collectivized and all pricing literally centralized, there is no scope left for a mechanism that can reproduce in any significant respect the functioning of competitive private enterprise.[5]

A more pungent summary of exactly the same point was made by an English financial journalist, Samuel Brittan, in an article published in *Encounter* in January 1980:

> To publish a set of rules asking the managers of state enterprises to behave *"as if"* they were profit-maximising entrepreneurs in competitive private industry ignores the actual personal motivations faced by these men. . . . You do not make a horse into a zebra merely by painting stripes on its back.[6]

---

[5] G. Warren Nutter, "Markets without Property: A Grand Illusion," in Nicholas A. Beadles and L. Aubrey Drewry, Jr., eds., *Money, the Market, and the State: Economic Essays in Honor of James Muir Waller* (Athens: University of Georgia Press, 1968), pp. 137–45 (quotation is from pp. 144–45).

[6] Samuel Brittan, "Hayek, the New Right, & the Crisis of Social Democracy," *Encounter*, January 1980, pp. 30–46 (quotation is from p. 38).

The fundamental problem with this approach is how to monitor performance. To state the central feature of a free-market system in a different way, it is a system under which each individual monitors his own performance and has an incentive to monitor it properly, a point that Thomas Sowell has developed with great insight in his recent book, *Knowledge and Decisions*.[7] The person who is using his own labor to produce goods for himself has a strong motivation to work hard and efficiently—as do those people tilling private plots in the Soviet Union and China. The person risking his own property has an incentive to make the best use of it. If he is using his property to hire others to produce a product or render a service, he has a strong incentive to monitor their labor; and, knowing that he is doing so and can reward or discharge them, the workers have a strong incentive to work efficiently. The consumer spending his own money has a strong incentive to spend it carefully. And so on.

Conversely, in a system in which managers of state enterprises are told to behave as if they were profit-making entrepreneurs, what incentive do they have to monitor themselves? Government officials will seek to monitor them, but what incentives do those officials have to monitor them properly? And how can they obtain the information to monitor the managers?

This problem can be brought out most clearly not by examining the routine day-to-day, repetitive operations of an enterprise, but rather by examining what in many ways is the most important single activity from the point of view of producing growth, development, and change, namely, innovation—deciding what new products to produce, what new methods to use in producing products, what new capital investment to undertake, and so on. Take a specific example. A person has an idea that, in his best judgment, has only one chance in ten of being successful. If successful, however, the financial return in the form of the value of the extra product produced or of the saving in production expenses would be, let us say, a hundred times the cost of introducing the idea. It is clearly desirable that this activity be undertaken. It is a good bet. If many such bets are taken, the end result will be highly favorable; the winners will more than make up for the losers.

In a market system in which the individual who makes the decision to undertake that venture receives all or a large fraction of the additional returns, he has an incentive to undertake it. He knows that

---

[7] Thomas Sowell, *Knowledge and Decisions* (New York: Basic Books, 1980).

there are nine chances out of ten that he will lose his money; yet the gain he will receive in the one case out of ten when his idea works is big enough to justify taking the risk.

Consider the same situation in a state-run enterprise. How can the manager of that enterprise persuade the people under whom he works that the odds and potential returns are what he believes them to be? He may have great confidence in his own judgment; yet he may have very great difficulty in persuading his superiors. In addition, the reward structure is likely to be very different. If the venture is successful, he will no doubt receive some extra compensation; he may be awarded a medal, receive kudos and honors, become a hero of the nation. If, however, the venture is a failure, as it will be in nine cases out of ten, he will almost surely be reprimanded and may lose his position and perhaps even his life and liberty. The reward in the case of success does not compensate for the loss in case of failure. His natural tendency is to avoid such risky enterprises, to play it safe, to undertake investments that are almost certain to yield returns. Who can blame such a manager? Considering the circumstances under which such managers operate, that is the reasonable, rational, human way to behave. For society as a whole, however, that kind of behavior is the road to stagnation and rigidity, and that in fact has been the outcome in collectivist societies.

Yugoslav Worker Cooperatives

A very different approach has been adopted in Yugoslavia, and it is the other main variant I want to discuss. The Yugoslav approach involves not playing at capitalism but establishing a restricted form of capitalism. This form operates on two different levels: strict capitalist private ownership and operation, that is, a real market; and worker cooperatives, a kind of halfway capitalist market.

Between 80 and 90 percent of the arable land in Yugoslavia is in strict private ownership. The peasant proprietors produce for the market. This sector of agriculture is comparable to the private plots that farmers in the Soviet Union or in China are permitted to cultivate.

Apart from agriculture, Yugoslavia permits—or at least it did when I was there some years back (I have not been there in recent years)—strict private ownership of all enterprises that employ fewer than five people other than family members. As I say, the exact numbers may be different now, but something like that is permitted. Although this keeps private enterprises relatively small, the cooperation of enterprises conducted by different members of the same family enables some to be fairly extensive while still remaining within the formal limits. Such enterprises have been particularly important in the tourist industry, where they have played a major role in providing Yugoslavia with a productive and financially rewarding industry.

For larger enterprises, Yugoslavia has adopted a form of worker cooperative in which the enterprises, instead of being explicitly owned by the state, supposedly are owned by the workers in the enterprises. I say "explicitly" and "supposedly" because the cooperatives involve the same mixture of collectivism and capitalism as do U.S. corporations. Who owns a U.S. corporation? The stockholders? Or is the owner the government, which receives 46 percent of the profits and bears 46 percent of the losses of all but relatively small corporations? Once when I was in Yugoslavia, I calculated that the difference between the degree of socialism in Yugoslavia and in the United States at that time was, if my memory is right, fourteen percentage points. In the United States, the corporate income tax was then 52 percent, and so the government owned 52 percent of every enterprise. In Yugoslavia, the central government was taking about 66 percent of the profits of the worker cooperatives. Thus there was only a fourteen-percentage-point difference in the degree of socialism. Just as we think of our enterprises as privately owned and operated, and this view contains an important element of validity, so in Yugoslavia these cooperative enterprises are regarded by the workers as being owned by the workers, a view that also contains a considerable element of validity.

This approach was adopted some decades ago after Yugoslavia had experimented with the rigid central planning methods of the Soviet Union. Those methods were very unsuccessful; and at about the same time that Yugoslavia broke politically with the Soviet Union, it abandoned them in favor of the worker cooperatives. The worker cooperatives have been far more successful than was rigid central planning. At the same time, they have been far less successful than a more nearly full-fledged free-market system. The first time we were in Yugoslavia, which was nearly twenty years ago, we were very much impressed by the contrast between our reaction and that of some other foreigners whom we met there. We went to Yugoslavia from the Soviet Union, and Yugoslavia struck us as a fairly prosperous and relatively open society. People we met there, however, who had gone to Yugoslavia from Austria thought that Yugoslavia was a very backward and unfree society.

It is worth examining more closely the problems with this approach because it seems very attractive. There has been much discussion in the West about the desirability of converting enterprises into worker-owned enterprises, and there have been a few examples in which such conversions have taken place. As you may know, when North West Industries owned the Chicago & North Western Railroad, which was losing money very rapidly, they found a profitable way to get rid of it by giving it to the workers, thereby establishing substantial tax reductions. As a result, the Chicago & North Western Railroad became a worker-owned enterprise, but not in the Yugoslav way because the workers actually had stock in the enterprise that they could dispose of and sell. In the Yugoslav case, workers do not have such shares.

The major defect of the Yugoslav approach arises from this difference in the linkage of property rights to employment status. Yugoslav workers have no separable or transferable rights to the productive enterprise. Workers are owners only as long as they are workers. If they terminate their employment, they no longer have any property rights or any rights to the income from the enterprise. As a result, a real capital market cannot exist. In line with the quotation that I read from Warren Nutter's article, both power and responsibility are dispersed; but there are no fully divisible and transferable property rights. The absence of such property rights rules out not only a capital market but also the possibility that private individuals can venture and innovate on anything but a minor scale, risking their own funds and reaping the rewards, without necessarily providing labor power themselves. That is possible in Yugoslavia on a very small scale, but nothing beyond that.

A few examples will show how this feature reduces the effectiveness of the system. Consider, for example, how workers are allocated among enterprises. Let us take an enterprise that happens to be highly successful. It is producing a product for which there is a good market; its receipts greatly exceed its costs. It is in the social interest that the enterprise be expanded, that it hire more workers. Each worker's reward consists not only of the value of the labor services that he contributes but also of his pro rata share of the returns attributable to the capital in the enterprise, whether that capital is in the tangible form of buildings and machines or in the intangible form of know-how and consumer goodwill. We can well understand that existing workers in such an enterprise will be reluctant to consent to the hiring of more workers because they will recognize that hiring additional workers would dilute the share of property income that each worker receives. As a result, successful enterprises are prevented from expanding. Workers who are not fortunate enough to be employed in such a successful enterprise must find employment in enterprises where their productive contribution is less. As an aside, we were fascinated to learn that one way in which managers of such enterprises have tried to offset this effect is by promoting nepotism; that is, when hiring additional workers, they give preference to the wives or the children of existing workers. In this way, they try to identify the incentives of the enterprise with the incentives of the workers.

Another aspect of the same problem is the absence of the right incentive for a worker to labor at the activity at which he is most productive. Consider a worker who could contribute more to the output of firm A, let us say, than to the output of firm B. Suppose, however, that firm A has little capital and earns little from its capital, whereas firm B has a great deal of capital and earns much that way. In consequence, if the worker can manage to work in firm B, he will have a higher income than if he works in firm A because he will share in a higher amount of property income, which will more than offset the lower value of the labor that he contributes. If he already works in firm B, he clearly has no incentive to shift to firm A, although that would be socially desirable.

A similar problem arises with respect to the use of the current profits of enterprises. A major decision that must be made by every enterprise is how to use its current profits, how much to devote to payments to its owners (in this case the workers), how much to set aside for investment and for building for the future. Under the Yugoslav system, current workers may not directly benefit from investment made for the future. That is especially true for older workers, and they are the ones who are likely to have achieved the greatest influence in the workers' councils. Who are the people who are elected to the workers' councils? They are not the young workers; they are the older workers. They are only going to work for a few more years, and so they are unlikely to favor investments that will not pay off for ten or fifteen years. As a result, workers have a strong incentive to press for the use of as large a fraction as possible of current profits for current benefits to current workers—in the form of direct bonuses, worker housing, or other benefits. Here again, one method that managers have tried to use to overcome this bias is nepotism. That is to say, enlisting the children of workers and the children's children in the enterprise provides the workers in the workers' council with an incentive to be concerned about the more distant future. That is far from a fully effective mechanism, however. The only fully effective mechanism would be to separate ownership from employment by giving the workers, or anyone else for that matter, transferable rights to the productive enterprise: that is, by making it a real, honest-to-God capitalist form of separable property right. Investment would then add to the value of these rights, and individuals could benefit currently from such investment.

Exactly the same problem limits the availability of risk capital. In general, investments in risky activities will pay off in the future and not in the present. Hence the bias against an investment in the future leads to a bias against investment of risk capital. Moreover, it is one thing for an individual by himself, or even for a few individuals who have common tastes and can join together, to undertake a major gamble. It is a very different thing for a large group of workers through a bureaucratic mechanism to justify engaging in risky activities. If one looks at Western capitalist societies, one sees that risky ventures have seldom been financed through banks; they have seldom been financed through major bureaucratic organizations, including the government—except, I should add, for some risky ventures that are almost sure to fail but that have strong political appeal. Risky ventures that seem to hold good promise of success but that are also very uncertain have almost invariably been financed by a small group of individuals risking their own funds or the funds of their relatives and friends.

The Yugoslavs have used banks and bank loans as a means of distributing capital. This arrangement does help; it does facilitate capital mobility and enable funds from a successful enterprise to be transferred to some extent to other enterprises that have promise of success but do not have the funds available. It is only a very partial substitute for a fully effective capital market, nonetheless. After all, the banks themselves are also worker cooperatives, and their employees have the same kinds of incentives to avoid risk as do the other bureaucratic enterprises.

Some Conclusions

Let me now try to draw some conclusions from these comments about the operation of the market and about what I think are the two leading methods proposed for giving market mechanisms a greater role in a centrally planned society—trying to have the enterprises play at capitalism, and trying to construct a restricted and modified form of capitalism.

Basically, the conclusion is that there is no really satisfactory substitute for a full-scale use of a free market. It does not follow, however, that it may not be desirable to depart from a completely free market. In the first place, efficiency in production is not the only goal that people have. All of us are willing to sacrifice some efficiency for other goals. In the second place, the market is simply incapable of doing some things. The market cannot provide national defense. For that purpose, it is essential to depart from the market, which also involves further interference with the market through the effects of the methods used for raising funds to finance national defense. Third, as we are all aware, the market operates defectively in those cases in which an important part of the effects of any transaction—either benefits or costs—impinges on parties other than those directly involved in the transaction, parties whom it is difficult to identify. This third factor, which has been labeled "neighborhood effects" or "externalities," is particularly troublesome because government attempts to deal with such externalities have typically turned out to do more harm than good. In principle, nonetheless, we cannot deny that there is a case for that kind of intervention.

There are no completely pure systems; every system is something of a mixed system that, on the one hand, includes command elements and, on the other, relies predominantly on voluntary cooperation. The problem is one of proportion, of keeping command elements to a minimum and, where they are introduced, of doing so in a way that interferes as little as possible with the operation of the market while achieving the objectives other than productive efficiency that are being sought.

I believe that the most important implication of this analysis is that even allegedly command economies will find it desirable to use free markets over as wide an area as is politically and economically possible. In particular, even for such collectivist societies as China, Russia, Yugoslavia, that area clearly includes much of agriculture and of retail trade, as well as small enterprises in manufacturing, mining, transportation, and communication. All three countries already practice this policy to some extent, but to a far smaller extent than would be feasible even while retaining centralized political control. Of course, every move in this direction does set up some sources of power independent of the central political authority, which is no doubt why collectivist countries have been so reluctant to move in this direction.

Second, insofar as the objective is to affect the distribution of income rather than to achieve particular production targets, the lesson of history is that it is better to do so through general taxes and subsidies rather than through interfering with the price system. That lesson applies to predominantly market economies such as our own as well as to command economies. In using taxes and subsidies, it is desirable to keep the marginal rates as low as possible. Countries in the West—the United States among others—have resorted to highly graduated rates; but although the rates are graduated on paper, they are not effective in practice. The millions of taxpayers, each seeking to reduce the taxes he must pay, have found effective ways to offset and evade the graduated rates.

The same principle applies to subsidization. Insofar as the political authorities want to assist particular groups of people, they should give them money rather than making available to them goods and services at artificially low prices. The groups will benefit more, and the system will be interfered with less. I may say that this point has been raising particular problems for China in the past year or two because their price structure is absurd, partly because they have tried to keep some prices of so-called necessities and the like very low. They have had great difficulty in trying to follow the Lange–Lerner advice to let those prices rise to more nearly what they would be in a free market. Their limited success in doing so has given rise to great complaints about inflation, a phenomenon with which we are all too familiar. If subsidies are given in money instead of in goods and services at artificially low prices, the recipients will benefit more, and the productive system will be interfered with less.

Third, for enterprises that remain state enterprises, the Lange–Lerner rule, although it cannot be fully effective because it cannot be properly monitored, nonetheless indicates the right direction for policy to take. Enterprises should be made responsible for their own behavior; their targets should be set in generalized terms of profits or money rather than in terms of specific physical outcomes. Let the enterprises bid separately for the resources they need, and let the prices be determined at a level that will equate demand and supply.

As I have already noted, the chief defect of all alternatives to an extensive use of free markets will be in the area of innovation, change, and progress, as we in the United States have been learning to our cost in recent years. Unfortunately or fortunately, depending on your point of view, in that area there is no effective substitute for permitting the private market really to flourish.

Finally, the major lesson that has impressed me as I have studied the economic policies and practices in various countries—whether fully capitalist, or mixed, or primarily collectivist—is that there is a difference between rhetoric and reality, between intentions and results. The prating in the collectivist economies about introducing market elements is mostly rhetoric. In China, we were enormously impressed by the contrast between rhetoric and reality. We read the pronouncements by Chairman Hua Guofeng about the plans for introducing greater market elements into the Chinese economy, about how enterprises were going to have greater freedom in distributing their products and in deciding what to invest, what to produce, and so on. In every factory we visited, we asked the people whom we interviewed —most were public relations people rather than the people who were really running the factory—"Do you know about the new economic policy that your government is proposing?" Yes, they all knew about it, and they were all able to describe it to me in great detail. Then I would ask the next question: "Tell me, how has that affected your particular firm?" "Oh," they would say, "it hasn't had a chance to affect us yet."

As the famous English writer Samuel Johnson put it two centuries ago, "the road to Hell is paved with good intentions." Or, if I may use one of my favorite quotations, as a deputy from Nemours at the French National Assembly at the time of the French Revolution put it in 1790 (I may add that deputy's name was Pierre S. Du Pont):

> Gentlemen, it is a disagreeable custom to which one is easily led by the harshness of the discussions, to assume evil intentions. It is necessary to be gracious as to intentions; one should believe them good, and apparently they are; but we do not have to be gracious at all to inconsistent logic or to absurd reasoning. Bad logicians have committed more involuntary crimes than bad men have done intentionally.

Thank you.

Questions and Answers

PROFESSOR SIDNEY HOOK, Hoover Institution: How would you evaluate the German and Scandinavian systems of co-determination? Isn't that a way of introducing a cooperative element affecting the structure of the economy?

PROFESSOR FRIEDMAN: If we carry it to its extreme, it would be the Yugoslav system. That is to say, in the Yugoslav system we have an elected workers' council that in principle is elected by the body of workers, and it appoints a manager. I must say, one of the fascinating things to me when we were in Yugoslavia and we walked around factories with the managers was that the deferential attitudes of the workers toward the managers seemed to me no whit different from what we would observe in a Western country when a boss is walking around the factory and the workers are kowtowing to him. I did not notice an iota of difference. The workers' council does appoint the manager, however—he is appointed for a specific term—and that is in principle where the German co-determination system would go if it were carried to its logical conclusion.

What has happened at the moment, as you know, is that in the German system the workers have a minority of the votes; they do not have the final deciding vote. They usually have a group of workers' representatives (they are really not workers' representatives but representatives of the trade union), and then they have managers' representatives. It is set up so that the managers' representatives hold the deciding votes. I believe, however, this system is a very undesirable one that has exactly the same kinds of problems as those I pointed out for Yugoslavia, except, at the moment, only to a partial extent. It is exactly the same problem that we have in this country with Mr. Frazer on the board of the Chrysler Corporation. He has conflicting interests, and he cannot represent both parties. Exactly that same conflict arises with the workers in co-determination. Take a case in which an enterprise in Germany is doing very well and has good profits, and it would be desirable for it to hire more workers. If it hires more workers, that will dilute the amount of money that it will be able to pay existing workers. Which option will the workers' representatives go for: a higher wage for the workers now there, or a larger number of workers at a lower wage? Still, the wage for the additional workers would be higher than that which those workers could get in second or third industries.

PROFESSOR HOOK: Presumably if they are going to hire more workers, it is in the expectation of making more money.

PROFESSOR FRIEDMAN: It depends on what wage they are paid. You cannot get out of it that way. You have an alternative, Professor Hook. You are running the factory, and you can either keep the price high, pay a high wage to a limited number of workers, and sell a small amount, or you can lower the price, sell a larger amount, and hire more workers at a relatively lower wage. You cannot get something for nothing out of that. What would the workers' representatives favor? They will be in favor of promoting the interests of current workers. It is not an accident that the two industries in the United States that are in the greatest difficulties, namely, automobiles and steel, are both strongly unionized; and both have wages that on the average are roughly twice as high as the average wage of all the other workers in the country. That wage may have been appropriate at one time, but it is no longer appropriate in the present competitive situation. The unions are very resistant to what would be an appropriate solution from the point of view of the country as a whole.

Sweden represents a more complicated situation because until a few years ago it was essentially a free-trade country that had very low tariffs. International competition was providing the same discipline that competition within a nation provides. In the past five or six years, however, Sweden has experienced increasingly greater difficulties. The government has been bailing out enterprises, and the system of so-called joint worker-employer-government negotiation of wage rates and so on has been coming apart at the seams.

I think the evidence is very unfavorable both to the German system of co-determination and to the Swedish system of joint bargaining by employer and employees.

QUESTION: Perhaps the greatest success story of the past twenty-five years is Japan, and they have neither a classical labor market nor a capital market, I would think. What is your comment on that?

PROFESSOR FRIEDMAN: I do not believe you are right. I believe they have both a labor market and a capital market. Whether it is a "classical" market is a question of semantics. As I emphasized, all systems are mixed. As it happens, I know the Japanese situation rather well. My basic conclusion about Japan is that any statement we make about Japan that is true has an opposite statement that is equally true. If we say that Japan does not have a classical labor market, we are right. They do have lifetime employment in a certain class of enterprise. If we say they have a classical labor market, we are also right. It turns out that they are able to maintain lifetime employment because those enterprises engage in a great deal of subcontracting and buying from suppliers. Those smaller enterprises, subcontractors, and suppliers do not themselves have lifetime employment. They have an essentially classical labor market. In addition, Japan practices retirement at age fifty-five, a very early age. After retirement at age fifty-five, people typically do not go out of the labor market. They remain in the labor market, but they then are paid wages that are in accordance with their productivity in an essentially free labor market rather than in the other kind of labor market.

Similarly, when we come to capital, there is a big difference among the institutions in Japan. Banks have played a different role in Japan than they have played in the United States; they have been active participants in the financing of many enterprises. This is really a carry-over from the Zaibatsu organizations in which a group of enterprises, of banks and so on, worked together to form a close conglomerate. At the same time, it is fascinating to look at some of the real success stories in Japan. For example, Honda, Sony, and quite a number of the other successful enterprises were not financed by banks at all. They are typical of the ordinary American kind of development in which a private entrepreneur develops a small enterprise into a large enterprise by being successful. Bank financing has tended to dominate the older, more established, more basic industries.

We have an image of Japan Incorporated as being government-industry collaboration. Again, that is true, and the opposite is also true. A very simple thing makes that arrangement work in Japan: It is retirement at age fifty-five, with the top officials in the government bureaus then going to work for the private enterprises they were connected with before. That is what transfers the private incentives to the political level.

It is a very much more complicated picture than it looks on the surface. The success of Japan, in my opinion, has unquestionably been associated not with the elements that seem deviant from the market but with those that are like it. When we look at the history of Japanese growth, for example, we find that the period from 1867 to 1914 —that is, the period after the Meiji Restoration—was a time of very rapid growth. The interwar period was a time of slow growth or stagnation. The period after World War II shows a resumption of the rapid growth that prevailed before World War I.

The years before World War I were a time of essentially free trade and of very little government involvement or intervention. From 1867 to 1897, Japan was prevented by international treaty from imposing tariffs of more than 5 percent, and so it was an essentially free market. Between the wars, the militarists took over and ran a collectivist society. There were severe restrictions on the free market, and there was slow growth. In the postwar period, particularly after 1950 when the Dodge Plan was implemented, there was again very rapid growth; and I believe that is again attributable to the prevalence of a predominantly free market with relatively limited intervention by the state.

QUESTION: What was the reaction of your Chinese audience to this lecture?

PROFESSOR FRIEDMAN: They were very much interested in it. In fact, I gave four lectures there; and this was by all odds the one in which they were most interested because it was most immediately relevant to their situation, although they were also very much interested in the discussion of inflation because that is also a current problem for them. It is hard to answer your question about their reaction, however, because appearances are so deceptive. When you are there and are standing before a group, your first impression is that everybody is speaking freely, that you are having the kind of discussion you might have here, with a wide range of opinions being expressed. Then, if you compare what is being said with the published statements about policy, you discover that it is all within very firm guidelines. At the time we were there, to an even greater extent than now because there has been some backsliding, those guidelines stressed the importance of introducing greater market elements into the economy. Thus they were very much interested in those elements, and they were particularly taken with the Yugoslav example. That has a strong appeal to them, much more than the Lange–Lerner approach does. In this sense, they were very much interested; but I cannot say that I got any valid feeling for what their true beliefs or values were.

ROSE FRIEDMAN: The other point is that they really did not know what a free market is, even after your lecture.

PROFESSOR FRIEDMAN: That's true—and I hope not because of the lecture. My wife's and my favorite story about that has to do with a minister from the Ministry for Materials Distribution and his chief associate who came to the lecture and subsequently took us to lunch because they were scheduled to be part of a group that was coming to the United States shortly thereafter. They did come and indeed visited the Hoover Institution. Some of you may have spoken with them. During our lunch after the lecture, they wanted to know whom they should see and talk to in the United States. The first question they asked us was: "Tell us, who in the United States is responsible for the distribution of materials?" Now as my wife says, that really showed an understanding of a market system. Dr. Freeman?

DR. ROGER FREEMAN, Hoover Institution: It is my impression that in China there has been very little practical progress toward establishing a market system in large enterprises, but there have been a few approaches in smaller ones. Most of the restaurants now are worker cooperatives, and it was my impression that they really tried very hard to attract customers and to please them. It is also true in small repair shops. It is true in agricultural co-ops. They are also, of course, very interested in producing the most because everybody participates in it. In the Soviet Union there were attempts, as you know, under the Liberman system fifteen years ago, to provide some incentives. I would appreciate hearing your impressions of what the varying effects of the Liberman initiatives have been where, of course, the bureaucracy at first pulled back and then after a few years again charged in and took over.

PROFESSOR FRIEDMAN: I cannot answer your question about the Soviet Union. I only know very vaguely that the most successful applications of the Liberman or Lange–Lerner approaches seem not to have been in the Soviet Union but in Hungary. I gather that Hungary has gone farther in this respect than most of the others, but this is all very secondhand. I have no direct evidence. I have not been in the Soviet Union for eighteen years; I have never been in Hungary; I do not read either Hungarian or Russian; and so I have no confidence whatsoever in anything I could say about that. If there were any good results, they seem not to have had any very long-lasting impact, certainly not in the Soviet Union.

DR. FREEMAN: Where they have had it is in some of their state-run stores. The bonus system has had considerable impact there in interesting the clerks and the managers.

PROFESSOR FRIEDMAN: In China we were interested in many of the same things that you are talking about. First of all, apparently for the first time, we were told, there were people on the streets who were selling something. They were very few and far between. They had to get a permit to do so, and we were told that the permits were being given to two classes of people. They have no unemployment; they only have "pre-employed" youth. Permits were being given to the pre-employed youth and also to the superannuated, and they were being permitted to sell at these street markets. They also had small-scale free markets, as you know. There was a very active outside market in the cooperative that we visited and also at several other places. So you are quite right that there is some element of this kind; but it is, as you say, very much limited to small enterprises. We could see almost no effect in the small number of larger enterprises that we visited. There it was all talk and no substance.

QUESTION: It may interest you to know that probably some of the same people you met in China came to the United States and went to the Department of Commerce with the same question. Their hosts were somewhat nonplussed when they insisted; and they were finally shown one spot, the General Services Administration.

PROFESSOR FRIEDMAN: Well I will tell you the answer I gave to them. I told them they should go to the Chicago Board of Trade and watch the trading for corn. I don't know whether they did that; but I can well believe that if they were shown the GSA, they had our very best example, and so that's good.

PROFESSOR CAMPBELL: It appears to me that the argument really boils down to how much of a command you have to have in a market system if you want to have national security and you want to have roads. Right now we have a system set up that attempts to determine how much command ought to be in the system; and they sit in Washington, D.C., and make decisions with which we may or may not agree. The real question is, What kind of system can we put to our representatives that tells them how far they ought to go, what method they ought to use when the market will not work for them, and how they can sell it to a constituency?

PROFESSOR FRIEDMAN: I think the founding fathers who drew up our Constitution tried to answer your question at the Constitutional Convention. I believe that fundamentally the only answer is to try to establish a self-denying ordinance on the part of the populace at large, narrowly limiting activities to certain areas through political mechanisms. I believe the attempt was made under the Constitution, through a whole series of measures, to restrict the scope and power of the federal government, certainly in comparison with the state and local governments. That attempt was very successful until about fifty years ago when it began to break down. I am no lawyer, but many legal scholars will say that it has broken down because of a defect not in the Constitution but rather in the way in which the Constitution was interpreted in the courts. Of course, as Mr. Dooley said, the Supreme Court follows the election returns; and so the breakdown, if it was a breakdown, was not because of any evil people trying to change the character of the system; it was in response to popular will. That is why the fundamental self-denying ordinance is not expressed on a piece of paper. It is expressed in the attitudes and the beliefs of the populace. Unless the populace at large accepts the idea that the role of government should be very narrowly limited to certain specific functions such as national defense, I do not think that you can achieve those limits with any pieces of paper or by giving power to a court or anything like that. I think it has to come out of the general will.

PROFESSOR CAMPBELL: The real problem comes once you have admitted that there is something the government has to do that is not a pricing mechanism within the overall system and that it has to provide national defense and that it has to provide roads. Then, let us say, we cannot retrain workers as fast as the ideal system would when we dislocate them; and perhaps we have to give them some money. The question is, How do we know where to stop?

PROFESSOR FRIEDMAN: We cannot. I do not believe that there is any way in which we can have a hard-and-fast formula. I think we can state the principles on which we want to judge the activities (they can be hard-and-fast), but I think in any particular case we are always in the position of drawing up a balance sheet. I cannot go along with the people who believe that it would be possible to abolish the government altogether and to have a completely anarchist-capitalist system. I wish I could believe it, but I do not believe it. I do not think it can be done. I think you are asking for a hard-and-fast formula where a hard-and-fast formula is not possible. For example, consider the kind of activity you are talking about—training dislocated workers. Surely your attitude toward it would be one thing if government was absorbing 5 percent of the national income and a very different thing if government was already absorbing 35 percent.

The problem is that it is easier to avoid an activity than to eliminate one already undertaken. Every time government undertakes an activity, that tends to create a class of people with strong vested interests in the activity's continuation. There are always many apparently worthy proposals; and so if even a small fraction are accepted, government tends to grow and grow. Now for that very reason many people have believed that a free market and a free society are fundamentally unstable positions of equilibrium, and that may be true. I do not think we can rule out that possibility. If we look back in history, we have had free markets and free societies only over a very small part of the globe at any time and only for very short periods in any one part of the globe. We know that just simply writing a constitution doesn't do it. Some of the South American countries have constitutions that are word for word identical with ours, but the results are vastly different. We cannot rule out the possibility that, for the kinds of reasons you are citing, it is an accident and an aberration if we happen to get a free society and that it is an unstable state of equilibrium that will sooner or later change. I trust that is not true, obviously; and all of us in this room have been working as hard as we can to see that it is not true. I must say I think that many of the fears that people have are not confirmed by the evidence. The great fear has always been that the have-nots would vote themselves benefits at the expense of the haves, and that is not what has happened. Look at the referendums, which are a sign of public opinion. If we look at the referendums on state constitutional amendments and so on that have been conducted around the country during the past fifty years, we see on the whole that they have been less redistributionist and much more in line with limiting government than the actual actions of legislatures have been. In the past few years, for example, a number of states have had measures on the ballot to increase the graduation of the income tax, and they invariably have been defeated. Connecticut had a measure on the ballot to impose a graduated income tax, and it was voted down. Massachusetts had a measure that would have increased the graduation; it was voted down; and so on down the line. I do not think that one needs to despair of the possibility of having a public understanding of what is involved. We are having another test right now, I think. One more question, and then we had better stop.

QUESTION: You drew a sharp distinction between a command economy and a price economy. I am just wondering whether on the theoretical level there really is such a sharp distinction. Suppose you were a Martian, and you came down to Earth. You couldn't really land on Earth; you could only hover. You couldn't see too well or hear, and you couldn't see that money was being exchanged. You would look at Russia and would see people taking part in their little activities, and in America they would be doing that, too. You could not tell, really, which country had a price system. The question occurs to me whether you think a command economy has an implicit price system there in the background. Even in the United States a lot of people will say that there is something like an auctioneer behind those people and will wonder whether it is not an implicit price system. Then the question is, If those are really thought of as price systems, what is really different about those two systems?

PROFESSOR FRIEDMAN: I did not make the distinction between a command system and a price system. I made the distinction between a command system and a market system. In a market system, prices serve certain functions. In a command system, one may also have prices that serve functions; one has shadow prices of the kind about which you are talking. The distinction I made was not at all command versus price; it was command versus market. For example, I regard the system for the development of scientific knowledge as a market system, but it is not a price system. If we look at it, the development of science has not come from commands given by a central authority concerning who should work on what topic. The development has come from the voluntary cooperation of people who were pursuing their own self-interest. That is a market system, but it is definitely not a price system in the ordinary sense.

Concerning your question, I am not sure a Martian can tell the difference because I do not think the difference is manifest in the things that a Martian could observe. That does not mean there is not any difference. I cannot even see those Martians on Mars, but that does not mean they are not there. I believe you are making a more fundamental point that I will agree with, and it is that in a static, repetitive system, you could not tell the difference; nobody could tell the difference. If we had a system in which the basic conditions remained unchanged and in which life was a simple repetition of one cycle after another, there would be absolutely no way whatsoever that we could tell the difference between a command economy, a price system, a market system, or any other system. All we would observe would be the same phenomena repeating themselves ad infinitum. There would be no money in such a system, of course; so we would not observe any money flows. All we would have would be flows of services and goods. I have tended to emphasize the role of innovation, change, and development because I think we tend to see the difference more clearly in a world that is dynamic and subject to change and not static, stationary, and repetitive. In this case the fundamental question is whether or not the acts that people undertake are voluntary, and the answer is not going to be observed in the flows of goods and services. The answer must be found in a different dimension of observation.

How Should Economists Choose?

R. H. Coase

November 18, 1981

R. H. COASE was on the faculty of the London School of Economics from 1935 to 1951. He then migrated to the United States to become professor of economics at the University of Buffalo. In 1959 he became professor of economics at the University of Virginia and in 1964 professor of economics at the University of Chicago Law School. He is now Clifton R. Musser Professor emeritus.

Introduction

Kenneth G. Elzinga

I count it a privilege to introduce the speaker for the third G. Warren Nutter Lecture in Political Economy, sponsored jointly by the Thomas Jefferson Center Foundation and the American Enterprise Institute.

Our speaker is Professor Ronald Coase of the University of Chicago.

Ronald Coase was born in Willesden, England, on December 29, 1910, and was educated at the London School of Economics. There he enrolled in the industry and trade curriculum, which exposed him to both economic theory and the detailed study of business and legal institutions. Apart from wartime service with the British government, Coase has spent his career in the world of books and ideas. In Britain he served on the faculties of the Dundee School of Economics and Commerce, the University of Liverpool, and his alma mater. In 1951 Coase moved to the United States, where he has held appointments at the University of Buffalo, the University of Virginia, and the University of Chicago.

For me to review Ronald Coase's academic accomplishments, for this audience, is probably pointless. We all know that he is one of the founders of the discipline of law and economics. It is no revelation to us that he recently became a distinguished fellow of the American Economic Association. No one here would be surprised to learn that his article on social cost[1] is one of the two most frequently cited scholarly papers in all of economics literature. The stature becoming the *Journal of Law and Economics* during Coase's editorship is obvious. And many of us probably know that when an all-star football team of economists, drawn from all generations, was selected, it was only natural for the "coach" to select Coase as the

---

1. "The Problem of Social Cost," *Journal of Law and Economics*, vol. 3, no. 1 (1960).

quarterback because of his knowledge of the game and overall versatility.[2]

But there is a personal side to our speaker that I want to address briefly in my introduction as well.

Ronald, perhaps more than any living economist, understands cost, and not only academically. There is an episode in his life that is sobering to hear if you are an admirer of the Chicago school. Coase once lunched at the faculty club of the University of Chicago and heard some economic eminences announce that because of certain ongoing events in financial markets and because of the quantity theory of money, it was inevitable that interest rates would soon go down. Coase listened attentively and after lunch bought bonds. Lots of bonds. Almost before he hung up the phone, interest rates rose smartly and stayed there. Coase, economist to the end, recognized that as the most expensive lunch he had ever had.

More than most economists today, Coase is widely read. I recall a time when I saw on a bookshelf in his office a two-volume work by Chadwick entitled *The Health of Nations*. A catchy title, I thought, and I asked our speaker about the book. Coase inquired whether it was really true that I did not know Chadwick's work. I said I did not. Whereupon Coase, frank in a manner that only the English can be, simply said, "That's a weakness, you know." I must confess it is one I still have.

Ronald Coase has a nose for facts, especially if they pertain to his heroes Adam Smith and Alfred Marshall. He considers one of his main contributions to economic thought correcting the date of a photograph of Marshall in an edition of Marshall's *Principles*. Ronald knew that the date shown could not be correct because Marshall, during that year, was not sporting the shape of moustache shown by the picture.

In Ronald Coase, the economics profession has a member who combines mental prowess and originality with personal charm and a prepossessing demeanor.

The talk our speaker will give is in honor of G. Warren Nutter—at one time a friend, or a teacher, or a colleague of each of us here. Ronald Coase is a fitting speaker for this lecture series. Coase and Nutter were colleagues at the University of Virginia for several years and remained friends after Coase went to Chicago. Each very much admired the work of the other. In thinking about these introductory

---

2. S. C. Littlechild, "Economics All-Stars v. Rest of the World," Inaugural Lecture, October 25, 1973.

remarks, I got out some notes Warren had written to me concerning some research I was doing about Coase. And I was reminded of the high regard Nutter had for Coase, as economist and friend.

We continue to miss Warren, as a friend, as a scholar and counselor, and as a champion of liberty. But in his untimely absence it is apt that he can be honored today with the G. Warren Nutter memorial lecture being presented by his friend Ronald Coase.

Professor Coase will speak to us on the question: How Should Economists Choose?

How Should Economists Choose?

R. H. Coase

I had a close relationship with Warren Nutter at the University of Virginia. I came to admire him for the thoroughness with which he carried out his researches, for the conscientiousness with which he performed his academic duties, and for the courage he displayed in doing what he believed to be right. Warren Nutter was an excellent economist, which is rare, but he was something rarer still, a truly moral man. Frank Knight, who was so much admired by Warren Nutter, tells us that the "basic principle of science—truth or objectivity—is essentially a moral principle, in opposition to any form of self-interest. The presuppositions of objectivity are integrity, competence and humility."[1] Integrity, competence, and humility—these three qualities sum up Warren Nutter's character. He knew that in economic affairs people are mainly motivated by self-interest, but he did not believe that this was their sole motivation and certainly he thought it should not be. In his own actions, Warren Nutter cared as much for others as he did for himself. As a colleague and friend, I knew him to be utterly reliable. It is our good fortune that he devoted himself to the service of economics. We are all in his debt. To have been asked to deliver one of the Warren Nutter memorial lectures is a great privilege. But it is not easy to prepare a lecture of a standard that will truly honor Warren Nutter's memory. There is also the problem of choosing a topic appropriate to the occasion. On this score, however, I believe I have succeeded and that Warren Nutter would have found the questions I will be discussing of great interest and would have treated my point of view with sympathy.

Many economists, perhaps most, think of economics as the sci-

---

1. Frank H. Knight, *Freedom and Reform* (New York: Harper & Brothers, 1947), p. 244.

ence of human choice, and it seems only proper that we should examine how economists themselves choose the theories they espouse. The best-known treatment of this question is that of Milton Friedman, who, in the "Methodology of Positive Economics," his most popular paper, in itself a somewhat suspicious circumstance, tells us "how to decide whether a suggested hypothesis or theory should be tentatively accepted as part of" the positive science of economics. As you all know, the answer he gives is that the worth of a theory "is to be judged by the precision, scope, and conformity with experience of the predictions it yields. . . . The ultimate goal of a positive science is the development of a 'theory' or 'hypothesis' that yields valid and meaningful . . . predictions about phenomena not yet observed."[2]

I should say at once that I do not consider Milton Friedman's answer satisfactory. At this point, I fear that many in this audience will be inclined to regard this statement as lese majesty. But I hasten to reassure them by saying that it is my belief that my way of looking at this question is more consonant with Friedman's general position as expressed in *Capitalism and Freedom* or *Free to Choose* than with that found in "The Methodology of Positive Economics." I should add that I am in no sense well informed in the philosophy of science. Words like epistemology do not come tripping from my tongue. What I have to say consists of reflections based on what I have observed about the actual practice of economists.

The view that the worth of a theory is to be judged solely by the extent and accuracy of its predictions seems to me wrong. Of course, any theory has implications: it tells us that if something happens, something else will follow, and it is true that most of us would not value the theory if we did not think these implications corresponded to happenings in the real economic system. But a theory is not like an airline or bus timetable. We are not interested simply in the accuracy of its predictions. A theory also serves as a base for thinking. It helps us to understand what is going on by enabling us to organize our thoughts. Faced with a choice between a theory which predicts well but gives us little insight into how the system works and one which gives us this insight but predicts badly, I would choose the latter, and I am inclined to think that most economists would do the same. No doubt it would be their belief that ultimately this theory would enable us to make predictions about

---

2. Milton Friedman, "The Methodology of Positive Economics," in *Essays in Positive Economics* (Chicago: University of Chicago Press, 1953), pp. 3, 4, 7.

what would happen in the real world; but since these predictions would emerge at a later date (and probably would also be about different things), to assert that the choice between theories depends on their predictive powers becomes completely ambiguous.

Friedman enlarges his argument by maintaining that theories are not to be judged by whether their assumptions are realistic. Let me quote what he says:

> Consider the density of leaves around a tree. I suggest the hypothesis that the leaves are positioned as if each leaf deliberately sought to maximize the amount of sunlight it receives, given the position of its neighbors, as if it knew the physical laws determining the amount of sunlight that would be received in various positions and could move rapidly or instantaneously from any one position to any other desired and unoccupied position. . . . Despite the apparent falsity of the "assumptions" of the hypothesis, it has great plausibility because of the conformity of its implications with observation.[3]

Let us suppose that it is true that the assumption that a leaf subscribes to *Scientific American* and the *Journal of Molecular Biology* and that it understands what is contained therein enables us to predict what the distribution of leaves around a tree will be. Such a theory nonetheless provides a very poor basis for thinking about leaves (or trees). Our problem is to explain how leaves come to be distributed on a tree given that a leaf does not have a brain. Similarly, to take an example in economics, we could have predicted over the last few years what the American government's policies on oil and natural gas would be if we had assumed that the aim of the American government was to increase the power and income of the OPEC countries and to reduce the standard of living in the United States. But I am sure that we would prefer a theory that explains why the American government, which presumably did not want to bring about these results, was led to adopt policies which harmed American interests. Testable predictions are not all that matters. And realism in our assumptions is needed if our theories are ever to help us understand why the system works in the way it does. Realism in assumptions forces us to analyze the world that exists, not some imaginary world that does not.

It is, of course, true that our assumptions should not be com-

3. Ibid., pp. 19, 20.

pletely realistic. There are factors we leave out because we do not know how to handle them. There are others we exclude because we do not feel the benefits of a more complete theory would be worth the costs involved in including them. Their inclusion might, for example, greatly complicate the analysis without giving us greater understanding about what is going on. Again, assumptions about other factors do not need to be realistic because they are completely irrelevant. If we wish to show that enforcement of a minimum wage will lead to unemployment among less productive workers, it is unnecessary to be accurate about the exact way in which capital gains are taxed. There are good reasons why the assumptions of our theories should not be completely realistic, but this does not mean that we should lose touch with reality.

I now turn to what is, from my point of view, the strangest aspect of "The Methodology of Positive Economics." It is that what we are given is not a positive theory at all. It is, I believe, best interpreted as a normative theory. What we are given is not a theory of how economists, in fact, choose between competing theories but, unless I am completely mistaken, how they ought to choose. When Friedman says that the "ultimate goal of a positive science is the development of a 'theory' or 'hypothesis' that yields valid and mean-ingful . . . predictions about phenomena not yet observed," I cannot help mentioning that a science has no goals, only individuals have goals. What has to be shown if Friedman's criteria are to be accepted as a positive theory is that individual economists actually choose among competing theories according to these criteria. I will show the difficulty of interpreting Friedman's argument in this way by considering three episodes, all of which occurred in my youth and which, unlike more recent events, I remember vividly. These are episodes in the 1930s in which economists changed their views, that is, changed the theories they espoused. I will mainly be discussing what happened in economics in England, but these were times when, to a very considerable extent, this was what happened in economics.

The first episode I will discuss is local, but the economists in-volved were among the best in the world. In February 1931 Hayek gave a series of public lectures, entitled "Prices and Production," at the London School of Economics, and in September 1931 these lec-tures were published as a book. They were undoubtedly the most successful set of public lectures given at LSE during my time there, even surpassing the brilliant lectures Viner gave on international trade theory. The audience, notwithstanding the difficulties of under-standing Hayek, was enthralled. What was said seemed to us of great importance and made us see things of which we had previously been unaware. After hearing these lectures, we knew why there was a depression. Most students of economics at LSE and many members of the staff became Hayekians or, at any rate, incorporated elements of Hayek's approach in their own thinking. With the arrogance of youth, I myself expounded the Hayekian analysis to the faculty and students at Columbia University in the fall of 1931. What now strikes me as odd is the ease with which Hayek conquered LSE. I think this was in part the result of a lack of precision in the existing analysis or, at any rate, in our grasp of it, so that Hayek's analysis seemed to give a well-organized and fruitful way of thinking about the working of the economic system as a whole. As far as I can see, the Hayekian analysis did not make predictions except in the sense that it explained why there was a depression. What can be said is that the analysis seemed to be consistent with everything we observed. To show that this was so, Robbins published in 1934 *The Great Depression*, the only one of his works, as he tells us, that he wishes he had not written.[4]

The next episode I will consider was by no means local, although I viewed it from the London School of Economics. It was a worldwide phenomenon. This was the Keynesian revolution. I will not labor its importance—that is conceded by the great majority of economists. I need only quote the statement of Hicks: "The Keynesian revolution is the obvious example of a big revolution [in economics]; there are not more than two or three others which might conceivably be compared to it."[5] While in the case of Hayek I thought (incorrectly) that I understood what was going on, I was never under such an illusion in the case of Keynes. By that time, I was wholly absorbed in what is now called microeconomics. What I mainly remember from this period is that everything I said on the subject was wrong because savings equaled investment. Fortunately I am not concerned so much with the substance of Keynes's *General Theory* as with the circumstances of its acceptance by the economics profession. For there can be no question that Keynes triumphed. Nor did it take very long. The *General Theory* was published in February 1936. Although some of the early reviews were hostile or lukewarm, it was soon apparent that the economics profession was, for the most part, going to adopt the Keynesian approach. Lerner, for example, published his influ-

4. Lord Robbins, *Autobiography of an Economist* (London: Macmillan, 1971), pp. 154, 160.

5. Sir John Hicks, " 'Revolutions' in Economics," in Spiro Latsis, ed., *Method and Appraisal in Economics* (Cambridge: Cambridge University Press, 1976), p. 208.

ential account of the Keynesian system in the *International Labour Review* in October 1936. As Samuelson has said:

> The *General Theory* caught most economists under the age of thirty-five with the unexpected virulence of a disease first attacking and decimating an isolated tribe of South Sea islanders. Economists beyond fifty turned out to be quite immune to the ailment. With time, most economists in between began to run the fever, often without knowing or admitting their condition.[6]

I cannot vouch for the accuracy of Samuelson's account of the difference in the response of economists in the United States to Keynes's *General Theory* according to their age, but it has very little relevance to events in England; there were, in fact, very few economists there who were older than fifty in 1936. Among those who were at Cambridge or were associated with Keynes when the *General Theory* appeared, apart from Keynes himself, who was fifty-two, only Pigou was over fifty, and he proved not to be immune to the Keynesian disease, as Samuelson describes it. Robertson was then forty-five, Harrod thirty-six, Mrs. Robinson thirty-two, Kahn thirty, Meade twenty-eight. The economists at the London School of Economics were even younger. Robbins was thirty-seven, Hayek thirty-six, Hicks thirty-one, Lerner thirty-two, and Kaldor twenty-seven at the time the *General Theory* was published. Whether the acceptance of Keynes's system of analysis was or was not affected by the age distribution of economists in Britain, its success was such that by the outbreak of war in 1939, it could be said to be the orthodox approach among British economists. In fact, Robbins, as director of the Economics Section of the War Cabinet Office, enthusiastically supported the proposals in the White Paper on Employment Policy, issued in 1944. And Beveridge, who had attacked the *General Theory* in 1937 as theory untested by facts, was to publish his *Full Employment in a Free Society*, also in 1944, assisted by a number of Keynesians, including Kaldor.

This swift adoption of the Keynesian system came about, I believe, because its analysis in terms of the determinants of effective demand seemed to get to the essence of what was going on in the economic system and was easier to understand (at least in its broad outlines) than alternative theories. That the Keynesian system offered a cure for unemployment without requiring any sacrifices, provided

---

6. Paul A. Samuelson, "The General Theory," in Robert Lekachman, ed., *Keynes' General Theory: Reports of Three Decades* (New York: St. Martin's Press, 1964), pp. 315–16.

a clearly defined role for government and a policy easy to carry out (as it then appeared), added to its attractiveness. It can hardly be maintained that the Keynesian analysis was adopted because it yielded accurate "predictions about phenomena not yet observed." It is true that Keynes claimed to demonstrate that the economic system could function in such a way as to bring about persistent mass unemployment. But mass unemployment could not be described in the 1930s as a phenomenon "not yet observed." And it is not without relevance that the alternative theory that was displaced, at any rate at the London School of Economics, was that of Hayek, which also explained why the economic system could operate in such a way as to lead to mass unemployment. Keynes's analysis was adopted in the main because it seemed to make more sense to most economists. Or, as I put it earlier, it provided a better base for thinking about the problems of the working of the economic system as a whole. And to those economists who were less concerned about the niceties of the analysis, Keynes's policy recommendations undoubtedly provided a sufficient reason for many of them to adopt his theory and to reject that of Hayek.

The third episode is concerned with the change in the way in which economists analyzed the working of a competitive system following the publication in 1933 of Chamberlin's *Theory of Monopolistic Competition* and Mrs. Robinson's *Economics of Imperfect Competition*. These books were, as Stigler has said, "enthusiastically received."[7] Bishop exaggerated somewhat, but not perhaps a great deal, when he said, writing in 1964, that it was "the consensus of economists" that these two books "touched off, in 1933, a theoretical revolution whose relative importance in the microeconomic area was comparable to that of the Keynesian analysis in macroeconomics."[8] These books were certainly an instant success, and their contents were quickly absorbed and used by economists interested in price theory. As an example, although these books only appeared in 1933, I had completed by mid-1934 a paper in which I used the geometrical analysis of Mrs. Robinson to illuminate and extend Chamberlin's treatment of duopoly and had corresponded with both Chamberlin and Mrs. Robinson. This paper was published in the *Review of Economic Studies* in 1935. At about the same time Kaldor wrote his article

7. George J. Stigler, "Monopolistic Competition in Retrospect," in *Five Lectures on Economic Problems* (London: London School of Economics and Longmans, Green and Co., 1949), p. 12.

8. Robert L. Bishop, "The Theory of Imperfect Competition after Twenty Years: The Impact on General Theory," *American Economic Review*, vol. 54 (May 1964), p. 33.

on "Market Imperfection and Excess Capacity," which was also published in 1935, in *Economica*. I have no doubt that there was similar activity in the United States among economists writing on price theory.

The speedy adoption of these new approaches was in large part due to the very unsatisfactory state of the existing price theory. That this was so had been demonstrated beyond doubt by the controversies in the *Economic Journal* in the 1920s and perhaps above all by Sraffa's 1926 article. We were therefore looking for ways to solve the dilemmas these discussions revealed. These new books by Chamberlin and Mrs. Robinson, which started the analysis with the decisions of the individual firm and used new tools such as the marginal revenue schedule, seemed to offer the way out. They certainly gave us a lot to put on the blackboard and to explain to our students. They enlarged our analytical apparatus. They seemed to give us a better understanding of how a competitive system works, but whether this was really so is another matter.

My own view of the contribution of these books is not essentially different from that expressed by Stigler in his "Monopolistic Competition in Retrospect," published in 1949. But what is particularly interesting and useful, given the questions I am discussing, is that Stigler also appraised Chamberlin's theory of monopolistic competition using Friedman's methodological principles. He argued that Chamberlin's theory should be adopted "if it contains different or more accurate predictions (as tested by observation) than the theory of competition." His personal belief was that "the predictions of [the] standard model of monopolistic competition differ only in unimportant respects from those of the theory of competition." He added, however, that "this is a question of fact, and it must be resolved by empirical tests of the implications of the two theories (a task the supporters of the theory of monopolistic competition have not yet undertaken)."[9] The fact that supporters of the theory of monopolistic competition had not made empirical tests comparing the predictions of the alternative theories of competition (and, I may add, do not appear to have made such tests in the years since Stigler wrote) lends support to the view that Friedman's methodology is not a positive but a normative theory. Certainly this is the way that Stigler used it. Stigler was not saying that supporters of the theory of monopolistic competition made such tests but did them badly and so came to the wrong conclusion. He was saying that they did not make them at all. Since they should have done so, this merits our disapproval.

---

9. Stigler, "Monopolistic Competition," p. 24.

If choosing theories in accordance with Friedman's criteria is to be treated as a positive theory, economists would need to adopt a procedure somewhat similar to the following. When a new theory is advanced, economists would compare the accuracy of its predictions, preferably about "phenomena not yet observed," with those of the existing theory and would choose that theory which gave the best predictions. Nothing remotely resembling this procedure happened during the three episodes that I discussed, two of which are recognized as having involved very important changes indeed in economic theory. For one thing, in each case the new theory was adopted within a time period too short for such a procedure to be followed. I believe that these three cases will be found to be quite representative of the process by which one theory has displaced another in economics, in large part because I do not believe that the process could, in general, be otherwise. An insistence that the choice of theories be made in accordance with Friedman's criteria would paralyze scientific activity.

Except in the most exceptional circumstances, the data required to test the predictions of a new theory (statistics and other information) will not be available or, if available, will not be in the form required for the tests and, even when put into this form, will need a good deal of manipulation of one sort or another before they can be made to yield the requisite predictions. And who would be willing to undertake these arduous investigations? Someone who believed in a new theory might be willing to make these tests to convince unbelievers that the theory yielded correct predictions. And someone who did not believe in a new theory might be willing to make these tests to convince believers that the theory did not yield correct predictions. But for the tests to be worthwhile, someone has to believe in the theory, at least to the extent of believing that it might well be true. There is little profit in undertaking an investigation that is expected to show that a theory in which no one believes yields incorrect predictions, and I doubt whether any editor of a professional journal could be found who would be willing to publish a paper giving the results of such an investigation. If all economists followed Friedman's principles in choosing theories, no economist could be found who believed in a theory until it had been tested, which would have the paradoxical result that no tests would be carried out. This is what I meant when I said that acceptance of Friedman's methodology would result in the paralysis of scientific activity. Work could certainly continue, but no new theories would emerge.

But the world is not like that. Economists, or at any rate enough of them, do not wait to discover whether a theory's predictions are accurate before making up their minds. Given that this is so, what part does testing a theory's predictions play in economics? First of all, it very often plays either no part or a very minor part. A great deal of economic theory, so-called pure theory (and this is most of economic theory), consists of logical constructions based on assumptions about human nature so basic that they are difficult to question, assumptions such as that, faced with a choice between $100 and $10, very few people will choose $10. The kind of prediction that results is that if the price of a commodity is reduced, more will be demanded, or if the price is increased, more will be supplied. But, of course, that this is so must have been known before economics existed as an academic study. Other parts of theory, and this applies particularly to monopoly theory, tell us that if something happens, the price will go up, go down, or remain the same, depending on demand and cost conditions. It goes without saying that its predictions are always accurate. It might be argued that what this theory does is to tell us, given the demand and cost conditions, whether the price will go up, go down, or remain the same, but it is not easy to discover in practice what demand and cost conditions really are, and they are commonly inferred from the result rather than the other way round.

Some of you may be inclined to think that, while what I have been saying no doubt applies very well to the economic theory of my youth, things are very different in present-day economics with its massive use of quantitative methods. No doubt things are different. But in what way? What I have to say is largely based on the quantitative articles published in the *Journal of Law and Economics* when I was editor, but I have no doubt that what they reveal is representative of other quantitative studies in economics. First of all, many of these papers cannot be said to test a theory at all. They are measurements of an effect, the nature of which was already well established but of which the magnitude was unknown. For example, economists would expect that governmental control of entry into banking would reduce the number of banks, but without a quantitative study we would be unable to estimate the extent of the reduction.[10] Of course, later on, theories may be developed to explain why some magnitudes are greater than others, and then such studies

10. See Sam Peltzman, "Entry in Commercial Banking," *Journal of Law and Economics*, vol. 8 (October 1965), pp. 11–50.

could be used to test theories. But, generally speaking, this does not appear to be where we are at present. Other studies take the form of a test of the theory espoused by the author: there is a model, then regressions, followed by conclusions. In almost all cases it will be found that the statistical results confirm the theory. Sometimes it does happen that some of the expected relationships are not statistically significant, but they will usually be found to be in the right direction. And when results are obtained that do not square with the theory, which occasionally happens, these results are not usually treated as invalidating the theory but are left as something calling for further study. I would not claim that such studies have never led the investigators to modify their theories, but such cases appear to be rather uncommon. Some articles, of course, involve the testing of alternative theories, and this means that some theories are bound to come out worse. But I doubt whether such studies have often led to a change in the views of the authors. My impression is that these quantitative studies are almost invariably guided by a theory and that they may most aptly be described as explorations with the aid of a theory. In almost all cases, the theory exists before the statistical investigation is made and is not derived from the investigation.

I do not believe that, for the most part, economists could act in any other way. I am bolstered in this view because quantitative methods do not appear to be used in the natural sciences in a way essentially different from the way they are used in economics. At this point, I should acknowledge my indebtedness to Thomas Kuhn. I first heard Milton Friedman expound his views on the methodology of positive economics one evening in London in the company of Ralph Turvey, at a time before Friedman's essay had been published. My immediate response was unfavorable. I voiced various objections to Friedman's views. But Adam Smith's impartial spectator, asked to report on this debate, would have said that I lost every round. Whatever argument I put forward, Friedman had a more telling counterargument. And yet I was not convinced. It was not until 1958–1959, when Kuhn and I were both fellows at the Center for Advanced Study in the Behavioral Sciences at Stanford, that I learned about Kuhn's views and came to see exactly what it was about Friedman's methodological position that I did not like. But what most influenced me was not so much the argument that was later to appear in Kuhn's famous book *The Structure of Scientific Revolutions* (although I am in general agreement with its main thrust) as what he said in an earlier paper, published in 1961, "The Function of

Measurement in Modern Physical Science."[11] Among other things, this paper makes clear that quantitative methods are used in economics in essentially the same way as in the natural sciences.

I said that quantitative studies in economics are explorations with the aid of a theory. Consider what Kuhn says:

> *The road from scientific law to scientific measurement can rarely be traveled in the reverse direction.* To discover quantitative regularity one must normally know what regularity one is seeking and one's instruments must be designed accordingly; even then nature may not yield consistent or generalizable results without a struggle.[12]

I remarked earlier on the tendency of economists to get the result their theory tells them to expect. In a talk I gave at the University of Virginia in the early 1960s, at which Warren Nutter was, I think, present, I said that if you torture the data enough, nature will always confess, a saying which, in a somewhat altered form, has taken its place in the statistical literature. Kuhn puts the point more elegantly and makes the process sound more like a seduction: "nature undoubtedly responds to the theoretical predispositions with which she is approached by the measuring scientist."[13]

I observed that a failure to get an exact fit between the theory and the quantitative results is not generally treated as calling for the abandonment of the theory but the discrepancies are put on one side as something calling for further study. Kuhn says this: "Isolated discrepancies . . . occur so regularly that no scientist could bring his research problems to an end if he paused for many of them. In any case, experience has repeatedly shown that in overwhelming proportion, these discrepancies disappear upon closer scrutiny."[14] Because of this, Kuhn argues that "the efficient procedure" is to ignore them, a conclusion economists will find it easy to accept. Furthermore, Kuhn says:

> Anomalous observations . . . cannot tempt [a scientist] to abandon his theory until another one is suggested to replace it. . . . In scientific practice the real confirmation questions always involve the comparison of two theories with each

11. Thomas S. Kuhn, "The Function of Measurement in Modern Physical Science," reprinted in *The Essential Tension* (Chicago: University of Chicago Press, 1977), p. 178.

12. Ibid., p. 219.

13. Ibid., p. 200.

14. Ibid., p. 202.

other and with the world, not the comparison of a single theory with the world. In these three-way comparisons, measurement has a particular advantage.[15]

This last statement of Kuhn's has a special significance for economists. Quantitative studies, or qualitative studies for that matter, may give someone who believes in a theory a better idea of what that theory implies. But such studies, normally quantitative in the natural sciences and increasingly so in economics, also play, as Kuhn indicates, another and very important role. The choice economists face is a choice between competing theories. These studies, both quantitative and qualitative, perform a function similar to that of advertising and other promotional activities in the normal products market. They do not aim simply at enlarging the understanding of those who believe in the theory but also at attracting those who do not believe in it and at preventing the defection of existing believers. These studies demonstrate the power of the theory, and the definiteness of quantitative studies enables them to make their point in a particularly persuasive form. What we are dealing with is a competitive process in which purveyors of the various theories attempt to sell their wares.

Failure to realize that we are dealing with a competitive situation seems to have led astray even so accomplished an economist as Patinkin. Consider this remark of his:

> What generates in me a great deal of skepticism about the state of our discipline is the high positive correlation between the policy views of a researcher (or, what is worse, of his thesis director) and his empirical findings. I will begin to believe in economics as a science when out of Yale there comes an empirical Ph.D. thesis demonstrating the supremacy of monetary policy in some historical period and out of Chicago, one demonstrating the supremacy of fiscal policy.[16]

I assume that Patinkin did not mean that the empirical findings are fabricated. If this were so, it would be a cause for disquiet. While there is, I suppose, some fraud in economics, it must be quite rare and is certainly not common at either Yale or Chicago. Patinkin expressed concern about the high positive correlation between the policy views of a researcher and his empirical findings. But this is

15. Ibid., p. 211.

16. Don Patinkin, "Keynesian Monetary Theory and the Cambridge School," *Banca Nazionale del Lavoro Quarterly Review*, June 1972, p. 142.

how it should be. I would be very worried by a negative correlation: if, for example, an economist at Yale advocated reliance on fiscal policy while his Ph.D. thesis demonstrated the superiority of monetary policy. The policy views of an economist should accord with the results of his empirical investigations. What I think really worried Patinkin is that, according to his observations, the empirical findings at Yale and Chicago are not the same. Such differences could come about because researchers in the two universities used different methods for estimating the magnitudes of important variables in spheres in which measurement is very difficult. But I do not think that this is what Patinkin had in mind. Assuming that Patinkin is right and that the empirical findings of economists at Yale and Chicago are not the same, this undoubtedly reflects a difference in their view about how the economic system operates, a difference, that is, in the theories espoused at the two universities. As Kuhn explains, this will inevitably lead to differences in the empirical findings. A belief that the empirical findings by research workers in all economics departments should be the same might lead an arrogant and ignorant university administration to attempt to destroy an economics department that had a distinctive character and to attempt to remake it so as to be like Yale (few would want all economics departments to be like Chicago). But that would be the way to mediocrity for that university as well as impeding the search for truth by restraining the competitive process.

Some may think that I have treated somewhat too literally what Patinkin said and have therefore failed to deal with the serious issue that inspired it. This may well be right. Earlier I said that many, I thought most, economists would choose to employ one theory rather than another because it afforded them a better base for thinking. Economists who choose theories using this criterion will not necessarily choose the same theory. They may be interested in different problems or approach the same problem in rather different ways or use different techniques of analysis, and these factors may lead them to prefer one theory rather than another. This does not bother me. In such cases there is little that should be done other than to leave economists free to choose.

But there are motives for selecting one theory rather than another that are more worrying, and I think it was this concern that lay behind Patinkin's somewhat facetious remark. In public discussion, in the press, and in politics, theories and findings are adopted not to facilitate the search for truth but because they lead to certain policy conclusions. Theories and findings become weapons in a propaganda battle. In economics, whose subject matter has such a close connection with public policy, it would be surprising if some academic economists did not adopt the criteria of public discussion in selecting theories, that is, choose a theory because it lends support to a particular policy (perhaps the policy advocated by a particular political party). At the same time, they may belittle the work of other economists because it seems to have the wrong policy conclusions. Many of us will, I feel sure, be able to think of an instance of a scholar doing solid work who suffered because his policy conclusions were considered unacceptable at that time.

Yet, such instances notwithstanding, what is striking is how unimportant the influence of such behavior is over the long period. As an example, consider what has happened to academic opinion on government regulation. Some fifteen or twenty years ago, economists, under the influence of Pigou and others, thought of the government as waiting beneficently to put things right whenever the invisible hand pointed in the wrong direction. The conclusions they drew for policy involved extensive government regulation. The effect of studies made in the intervening years has been to show that such regulation often has no effect or has effects opposite to those expected and was commonly introduced to serve the interests of politically influential groups. What has happened is that most economists have changed their views on policy to fit the new findings. One might have expected, given the stakes involved, that the various groups active in the political arena could have procured economists to voice opinions which served their interests. There can be no question that the affiliation of economists with business or labor organizations or with political parties or even their engaging in consulting does threaten academic integrity. No doubt some economists have been corrupted. Yet my experience is that corruption of this sort, at any rate among economists of quality, is very uncommon or even nonexistent. As Stigler says: "I have seen silly people—public officials as well as private, by the way—try to buy opinions but I have not seen or even suspected any cases in which any important economist sold his professional convictions." Stigler is clearly troubled by the thought that this implies that economists are not maximizing their money incomes, and so he adds:

> When we strive to solve a scientific problem, is ambition for our own professional status completely overshadowed by our love of knowledge? . . . When we write an article to demonstrate the fallacies of someone else's work, is our

hatred for error never mixed with a tiny bit of glee at the display of our own cleverness?[17]

So if we have to admit that we are not maximizing our money incomes, we can at least console ourselves by claiming that we are maximizing our self-esteem.

It is also true that we value the respect of our colleagues. As Samuelson has said: "In the long run, the economic scholar works for the only coin worth having—our own applause."[18] The professional position of an economist depends on work that could not even be understood by the ordinary person. Samuelson does not owe his reputation to those of his writings that are read by the public but to papers that would be completely incomprehensible to them. Just as is true for those working in the natural sciences, the activities of economists are regulated by, or at least much influenced by, professional organizations (universities or societies), in such matters as the design of courses, the requirements for degrees, the allocation of research funds, the standards for publication, and qualifications for employment. Respect and position are obtained by doing work which meets the standards of the economics profession. This regulation through professional organizations means that we are to a very considerable extent insulated from outside pressures. But we avoid that danger only by creating another. This danger is that the implementation of such standards, through its influence on courses, research funds, publication, and employment, not necessarily completely unaffected by political considerations, may be so rigid as to impede the development of new approaches. If this happens, the likely response will be an attempt to form new professional groupings or to carry forward the work under other auspices. If professional organization is sufficiently loose, as it tends to be in the United States, and the new approach has real promise, such efforts will probably succeed. It is not without significance that the new group of studies that has come to be known as "law and economics" has to a very considerable extent been carried forward in law schools rather than in economics departments, where the economists' somewhat narrow conception of the scope of their subject led them to be, at least initially, largely uninterested in the field. For economists to be free to choose the theories that will be most helpful in guiding them in their work, and

---

17. George J. Stigler, *The Intellectual and the Market Place* (New York: Free Press of Glencoe, 1963), p. 92.

18. Paul A. Samuelson, "Economists and the History of Ideas," *American Economic Review*, vol. 52 (March 1962), p. 18.

to invent new theories when the existing ones seem unsatisfactory, research has to be carried on within a relatively free educational structure, with universities, research institutes, and the foundations and other bodies that finance research all following independent policies and even within universities allowing a considerable degree of autonomy for schools and departments.

I started this talk by asking, How should economists choose? I have ended by discussing the organization and finance of academic activities. I do not think that I have lost my way. Instead of confining ourselves to a discussion of the question of how economists ought to choose between theories, developing criteria, and relying on exhortation or perhaps regulation to induce them to use these criteria in making their choices, we should investigate the effect of alternative institutional arrangements for academic studies on the theories that are put into circulation and on the choices that are made. From these investigations we may hope to discover what arrangements governing the competition between theories are most likely to lead economists to make better choices. Paradoxically, the approach to the methodological problem in economics that is likely to be most useful is to transform it into an economic problem.

In carrying out this task, we may draw inspiration from the example of Warren Nutter. As I said at the beginning of this talk, he possessed what Knight considered the essential attributes of a good scholar: integrity, competence, and humility. But Warren Nutter added courage. Fearless in the defense of the causes in which he believed, he calls to mind that heroic figure in Bunyan's *Pilgrim's Progress*, Valiant-for-Truth. And it may surely be said of Warren Nutter, as it was of Valiant-for-Truth, that when "he passed over . . . all the trumpets sounded for him on the other side."

Economists
and
Public Policy

George J. Stigler

April 23, 1982

GEORGE J. STIGLER was Charles R. Walgreen Distinguished Service Professor of American Institutions, University of Chicago, from 1958 to 1981. He is now Charles R. Walgreen Distinguished Service Professor emeritus, Department of Economics and Graduate School of Business, University of Chicago. He was professor of economics at Columbia University from 1947 to 1958, and prior to 1947 he served on the faculties of Iowa State University, the University of Minnesota, and Brown University. He has been director of the Center for the Study of the Economy and the State, University of Chicago, since 1977, and editor, *Journal of Political Economy*, since 1974.

Introduction

Thomas F. Johnson

It is a pleasure to introduce our speaker this afternoon for the fourth G. Warren Nutter Memorial Lecture. George Stigler was one of Warren Nutter's longtime friends and is regarded as a prominent spokesman of the "Chicago School of Economics." For the economists present, it is superfluous for me to recount our speaker's background and accomplishments, but, for those from other disciplines, let me mention a few particulars.

George J. Stigler has been Walgreen Professor of American Institutions at the University of Chicago since 1958. He holds a Ph.D. in economics from the University of Chicago. Prior to 1958, he served as a faculty member at Iowa State University, the University of Minnesota, Brown University, and Columbia University. He has also been a member of the research staff of the National Bureau of Economic Research and is a past president of the American Economic Association. Professor Stigler served on President Nixon's Blue Ribbon Defense Panel to study the organization of the Department of Defense. Warren Nutter was instrumental in having Professor Stigler nominated for this panel.

Countless students of economics know George Stigler from working their way through *The Theory of Price*,[1] now in its third edition and sixth printing. As a graduate student at the University of Virginia after World War II, I remember enrolling in a course in price theory taught by Professor Rutledge Vining, and thinking when I acquired what Professor Vining stated was one of the major texts for the course: "Can we possibly spend an entire semester on this little book?" All of us in the course quickly learned that we could. In fact, it was very easy to do so because an awful lot of economics was

---

1. George J. Stigler, *The Theory of Price*, 3rd ed. (New York: Macmillan, 1966).

packed into that little book. My 1946 edition is a source I still refer to often.

This is not Professor Stigler's first visit to AEI. In the 1960s and early 1970s, AEI held a series of "Rational Debates" on major public policy issues at which Warren Nutter served as master of ceremonies and referee. In 1971, Professor Stigler came to AEI to take part in one of those debates, which was entitled, "Can Regulatory Agencies Protect the Consumer?" His opponent was Manuel F. Cohen, who had until recently been the chairman of the Securities and Exchange Commission. With his incisive reasoning, Dr. Stigler argued that public regulation weakens and sometimes destroys the consumer's traditional defenses against fraud and negligence in the marketplace without replacing the protections those defenses used to afford. He stated that "the doctrine of *caveat emptor* has not lost its force. The only change is that now the consumer must beware of different threats, and threats which he is less well equipped to defend against." Dr. Stigler concluded that, in his view, the consumer's best assurances of satisfaction are his own care and intelligence and "the most powerful of allies, competition." In the decade since those remarks were made, the idea of less regulation by government appears to have gained strength in our society.

We are delighted to have Professor George Stigler here this afternoon to address us on "Economists and Public Policy."

Economists and Public Policy

George J. Stigler

In the preceding memorial lecture for Warren Nutter, Ronald Coase presented a critique of the methodological writings of the lecturer who had preceded him in this series, Milton Friedman. My momentary temptation to confirm the tradition by devoting this lecture to a critique of Coase's work was easily resisted: there are better methods finding a vulnerable adversary. In fact I have been able to find a much more vulnerable target, and with well-placed confidence, because I am the target.

In a paper I once wrote, entitled "The Economist and the State,"[1] I proposed two main theses. The first was that economists had a deplorable habit of giving emphatic advice on public policy without bothering—even if they lived long after—to see whether their predictions of the effects of a policy were correct. Nassau Senior and Robert Torrens predicted dire consequences for the textile industry if Britain adopted the ten-hour day. In a characteristically terse eighty-page letter to Lord Ashley, the sponsor of the ten-hour bill, Torrens stated:

> I have not hesitated to address your Lordship, throughout the preceding pages, a free and unmitigated expression of my opinions in regard to a measure, the express object of which is to diminish the quantity of work performed within a given time, and of which, as I conceive, the necessary tendency would consequently be ... to effect a reduction of wages proportionate to the diminution in the quantity of work performed within a given time; and ultimately to create a bitter spirit of disappointment and despair, endan-

---

1. *American Economic Review*, March 1965.

gering the security of life and property, and terminating, it might be possible, in the horrors of a servile war.[2]

Senior's letter was little shorter, but I will quote only his conclusion, of which he said that he had no doubt, that "a Ten Hour Bill would be utterly ruinous." Each of these famous economists lived for seventeen years after the passage of the act, but neither found time in his busy life to examine the actual effects of the ten-hour law.

Near the end of the nineteenth century, again, there was substantial hostility or indifference by economists toward the passage of the Sherman Antitrust Act. Not one of the economists of the period made a study to confirm or deny the popular prediction that a mere statute could not retard the gigantic forces making for large business enterprises. My first thesis has surely been completely valid for most of our history as a science, and is still entirely too valid today.

The second thesis is the one I now wish partially to recant: it asserted that once the practice of testing our predictions by examining the evidence became general practice, economists' advice—that is, the advice that survived the empirical tests—would be heeded by the society. For truth, even temporary truth, is a God that the rational society must worship. And of course our society is rational, being constituted as it is of some 230 million utility-maximizing individuals.

My argument rested on the proposition that a society will not long challenge established truths about the real world because that is unwise behavior no matter what one is seeking to do. To disregard the real world is to act inefficiently. Suppose, for example, that economists demonstrate that a minimum-wage law is largely vitiated by the ability of employers to reduce fringe benefits and costly working conditions.[3] Then the labor unions that support such laws should surely address this method of frustrating their desired increase in the cost of employing workers who receive low wage rates. But I erred, I believe, in confusing truth with virtue. Let me go back to the beginning.

The Place for Hard Science

There are things that economists know with great confidence about the workings of an economic system. The price of a commodity will rise when its supply falls, even if the state passes a law against a price

---

2. *A Letter to Lord Ashley* (London, 1844), p. 78.

3. This is suggested by Walter J. Wessels, "The Effect of Minimum Wages in the Presence of Fringe Benefits," *Economic Inquiry*, vol. 18 (April 1980), pp. 293–313.

rise: the rise will then simply take the form of legal or illegal costs in getting the rationed commodity—waiting in line or buying in a black market. A large and rapid rise in the supply of money will lead to a rise in prices (again, possibly concealed but not avoided by public controls). A competitive industry will refuse in the long run to supply its product at less than a cost-remunerative price and will be unable to get much more. Such elementary and even platitudinous findings are deducible from first principles and illustrated by indefinitely many thousands of documentable instances.

These were the kinds of findings that I argued were inescapable and therefore irresistible to an intelligent society. I was saying, as Edwin Cannan once put it, "However lucky Error may be for a time, Truth keeps the bank, and wins in the long run."

I am still prepared to assert that such established economic principles are accepted by the society, whether a principle is liked or not, just as birds and stones accept gravity. When the society imposes a price ceiling that prevents a market from clearing, for example, that is not an act of defiance against the law of demand. Rather, it is a decision based upon a preference for another system of assigning goods and distributing income. The rent ceiling in effect assigns each property to the tenant already residing in it, and forces the later comers to take the leavings. The rent ceiling redistributes income from landlords to tenants and is a feasible policy because even neglected dwellings are fairly durable. These are known consequences, and if someone asserts that they were unknown consequences when rent control was first adopted in some Dark Age of long ago, will that person have the effrontery to say that the consequences are still unknown today? No, it will not do to say that rent control and its many brothers and cousins are adopted out of ignorance of their effects.

Indeed, if such policies were adopted in ignorance of their effects, we would be hard put to explain their form as well as their duration. If a rent ceiling were not anticipated to have the effects it does have, many aspects of the policy would be mysterious. If it were not expected that landlords would seek to escape the controls—that is, that the supply of rental housing has significant elasticity, then rent control laws would have placed no controls over conversions and demolitions. If the chilling effect of rent controls on new construction had not been anticipated, no one would have made the promise—however badly kept—to leave rents uncontrolled on buildings constructed thereafter. If queuing had not been expected, rent control laws would have paid little attention to the rights of tenants to sublease controlled properties.

I believe that if we look at any important economic policy of the state, we shall find that it takes account of whatever established knowledge economists possess, and perhaps of some that we do not yet possess. The theory of price discrimination, for example, emphasizes the possibility of profiting from differences among buyers in demand elasticities when the buyers can be prevented from reselling to one another. This theory is fully recognized in the regulation of the structure of public utility prices. Indeed, we may turn the situation around and assert that legislation we economists usually dislike is capable of teaching us economics. I conjecture, for example, that the early applications of a minimum-wage policy are to classes of workers most substitutable for the workers whose unions achieve passage of such laws, and only gradually is the law extended to workers with lesser substitution capabilities, or to closely substitutable workers with less political influence.

On this interpretation, economists have no great difficulty in having their solid new findings adopted: they do not even have to go abroad to be accepted as the discoverer of a new drug does, to escape FDA's formidable obstacle course. That part of the thesis I am recanting does not need to be withdrawn or qualified.

The Presence of Other Values

And now I come to the error of my ways, and indeed of economists' ways generally. We expect the society eventually to believe our case for free trade and our case against minimum wages and our case for free energy prices and our case against rent controls. Every one of these recommendations is based on a tolerably accurate analysis of the effects of the policies on aggregate social income, and yet the community often pursues very different economic policies. How can I still say that society accepts all the truly reliable findings of economics?

If "the society" (that is, the government) wishes to give more income to a class—say, tenants or farmers or producers of steel or teamsters—than the free market will afford, it seeks to contrive a policy that will accommodate that goal. There are numerous other goals of the state such as the moral improvement of the society's members, and they are implemented with instruments such as tax exemption for certain activities and legal prohibition for others.

Compared with income redistribution, however, these supplementary goals are unimportant in our society, and I shall put them aside in what follows.

These income redistribution goals, it must be pointed out, are not simply derived from some widely accepted ethic such as the moral value of redistributing income more equally, although there may be some of that in fact and certainly a great deal in rhetoric. The beneficiaries of income redistributions in a modern state include an unbelievably varied assortment of groups: oil millionaires, the largest banks in the nation, the elderly, families without male heads, airline pilots, Harvard professors, government employees, city landowners, and beekeepers. The losers include automobile drivers, small bank depositors, young workers, owners of television sets, landlords, nonminority students and employers, Grumman stockholders, and owners of some California coastal lands.

Whether any specific person gains or loses on balance by the sum total of all the redistributive measures that affect him is a question whose accurate answer would require perhaps several billion dollars of economic research. (In a time of less overwhelming concern with deficits I would of course propose such a research program.) Clearly on average we lose because there are no redistributive policies that simply transfer income: deadweight losses—costs without any corresponding benefits—are imposed by the costs of collecting and disbursing money and even more by the efforts of buyers and sellers of goods to try to get around the policies.

Quite evidently this immense smorgasbord of redistributive policies bears hardly any relationship to simple compassion for the poor or envy of the rich because there are dozens upon dozens of policies that injure the poor and as many that help the well-to-do. The political system responds to groups who can organize and raise funds to influence the politicians by votes and campaign contributions. We need not go into the precise factors that determine whether any particular group will have much, little, or no political clout, and that is a good thing for me because we still know very little of the answer. The fact that there are literally hundreds of political groups at various levels of government, that they vary greatly in political strength, and that this strength is not at all closely related to one's place on the income ladder—these facts are enough to show that political life displays a set of preferences for income distribution that fits no simple ethical or political theory.

Any thinking person surely disapproves of many of the redistributions engaged in by even the most democratic of societies, and economists are singularly agreed on their disapproval of many of them. (One is entitled to suspect that a person's disapproval is related to his circumstances: economists believe that federal support of their research is more desirable than federal support of industrial research.) The disapproval of the economists, however, is uninformed.

It is uninformed with respect to the reason that the disapproved policies are adopted—uninformed with respect to what the operative political desires of the community are. Clever economists have displayed an obtuseness in this matter that is difficult to believe. They will say, not year after year but generation after generation, "Parliament, do you not realize that free trade would increase the national income?" As if the Parliament did not know this! At their most sophisticated, these economists have added: "If you must aid farmers or whomever, tax a portion of the larger income obtained with free trade and give the revenue directly to the people the tariff was intended to help"—as if they had studied the comparative efficiency of subsidizing a given group by tariffs as compared with general taxes and selective subsidies.

The true account, then, is that the economists refused to listen to the society, not that the society refused to listen to the economists. What the economists had to say that was relevant was heard and acted upon, but the society insisted also on taking into account the realities of a political process that the economists persisted in viewing as an all-powerful God who shared the economists' preoccupation with efficiency. Nature was not stupid because it required so long for some of its methods to be disclosed to physicists, and society is not stupid because social scientists have been slow learners.

I explain the disregard of economists' policy advice by the fact that society pursues other values, and in particular income redistribution. The traditional explanation given by economists for the disregard of our advice is that the society does not comprehend the theories on which our evidence is based. I have already given my main answer to this alternative explanation: it fails to account for the efforts that are made to achieve precisely the effects we deplore. No one could support the thesis that societies make no mistakes, especially in this town [Washington, D.C.], which is the center of the mistake industry. To explain something by saying that it is a mistake, however, is on the same level as explaining it by the intervention of invisible spirits.

The Roles of the Economist

I have produced a paradox of sorts: the society, I say, knows what it wants and seeks it as efficiently as it knows how—but it continues to hire economists who tell it to do things differently. Are we court jesters? Or are we fulfilling some subtle social service quite divorced from the Pareto optimal solutions we are preaching?

Of the various roles of the economist in our society, let me put aside the one that employs most economists: the teaching of economics to the next generation. That is a useful activity to the degree that methods of economic thinking and theories constructed by economists and findings of economic research are useful to the society. For now I wish to concentrate on the economist's role as an adviser. Moreover, I wish to exclude the technical advice that the economist provides to (say) an antitrust case litigant or to a business through consulting. I am left for now, then, with the economist as a social reformer, or in short, as an advocate.

It is an interesting fact that people dislike private reformers but admire (some) public reformers. As to the private reformers, they are the people who in the petty details of life take most seriously the welfare of their associates—I do not say friends, for they usually have few friends. They reproach the cigarette smoker, comment on the richness of the dessert one is eating, urge the sedentary to jog, and assure the unthinking recipient of their advice—who by now may well have a headache—that all aspirin is the same, except in price. In a hundred other ways they seek to ameliorate or at least lengthen and generally tidy up the lives of their unwilling beneficiaries. Moreover, they do not charge for their advice.

Why is the situation different when a person addresses himself not to the foibles and follies of an individual but instead to the foibles and follies of his society? Heaven knows that such sermons also can be boring: there is enormous conformity among social critics in a society. Examine the mountains of paper devoted in the past twelve months to Reaganomics, composed 98 percent of repetition, 94 percent of malice, and about 2 percent of knowledge.

Yet we cannot label the social critics as intrusive, for they are invited into the house, though we are well aware of their nature. We buy their printed message or turn on the television or radio when they appear or even go to the meeting at which they will exhort us to social virtue.

The conventional answer to this impolite inquiry is that the society as a whole wishes to do good, and it seeks the instruction and advice of a class who by talents and specialization can accumulate the knowledge and analyze it competently to help us do that good. Yet there is the paradox to which we have referred: Why does the society pay Milton Friedman a lot more to be an eloquent spokesman of conservatism than to be a superb economic scholar—isn't it telling him to forget the scholarship? Nevertheless it does not hurry to adopt his policies.

The paradox is of course in one direction a most shallow one. "Society" is a bundle of interests and resources, not some single-minded collectivity. The people who demand the services of economic reformers are diverse interest groups in the society, and they have very different ideas of what reform is. The people who demand economic scholarship are a different, but overlapping, group.

I have already given my explanation for the demand for scholarship: the better we understand causal relationships, the more efficiently we can pursue our goals. It is true, of course, that a given piece of new scholarship may help one side of a policy argument more than another. The findings of labor economists have caused some trouble (but not a lot) for the AFL-CIO [American Federation of Labor–Congress of Industrial Organizations] in its pursuit of higher minimum wages. The development of the efficient market theory of organized markets has reduced the academic support for SEC-CFTC [Securities and Exchange Commission–Commodity Futures Trading Commission] regulations of the exchanges. The effects of the research, however, are usually not predictable. Often the new scholarship has led to surprising changes of attitude on policy. Chicago economists were once highly critical of retail price maintenance. Now on balance they favor legalizing it.

My paradox is shallow also in a second dimension: most economists, as I have noted, have nothing to do with economic reform. The vast majority of the profession do not appear before Congress, write for the popular press, ride the lecture circuit, or even send letters to the newspaper. Their primary task is teaching or applied research. In the classroom they will do a fair amount of preaching of reform, but it will not be very professional. If we study the views on economic policy that students adopt in college, and keep for a time thereafter, I believe that we will find that the major views—such as those on income equalization and antidiscrimination and maintenance of full employment—are not even part of technical economics. Indeed, I suspect that students get most of their new ideas on economic reform from members of the faculty who are not professional economists, indeed who are professional noneconomists.

The residual paradox is small indeed: the various interest groups wish support for their own views and even more do they wish skillful and effective attacks upon their rivals and opponents. The interventionists for the most part want from their economists repeated demonstrations of the inefficiency and immorality of business and of the helplessness of individuals in a competitive jungle. The conservatives wish from their economists demonstrations of the incompetence and venality of the political process and of the efficiency of unregulated markets.

Interest groups need this professional assistance especially in the attacks they make on their opponents. A labor union leader or a conservationist or a businessman is usually quite competent to determine where his self-interest lies. He is not necessarily skilled either in analyzing the objectionable economic effects of his opponents' policies or in presenting his own case attractively to those groups not directly affected by the disputed economic policies. This labor leader or conservationist or businessman employs economists—often by buying the books or attending the speeches of sympathetic economists—to assist him in these tasks.

The vestiges of the paradox can be explained away by one further consideration: there are precious few able economists who are first-class advocates, and just as few fine advocates who are outstanding economists. Indeed the number of economists who have been truly outstanding in both scholarship and public policy advocacy in this century can be counted on the thumbs of one person. Such scarce resources of course command high prices.

Reflections on a Chicago Credo

As far back as I can remember, the Chicago economists have nourished a credo: people act efficiently in their own interests. The people who make automobiles on average know better what to make and how to make it than the best industrial economists. The worker who chooses an education and a craft on average knows better how to choose than the best labor economist. The householder who buys a consumer good on average knows better what and where to buy than the best home economist.

This is not to say that the economic world is perfect—although it really is pretty impressive—or that its imperfections can never be discovered by an economist—although I am hard put to find an example. The credo does assert, however, that economic agents learn all the presently knowable things it pays them to know—always on average—and act with due regard for this knowledge. The credo asserts that nothing is easier than for an economist to be wiser in 1982 than the American automobile industry was in 1972, but no economist in 1982 is so wise as the automobile industry in 1982 or even in 1981.

Not only is this credo not owned by Chicago economists, but it was not even invented by them. Indeed it was the cornerstone of Adam Smith's *Wealth of Nations*—recall Smith's observation:

> The statesman, who should attempt to direct private people in what manner they ought to employ their capitals, would not only load himself with a most unnecessary attention, but assume an authority which could safely be trusted, not only to no single person, but to no council or senate whatever, and which would nowhere be so dangerous as in the hands of a man who had folly and presumption enough to fancy himself fit to exercise it.[4]

He would have been no kinder to presumptuous professors. The credo was given an elegant and powerful formulation in the famous essay of Friedrich von Hayek, "The Use of Knowledge in Society."[5] The basis of the credo is simply the fact that an economic actor on average knows better the environment in which he is acting and the probable consequences of his actions than an outsider, no matter how clever the outsider may be. I attribute the credo to Chicago only because that is where I learned it.

Whatever its proper name, the credo is often ignored by others. That professional reformer, John Kenneth Galbraith, has found time in his active life to instruct Detroit in the design of automobiles and Peoria in the correct amount of municipal services. An equally busy man, Irving Kristol, has been seeking to mend the public manners of corporations for years. At one point in the Nixon regime the leading economists of the administration were advising the public to eat cheese instead of meat, perhaps the most exotic monetary policy of recent times.

Even our acceptance of the credo in Chicago has been selective: we have ridiculed the advice an economist gives to a businessman

---

4. Adam Smith, *Wealth of Nations* (Glasgow, 1976), I, 456.

5. *American Economic Review*, September 1945.

about running his business, but have been quick to tell this same businessman how he should deal with public policies. The business-man is the best arbiter of whether to build a new plant to produce a new product, but—lacking as he does a Ph.D. in economics—he is less qualified to determine the effects of tariffs or the efficient methods of reducing environmental damage.

The inconsistency is evident. If the businessman will spend a dollar to get a dollar or more worth of information about affairs as complex as labor strife and new and untested technologies, why does he not do the same with respect to public policies that strongly affect him? A similar question can be asked of the worker or the investor or the consumer. A good many public policies will have consequences for the economic actor that are easier to estimate than the conse-quences of more narrowly economic decisions. It is easier to estimate the major effects of a rent control program, I suspect, than the out-come of an investment in a foreign country.

There is of course a conventional response: knowledge of particu-lar public policy proposals cannot sensibly be collected by any one person or company; the costs are usually too large relative to any one person's benefits. Hence there is underinvestment in knowledge of this sort. The argument does operate strongly to weaken the role of individual consumers in policy formation, although there are some defenses, including even professors of economics.

The argument does not fit businesses very well: they have formed thousands of associations precisely to deal with this problem. It is interesting that no one has yet produced an inventory of cases in which businesses neglected proposed legislation or administrative decrees of large potential influence on their affairs.

So I plead for consistency—and that means generality—in the application of the credo. Consistency demands, or at least requests, that we should not ascribe incompetence in acquiring information on policy positions, or in acting upon it, blithely and almost routinely to the various economic agents. That attribution of amateurism in public policy is an obstacle to understanding how people behave.

Academic Reformers

All active and ambitious economists—fully 2 or 3 percent of the pro-fession—are reformers in another area of life: the reform of economic science. Anyone who seeks to change the views, the techniques, or the theories of his fellow scientists is obviously seeking to reform them. Our journals would not need to change their editorial policies if they were titled *The American Economics Reformer* or the *Journal of Improvements in Political Economy*. We instruct our students that it is their *duty* to improve economics if they possibly can, and great rewards are reserved for those who apparently succeed. This duty is much younger in economics than the practice of being a political reformer.

Of course the academicians will point out that, in contrast to political reforms, scientific reform is always lofty in its goal—which is to increase knowledge—and the validity of each proposed reform is tested by logic and evidence. These self-serving remarks contain a measure of truth, but not so much as to exclude long fads in our science and no doubt in others. Still, I do not wish to dispute the propriety of scientific reform any more than that of political reform.

Scientific reformers, or scientists, as they prefer to be called, have one substantial difference from political reformers, and it is a difference that has been growing over time. A political reformer must be at least mildly comprehensible to his lay audience—I hope the word "mildly" is enough to cover Marx. A scientific reformer is permitted—and, it seems, often encouraged—to use esoteric and difficult ideas and methods. It follows that a society, when it decides to support economic or other scientific research, must allow the scholars a vast amount of self-determination in what should be studied and how. The society can tell rather quickly and accurately whether an advocate of policy is effective; but it must wait for decades to learn whether a discipline is pursuing fertile lines of inquiry. In principle that makes for less efficient direction of scientific reform than of political reform.

A second and lesser difference is that scientific reformers look down upon political reformers, and political reformers play their part by looking up to the scientists. We are entitled to believe that when Laplace gave the *Mécanique céleste* to Napoleon, Napoleon received it with envy. I conclude, not that it is easier to be a great political leader than a great scholar, but that the scholars have the prerogative of making the final assessment of the two.

Conclusion

The Chicago Credo—the extension of the theory of rational behavior to all areas of man's behavior—has one immense and decisive attraction. It arms the student of life with a powerful and versatile theory which can produce suggestive hypotheses to tackle new problems, and it provides also the methods to study these hypotheses. The ad hockery of special explanations and the easy recourse to exceptions that prove no rule are replaced by a tough logic.

The extension of this logic to political processes on a systematic and persistent basis is now only about twenty-five years old. This is of course the way in which I introduce the fact that the achievements of this approach are still meager, and the known unfilled tasks are manifold. I do not feel apologetic for the modest achievements—we have still been rather more successful in dealing with political events than have economists in previous centuries.

The credo has one substantial, but not wholly offsetting, disadvantage. Curiosity about a vice in the world and self-examination of the motives for mounting an attack against it are no sources of strength to a reformer. Worse yet, the message of a reformer who adopts the Chicago Credo loses a good deal of its appeal. He can no longer say,

> We know beyond reasonable doubt that free trade is good for the nation: let me explain the fallacies of protectionism and then I shall estimate for you the rise in our nation's income if we move to free trade.

Instead he must say,

> Will you supporters of protective tariffs and quotas please stop pursuing your own welfare, as you have been doing with insight and success? Become altruistic and abandon your trade barriers, and if we can also persuade the many other groups who have been feathering their nests to abandon those nests, it is probable that you will actually benefit from your altruism, and surely recoup at least a part of your losses.

It is indeed possible to advise people to stop being sensible, but it takes unusual skills to do it well.

Let me close on a truly old-fashioned note. I have raised doubts about the nature and role of economic reformers. They are not serious doubts, because I must assume that these reformers are employed by sensible, informed people, and they must be providing useful services. In any event, I have no doubts about the importance of increases in our understanding of the economic system. Ancient faith joins the Chicago Credo in saying that everyone will respect and use genuine scientific knowledge, and the society will be the better for every truth conquered or error vanquished.

Global Evolution since World War II

Thomas H. Moorer

November 16, 1982

THOMAS H. MOORER, after commanding the Seventh Fleet, the Pacific Fleet, and the Atlantic Fleet, became chief of naval operations in 1967 and chairman, Joint Chiefs of Staff, in 1970. He retired in 1974. Admiral Moorer is now affiliated with the Center for Strategic and International Studies at Georgetown University.

Introduction

Richard A. Ware

I join in a welcome to all of you and especially to Admiral Moorer and his gracious lady, Carrie.

These late afternoon talks and conversations, followed by an informal dinner, are designed as gatherings of Warren Nutter's friends to respond to the challenges of ideas, to visit over our recollections of Warren and his works. I like to believe these events would have been enjoyed by Warren as instructive intellectual exchanges in a setting of good cheer.

Those who have preceded me in offering a few words of introduction to the lecturers have been either colleagues or students of Mr. Nutter the political economist. Those introduced have been distinguished scholars of the economic affairs of mankind—Professors Frankel, Friedman, Coase, and Stigler, two of them Nobel Laureates. This fifth occasion is of a different character and relates to another facet of Professor Nutter's career. Our lecturer today comes from the world of political-military affairs, his last active duty post having been four years as senior officer of all American armed forces and chief military adviser to the Congress and the president.

The introduction today is presented by a practitioner who once served as principal deputy to and comrade of the Honorable G. Warren Nutter, assistant secretary of defense, international security affairs. Two of the great opportunities that have come to me were those of serving with Secretary Nutter and with Admiral Moorer. Perhaps you will not consider it presumptuous of me to offer a few personal remarks.

My first must be to acknowledge the opportunity Warren Nutter gave me to serve with him. The memories are precious ones. I have continued to find joy in sharing them with Jane Nutter. I am grateful for the trust Warren placed in me.

Second, I recall the day early in 1969 when Secretary Nutter held the Bible and Secretary Laird administered to me the oath of office. Since I am not a person enamored of public office, this was a new experience for me. The chief of naval operations was interested enough to attend. He probably wanted to take the measure of a chap from Michigan.

When Admiral Moorer congratulated me, he displayed his skill in human management by inquiring whether I was related to the naval officer after whom the USS *Ware* was named. Although my response had to be negative, some months later I was presented with a striking aerial photograph of this ship at sea. With its inscription from Admiral Moorer, the photograph now graces the wall of my study. What a fine lesson on how to establish relationships in Washington!

Finally, one of the few instructions issued by Secretary Laird to Mr. Nutter said something about bringing to an end the "cannonading on the fourth floor of E Ring"—that it was time to establish harmonious and productive relations between the civilians and the military. Admiral Moorer was one of those who made such relations possible. He worked closely with us on many occasions and on many problems.

I recollect also that Admiral Moorer always proceeded at flank speed. He and I attended National Security Council committee meetings in the Situation Room when I acted for Secretary Nutter. Somehow after the meeting the admiral always managed to arrive ahead of me at General Pershing's desk to report to Secretary Laird. Apparently, he had a better located parking place and a more adroit driver than I. I finally overcame this handicap by thumbing a ride with the admiral. It solved what could have been a serious problem for me in terms of Secretary Laird's perception of my bureaucratic capabilities. The admiral also taught me the value of note taking; he is a master of the art.

These informal recollections are my attempt to convey my esteem for a military statesman with whom I share a love of the man to whom these lectures do honor.

Admiral Thomas Hinman Moorer of Alabama graduated from the Naval Academy in 1933 with a solid record of academic achievement and football prowess. "Dead Eye" was his acquired nickname. One of the limited number of Great Depression graduates offered commissions, he served at sea, took flight training, and was awarded his gold wings in 1936. In that year he and Mrs. Moorer made the first of twenty-six moves in their years of active duty.

On December 7, 1941, Lieutenant Moorer was at Pearl Harbor. A few weeks later he was in the Dutch East Indies attempting to stem the Japanese push. In February 1942 his PBY reconnaissance plane was shot down, and he was wounded. He landed his crew safely; they took to a life raft and were picked up by a freighter later sunk by the enemy; under Moorer's leadership the forty survivors made their way to an island and were rescued. Lieutenant Moorer was cited for "gallant and intrepid conduct."

By July 1942 Tom Moorer was serving in Europe with the Royal Navy, and at the end of the war he was a tried and true officer, thirty-three years of age, with service in the Pacific, the Atlantic, the Caribbean, and also in Australia, England, and Africa. He knows the sea lanes and harbors of the world.

In 1945 he was assigned to the now famous Strategic Bombing Survey in Japan and then to various tours at sea, at naval installations ashore, and in the office of the chief of naval operations. He was selected for rear admiral in 1957, vice admiral in 1962, and admiral in 1964. He commanded the Seventh Fleet, the Pacific Fleet, and the Atlantic Fleet and became chief of naval operations in 1967 and chairman, Joint Chiefs of Staff, in 1970. He retired in 1974 after forty-five years of service to the Republic as a midshipman and sailor, naval aviator, sea commander, staff officer, military statesman, and student of political-military affairs. He continues to serve his country in the last role, especially in association with the Center for Strategic and International Studies at Georgetown University. He has a rich experience as the basis for his wise counsel.

Admiral Moorer has been awarded four Distinguished Service Medals, the Silver Star, the Legion of Merit, the Distinguished Flying Cross, the Purple Heart, a Presidential Unit Citation, many campaign and theater medals, and the decorations of ten foreign governments.

I present Thomas H. Moorer of Alabama, Admiral, United States Navy, Retired.

Global Evolution
since World War II

Thomas H. Moorer

I⊤ is a high honor for me to join the distinguished speakers who have preceded me in the G. Warren Nutter Memorial Lectures sponsored by the Thomas Jefferson Center Foundation and presented by the American Enterprise Institute. I believe I am unique among these speakers in that my warm friendship with Dr. Nutter was developed in an environment somewhat different from the academic world: the Pentagon. Of all the civilian officials I encountered in the Pentagon during the long years I spent there, I found Warren Nutter one of the most intelligent, most dedicated, and most profound. While he was assistant secretary of defense for international security affairs, I was chairman of the Joint Chiefs of Staff, and we had almost daily contact over issues of mutual interest, in addition to a periodic luncheon engagement in the privacy of my office. Many times we went together to the White House to participate in what was called at that time the Washington Special Action Group, chaired by Henry Kissinger, which was in effect the White House instrument for crisis management. Warren would sit in these meetings paying close attention and saying little until the final wrap-up. At that time he would express in the most succinct and, in my view, sound terms the factors involved and the best course of action to follow.

Perhaps my most lasting memory of Warren Nutter is founded in the long discussion we once had over the future of the world as he saw it. This afternoon I propose to structure my remarks around the comments made by Warren at that time. He clearly saw the effects of the worldwide population explosion, the emergence of third world nations, and the attitude of many politicians that the world owed all citizens a living and would take care of them from the cradle to the grave regardless of any efforts they might put forward. In particular he suggested that democracy in the United

States would be replaced by a conglomerate of special interests, each bringing pressure to bear on the policy of our government. Throughout these discussions he frequently expressed his concern that Americans soon forget history and the lessons learned from it. But the matters we discussed at greater length dealt with national security, with which we were involved on a day-to-day basis.

Warren pointed out three significant conditions, developed at the end of World War II, that would affect international relations and confrontations for many years to come: First, it was clear that no matter where a problem arose throughout the world, the United States would be immediately involved. Second, nuclear weapons had imposed a new dimension on warfare, which would bring about vast change in military relations and military balances. Third, it was clear before the guns ceased firing that the Soviet Union had embarked on a grand design of world conquest—conquest in the sense that their objective was not so much to destroy us as to defeat us in terms of national will and international influence throughout the world. Let me discuss the conclusions drawn by Dr. Nutter in somewhat more detail.

First, with respect to the international involvement of the United States, nations that were once our allies with worldwide influence no longer find themselves in that position. The Netherlands, a world power before World War II, lost access to the vast areas packed with valuable raw materials now known as Indonesia, as well as to other territories; it has withdrawn to become a very small nation in Europe. The British, who at one time boasted the sun never set on the British Empire, have withdrawn not just east of Suez but also east of Gibraltar; they have very little strength dispersed around the world, as the Falkland Islands incident so well demonstrated.

In the Pacific the Japanese, who with our assistance have developed into one of the world's leading economic powers, have spent very little of their gross national product on defense and rely on the United States to provide their nuclear umbrella and their overall national security. The other nations of the world look to the United States to take a leading position in every crisis.

In the Middle East we are, of course, heavily involved and will be for some time to come. We have made a major commitment to Israel, having provided about $21 billion of aid since 1970; $6 billion of that has been economic aid, of which 90 percent has been forgiven, and $15 billion has been military aid, which either has been forgiven or is supported by most favorable terms.

In Africa, where a confrontation has existed, particularly with respect to Namibia, all nations look to the United States to settle this difficult problem. When one looks at the natural catastrophes of the world—famine, or volcanic eruptions, or floods—here again it is the United States that is expected to rush to the rescue. In Central America the United States is heavily burdened in an effort to improve the economy and at the same time put a stop to the conflicts that are continually funded and promoted by the Soviets through their surrogate Cuba.

There is thus no question that the United States is involved worldwide. This involvement is made more difficult because we no longer have bipartisan support of foreign policy in the Congress. The result is that each administration has taken its own position, which has often been reversed as soon as the next administration moved into the White House or to Capitol Hill.

Another problem for our country revolves around the acquisition of raw materials, which are being rapidly depleted. These resources are located primarily in the undeveloped countries. Petroleum, which has held our attention so strongly since 1973, is typical of such resources. I believe that military confrontation over the access to critical raw materials is far more likely in the future than a major confrontation with Soviet Russia in Western Europe.

Second, let me discuss the effect of the advent of nuclear weapons and the delivery vehicles that can transport them quickly across the oceans. No longer can the United States hide behind these oceans, as we did in World War I and World War II, while our great industrial machine, which has been decisive in both world wars, is geared up for full production. Today we must be ready at the very outset and maintain a permanent ready force, both nuclear and conventional. This force must have the capability of inflicting unacceptable damage on the other side, no matter what preemptive action they choose to take against us. This position, commonly known as deterrence, certainly has worked so far. So long as the United States maintains a modern force with a secure command and control system, I am confident that the Soviets, faced with such a U.S. capability, will recognize that there can be no winner in a nuclear war. Consequently they will be deterred from starting such a war. They will not be deterred, however, if through actions on our part they come to believe that they can succeed and win. I cannot emphasize too much that deterrence depends on a perception by the leaders of the hostile nation about their chances of winning.

This idea of perception was brought very forcefully home to me at the end of World War II when I had an opportunity to question the Japanese leaders about why they had attacked Pearl Harbor. The answer was the same from all. They pointed out that we had passed the draft law by only one vote, that we had failed to fortify Wake and Guam islands, and that we had our army in Louisiana training with wooden guns. In the general perception of the United States built up in the minds of the Japanese, we did not have the will to defend ourselves, so they made the decision to attack our sovereign territory. Never mind that this was a major mistake; it did result in a major war.

For this reason I am very concerned about the nuclear freeze movement, which is gaining momentum. President Reagan is absolutely right in taking the position that we are for verifiable reductions but against a freeze at the current state of our strategic forces. Our forces were allowed to deteriorate for the past ten years while the Soviets were carrying out a major buildup of their large strategic missiles, such as the SS-17, SS-18, and SS-19. Unfortunately, we are becoming a nation ruled by placards and demonstrations. Consequently, the federal government is severely handicapped in its efforts to provide for the nation's security. There is certainly no question that such groups as the American Peace Council and others are in full support of the nuclear freeze movement. It is an emotional movement, fueled by fear of the unknown. A study of the facts will, however, prove the fallacy of this effort by so many well-meaning but confused citizens, aided and abetted by some whose basic objective is unilateral disarmament by the United States. Certainly much about this will be expressed—in some cases, acrimoniously expressed—during the forthcoming debates on the defense budget in Congress.

Finally, I do not think that any sane person can quarrel with Dr. Nutter's statement that the Soviets have embarked on a grand design of world conquest. From the very outset, Dr. Nutter pointed out, the Bolshevik ideologists were aware that people become gullible and irrational when offered the slightest temptation to believe that peace and the absence of confrontation are at hand. Lenin said: "As an ultimate objective, peace simply means Communist world control."

To understand how the Communist dogma operates, one has only to examine the Soviets' rapid shifts of position at the beginning of World War II. Before the Molotov-Ribbentrop Pact was signed in

1939, all Communists were mobilized against Facism, whether in Spain, Italy, or Germany; but as soon as the pact was signed, their notions of what was progressive and what was not changed dramatically. In 1940 the German Communist leader Walter Ulbricht, later to become head of the East German state, published an article in which he said: "Those who intrigue against the friendship of the German and Soviet people are enemies of the German people and accomplices of the British Imperialists." The British *Daily Worker* adopted a similar line and greeted the new alliance as a victory for peace. So did the American *Daily Worker*, which proclaimed that the war declared by France and Britain on Nazi Germany was an imperialist war and should be opposed by the workers. Trade unions were called upon to sabotage production in munitions factories.

This struggle for peace was particularly influential in France, where the Communist party and its fellow travelers were openly defeatist before the Nazi invasion of France. As soon as Nazi Germany turned against its great eastern ally and invaded Russia, however, the so-called struggle for peace was instantly terminated. For the remainder of World War II the Allies were to enjoy a relaxation of what the Communists like to call the "class struggle."

The Soviet "peace offensive" has been resumed with significant success. The Western governments insisted on linking participation in the Helsinki Agreement to the observance of human rights agreements inside the Communist bloc. The idea was to bring about the internal relaxation of the Soviet regime and so make it open and less oppressive. In exchange the West provided everything Brezhnev had demanded in his peace program of the Twenty-fourth Party Congress in 1971: the inviolability of the postwar frontiers in Europe, that is, legitimation of the Soviet territorial annexations between 1939 and 1948; and a commitment to a substantial increase in economic, scientific, and cultural cooperation. We had earlier agreed to a division of Germany without raising the issue of the Berlin wall.

Far from making the Soviets more dependent, increased trade and huge Western credits have made the West more and more dependent on the Soviet Union, as shown in the dispute between the United States and European nations over the sanctions against the pipeline. In addition, as the press has reported, we have had a devastating flow of technology into Russia, which has been used primarily to enhance its military capability. The Soviets invariably put this technology to military use. The Kama River truck factory built by Americans in the 1970s, for example, manufactured the trucks used during the Soviet invasion of Afghanistan.

After the invasion, which brought about so much negative reaction in and outside Russia, the Soviets accelerated their peace movement. The World Peace Council declared that the people of the world are alarmed, that never before has there been so great a danger of a world nuclear holocaust. This alarm has spread to our country, where we now have all kinds of reactions. The amazing thing about the nuclear freeze movement in both Europe and the United States is that millions of people supposedly of sound mind march about claiming that the threat of war comes from their own governments rather than from the Soviet Union. No matter what one may think of President Reagan, he was elected by the majority of our population, to whom he is fully accountable. He cannot declare war on his own. One should look for the real source of aggression. Was it American or Soviet troops who occupied half of Germany and built a wall in Berlin? Is it not the Soviets who still occupy Hungary, Czechoslovakia, and the Balkan states, not to mention Afghanistan, very much against the wishes of the people in those countries? Was it East or West German troops who took part in the occupation of Czechoslovakia and who are prepared to help subjugate Poland? What do we really know about the decision-making process of the fourteen old terrorists in the Politburo, who were never elected by anyone and who are not accountable to anyone? No press is allowed to criticize them; no demonstrations can be held to protest against their orders. Anyone who refused to obey the orders would disappear forever. There is no real difference between the Soviet system today and Nazi Germany under Hitler.

Dr. Nutter was correct when he called attention to the fact that the Soviets have embarked on a grand design of world conquest, supported by a system completely foreign to ours. In that connection let us examine some of the external activities of the Soviet armed forces after World War II.

Before the guns had even stopped firing, the Soviets were moving into Iran. According to some sources, President Truman told Stalin he would drop the bomb on them if they did not get out—and I emphasize that this was at a time when the United States had a monopoly on nuclear weapons. Only then did the Soviets withdraw from Iran, but shortly thereafter they were in Greece. There followed the very difficult positions the Soviets took that resulted in the Berlin airlift. Shortly thereafter came the Korean War, in which the Soviets fully supported the North Koreans and the Red Chinese. And, of course, everyone knows the Soviets' contribution to the continuation of the Vietnam War, when they were providing approximately $1 billion a year in military supplies to North Vietnam.

Then there was the Cuban crisis, in which the Soviets endeavored to plant missiles on our very doorstep. But perhaps even worse, they have succeeded in maintaining control of Cuba and have used Cuban troops to infiltrate and subjugate many areas in Africa and the Middle East: Angola, Mozambique, Ethiopia, South Yemen, and others.

After the Cuban crisis, at which time we had clear superiority in nuclear weapons as well as in naval forces, the Soviets embarked on a major weapons buildup; today they have without a doubt the largest strategic nuclear force in the world. They exceed us in the number of large missiles, their throwweight, the number of submarines, and the number of tactical nuclear weapons. They have clearly made a major effort to increase both their strategic and their conventional military strength. In a comment on the death of Brezhnev, a Soviet expert pointed out that although Brezhnev had been a total failure in the development of his own economy and in feeding his people, he had nevertheless presided over the most accelerated and largest buildup of military strength in the history of the world. That is the situation we face today.

Let us be hopeful that the advances being made by Secretary Shultz and Vice President Bush will show the Soviets that some kind of accommodation must be reached between the United States and the Soviet nation. As Secretary Shultz has clearly said, however, and as President Reagan has stated over and over again, the United States does have the will and the determination to stay the course despite the storms and the rocks and the shoals that the ship of state faces. Certainly that determination is due in large part to our having men such as Dr. Warren Nutter, who have served their country well and who have been able to state clearly and succinctly the nature of the problems we face.

I repeat that it was a great honor and an education for me to have known my good friend G. Warren Nutter.

Political Economy
1957-1982

James M. Buchanan

April 20, 1983

James M. Buchanan is University Professor at George Mason University, Fairfax, Virginia, and general director of the Center for Study of Public Choice at the University. He was professor of economics from 1951 to 1956 and chairman of the Department of Economics at Florida State University, 1954–1956; chairman of the James Wilson Department of Economics, University of Virginia, 1956–1961; Paul G. McIntire Professor of Economics, University of Virginia, 1962–1968; director of the Thomas Jefferson Center for Political Economy, University of Virginia, 1958–1968; and University Distinguished Professor at the Virginia Polytechnic Institute and State University and general director of its Center for Study of Public Choice, 1969–1983.

Introduction

William Breit

To introduce James Buchanan would be an honor on any occasion, but is a most special honor to me on this one. For Warren Nutter and James Buchanan were the leading luminaries of the University of Virginia's economics department when I arrived there as an untenured faculty member in 1965. Both of them had been names on my reading lists in graduate school. They had made the University of Virginia's economics department famous on the national scene as being unique. The word was out that political economy was being resuscitated at Virginia, and the Thomas Jefferson Center for the Study of Political Economy, which Jim Buchanan and Warren Nutter had founded, was a beehive of scholarly activity investigating the new political economy and its ramifications. The opportunity to join them as a colleague at Virginia I found impossible to resist.

Excitement was in the air. The controversy stirred up by Nutter's recently published book on the Soviet economy, challenging the Establishment view of Soviet industrial growth, was still reverberating from the rafters. I remember well from those days the embattled, tough-minded Warren Nutter, with his soft-spoken manner, his keen sense of humor, the easy laugh, the penetrating insight. Down the hall a bit was James Buchanan, slightly more aloof than Warren Nutter, at first seemingly less approachable. Often the two would huddle together to discuss policy matters, exchange a bit of professional gossip, or more often, to argue some point of economics. I was fortunate to be in on the beginning of the journal *Public Choice*, then called rather infelicitously, *Papers on Non-Market Decision Making*. Other members of the Thomas Jefferson Center were Alexandre Kafka, Gordon Tullock, and Leland Yeager, no slouches as scholars in their own right.

The graduate students were almost uniformly excellent, having been attracted by the stimulating atmosphere that was widely known to prevail in Charlottesville in that department at that time. Best of all I became the personal friend of both Nutter and Buchanan. My most vivid recollection from those days involves the daily lunch period. The topic for discussion typically centered on a recent issue of the *American Economic Review* or *Journal of Political Economy*. It was automatically assumed each individual had read the latest articles in his field. You were certain to be asked your opinion, and it was not considered good form to stare back blankly when your turn came.

At Virginia my education in economics began all over again. Or, as some at Virginia would have said, my education in economics began.

In introducing James Buchanan to this audience I will use a technique that is the counterpart of what in art is called pointillism. Since we do not see others "as complete images but as processions of flashing points,"[1] I shall give you my portrait of Buchanan in a pointillistic fashion, with each fact a dot. That is the way my own image of Buchanan was formed.

- He is five feet, ten inches in height and stands very straight.
- His father was a farmer, and he grew up in rural Tennessee.
- He believes that being a college professor is better work than following a plow.
- He sports a mustache and combs his hair back in a way that makes him look as if he might be playing the part of the heroic general in a war movie.
- He does not suffer fools gladly, and he starts with the assumption that everything he reads in economics is chock full of flaws.
- He is an excellent host, and he and his wife, Ann, serve the best victuals in town.
- He is a prodigious worker and can write a twenty-page article, ready for publication in a leading journal, in a single afternoon.
- He is a considerate referee and will return a manuscript with detailed comments on the day he receives it.
- He was once a flaming socialist.
- He thinks that Knut Wicksell was the greatest economist of all time.
- He is the author or coauthor of fifteen books, the most famous

---

[1] Owen Hatteras, *Pistols for Two* (New York: Alfred A. Knopf, 1917).

of which is *The Calculus of Consent,* written with Gordon Tullock.

- His favorite dish is fried white corn.
- He recently received an honorary doctorate from the University of Giessen in Germany.
- He believes there is no such thing as a benevolent government.
- He is a fellow of the American Academy of Arts and Sciences.
- He considers Frank Knight his greatest teacher.
- His secretary, Betty Tillman Ross, has an efficiency that is legendary, and she is usually mentioned in the prefaces of his books.
- He believes that to have true bureaucratic change you must change the rules, not the personnel, in government. This is called the "constitutional approach." He is its most eminent expositor.
- He has written so much that all alone he would be one of the best economics departments in the country.
- His life is shared with his wife, Ann, six cats, three dogs, and a donkey.
- He makes excellent blackberry wine.

It is my pleasure to present him to you now—James M. Buchanan.

Political Economy: 1957-1982

James M. Buchanan

Introduction

I have chosen my title with deliberation. The symmetry of a quarter-century has an appeal all its own, but my choice was also prompted by events at the beginning and the end years of the period selected. It was in 1957 that Warren Nutter and I founded the Thomas Jefferson Center for Studies in Political Economy at the University of Virginia. It was in 1982 that I engaged in a modern struggle to sustain an institutional setting for a political economy that Warren Nutter would have endorsed enthusiastically. I want to trace the lineage between these terminal points of my narrative. In so doing, I shall be largely concerned with what members of the nation's academies were and are doing and how they interpret their own social, scientific, and philosophical roles. I do not apologize for this emphasis to those among my audience who are not of the academy. I remain convinced that what goes on in the groves has profound effects on the development and transmission of ideas and, ultimately, on the translation of these ideas into practice. I think Warren Nutter might have agreed with me on this point, regardless of what George Stigler, one of my predecessors in this lecture series, has argued.

Political Economy: 1957

In 1957, the implicit socialists were in the ascendancy in the academies of the land. By implicit socialists I refer to those who were driven by an ideological commitment to the benevolent leadership of the national state on all matters economic. (The French have a more suitably descriptive word, *dirigistes*.) In 1957, the Keynesian diversion, to employ Leland Yeager's apt phraseology, was still accelerating if measured by its acceptance in the universities. Those were the days before the Stalinist terror had fully seeped into modern intellectual consciousness. The debacle of postwar socialist experiments elsewhere had not then been fully recognized. The dirigistes in the academic establishment, those who would have run our lives for us, were in positions of dominance. They controlled major departmental programs; they made basic decisions on who should be appointed, tenured, and promoted; they approved what was to be published; they controlled the flow of funds from the major foundations, which had by that time floated free of any desires of the initial donors.

When Warren Nutter and I joined the faculty at the University of Virginia in late 1956 and early 1957, we found, I think to our own surprise, an academic setting that was genuinely different, in a commonwealth with a history that was different in a way that mattered for its academies. Under the leadership of T. R. Snavely, and bolstered by the imaginative ideas of David McCord Wright and Rutledge Vining, the economics program at Virginia had already become different from its counterparts. The University of Virginia administration was more than passively receptive to our announced intention to make some effort to counter more explicitly the dominating thrust in economics, and in political economy, *circa* 1957. (Almost surely, any statement of such an intention would have met immediate resistance at most of the leading universities in the country at that time.) I recall vividly the meeting with William Duren, then dean of the College of Arts and Sciences, and Colgate Darden, then president of the University. When I somewhat hesitantly put forward the notion that Warren and I had discussed about establishing a Political Economy Center, the simple response was go ahead. Given this lead, we waxed enthusiastic, and establish such a Center we did.

In the initial brochure for the Thomas Jefferson Center for Studies in Political Economy that Warren and I jointly prepared, we stated that our purpose was to set up a "community of scholars who wish to preserve a social order based on individual liberty." Little did we reckon on the difficulties that the phrase "individual liberty" would cause us in the intellectual-academic atmosphere of that time. We were told, quite openly, by an officer of a major foundation, that the explicit encouragement of scholars who believed in individual liberty, as implied in the brochure, was "particularly objectionable," and that the Thomas Jefferson Center's stated purpose reflected a clearly defined ideological bias. We were placed under suspicion precisely because we had indicated our intention to study the problems of a free society.

In retrospect, I can recognize our naiveté in thinking that rational argument could have been effective in countering the dominant mind-set of the time. But we did make such argument, and, to this day, I remain pleased with one of my own statements included in a letter to Kermit Gordon, our primary adversary:

> I categorically refuse to acknowledge or to believe that a program such as ours, one that is unique only in its examination of the search of free men for consensus on social issues and which assumes that individuals are free to discuss all issues openly and fully, violates in even the slightest way the Jeffersonian spirit.

But all of this belongs in a much longer story than I can narrate here, a story that would not be appropriate in this lecture.

Let me then shift my level of discourse and try to outline our thinking in establishing the Thomas Jefferson Center. What differences in program did we have in mind? How did Warren Nutter and I aim to make the Virginia program in political economy distinct?

We were concerned, first of all, by what seemed to us to be a developing neglect of the basics of economics. Both Warren Nutter and I were Chicago economists, and Chicago economists of the Frank Knight, Henry Simons, Lloyd Mints, Aaron Director vintage. The basics of economics were those of price theory, not formal mathematics, and price theory applied to real world issues. The economic organization, the market process, was the focus of attention, and the working of this organization operating through the pricing structure was the subject matter of the discipline. Political economy was nothing more than this subject matter embedded within the framework of society, described by the "laws and institutions" about which Adam Smith wrote. To us, quite simply, political economy meant nothing more than a return to the stance of the classical political economists. Aside from Chicago, we saw programs elsewhere in economics neglecting these very foundations of our discipline.

Let me also admit, openly and without apology then or now, that we were motivated by our conviction that if these foundations are neglected, a society in which individuals retain their liberties is not sustainable. We had faith that an understanding of the price system offered the best possible avenue for the generation of support for free institutions. We did not feel any need for explicitly ideological polemic. Our faith in understanding was intensely personal. Both Warren Nutter and I had become economists when we were dedicated socialists. We experienced "conversion" as a result of our own enlightenment through an understanding of market process, and we translated our own shared experience into the positions of our peers and students. We were convinced that the socialist arguments seemed persuasive only to those who were ignorant in economics. Our ultimate purpose was to enlighten prospective graduate students, to help them reach an understanding comparable to our own, to produce economists who knew what their proper subject matter was all about—economists who might then be able, by presenting their own hard-nosed analysis, to lead other generations to their own enlightenment. It was as simple as that, even if we then could not state our purpose so straightforwardly as I now can do. And let me also now acknowledge that, in the dominant mind-set of the late 1950s, our purpose was indeed *subversive.*

The Charlottesville Decade: 1957–1967

Both by our own and by external standards, the Virginia School, over the decade 1957–1967, was highly successful. The Thomas Jefferson Center for Studies in Political Economy was generously supported by several special, nonmainstream foundations, as well as by the University and the Commonwealth. The graduate program was expanded. Leland Yeager, Ronald Coase, Alexandre Kafka, Andrew Whinston, Gordon Tullock, and William Breit were added to the faculty. Visiting scholars, political economists all, and all of worldwide eminence, come to the Center for extended half-year visits. These included Frank Knight, F. A. Hayek, Michael Polanyi, Bertil Ohlin, Bruno Leoni, Terence Hutchison, Maurice Allais, Duncan Black, and O. H. Taylor.

We commenced to attract outstanding graduate students. For a period, our graduate students were among the best in the land. Out of several cohort groups (and with my apologies to an equally large number whose names could well be added), let me mention only a few here: Otto Davis, Charles Goetz, Matt Lindsay, Charles Meiburg, Jim Miller, John Moore, Mark Pauly, John Peterman, Charles Plott, Paul Craig Roberts, Craig Stubblebine, Bob Tollison, Dick Wagner,

Tom Willett. These were all products of the Virginia School of Political Economy. A mere listing of these names is sufficient without elaboration on my part. The Virginia initiative was successful.

During this Charlottesville decade, which seems so productive when viewed retrospectively, things were, of course, happening in economics and in political economy, both in and out of the academies. As I noted earlier, the socialist ideal, as a motive force for intellectual-moral-emotional energies, was perhaps at its zenith in the 1950s. This force was spent by the middle of the 1960s. The somewhat lagging Keynesian apogee was attained in the early 1960s, and fine tuning went the way of all flesh in the latter part of the decade.

The dirigistes of our discipline shifted into neutral or joined the flower children. The Virginia program in political economy lost any putative ideological taint it might have had to external observers as its scholars and students produced ideas that came to command respect and attention. There came to be an increasing awareness of the importance of the institutional setting and of institutional constraints for the operation of an economy. Property rights economics, law and economics, public choice—these three closely related but distinct subdisciplines emerged, each of which is derivative from political economy, broadly defined, and each of which also finds some of its origins in the work of scholars then associated with the Virginia School.

The active and identifiable program at the University of Virginia was not, however, destined to persevere much beyond the decade. Despite its dramatic success story, the program was too different from mainstream academic attitudes within the University itself, and notably to attitudes held by those outside economics. At the same time that the graduate program was being so widely praised for its success by those beyond The Lawn, there were active internal efforts aimed at its destruction. I personally recall that one of my proudest moments was recorded when Jack Gurley, then editor of the *American Economic Review*, in 1963 or 1964, stated in a general meeting of the American Economic Association that Virginia's graduate students were submitting more interesting manuscripts than those of any other institution in the country. At almost the same time, however, and unknown both to Warren Nutter and to me, the university had, in 1963, organized a secret study of our program, by a committee seeking to offset the "political motivation" of the Center. The committee's report concluded with a description of the Department of Economics as "rigidly committed to a single point of view," which it labeled "nineteenth century ultra-conservatism." All of this was produced without consultation with the Department or the Center. The committee went on to recommend, of course, that economists of a "modern outlook" be appointed.

In 1983, twenty years after, this whole episode places the University of Virginia in an extremely bad light. By the mid-1960s, the University, which had indeed been so different in the 1950s, had joined the ranks of academic orthodoxy, albeit belatedly, when it was almost out of date. It is difficult for us to understand the petty ideological envy of the period, and the inability of the University's administrators to separate ideological rancor from standards of scholarship remains incomprehensible to those of us most closely affected.

But the enemies within held the trumps. Over a period of some four years, from 1964 through 1968, the university made no effort to hold onto members of the dramatically successful research-educational unit that we had so fortunately managed to organize at Virginia. Through a policy of deliberate neglect and even active encouragement, scholars were allowed to shift to other institutions. By 1968, Coase, Whinston, Tullock, and Buchanan had moved to other universities, and, in 1969, Warren Nutter became a participating rather than an academic political economist.

At this point my necessarily autobiographical narrative loses direct contact with Warren Nutter. I saw him only rarely after I left Charlottesville in 1968, and after he joined the Department of Defense in 1969. I cannot, therefore, bear personal witness to the continuing struggle within the University that was waged by Warren Nutter after his return to academia. Warren was joined by Leland Yeager, William Breit, and others in this struggle, which continued over the decade of the 1970s. On the few occasions that Warren and I did meet, however, I felt that there had been no change in our long-standing agreement on the purpose and objective of any program in political economy. There was really no need for us to discuss this commonly held commitment to what we considered to be the moral obligation of those in our discipline. For this reason, I feel that it remains appropriate for me, in this memorial lecture, to continue my personal approach to developments in political economy after 1968.

Public Choice—The New Virginia School: 1969-1982

As I noted above, public choice emerged as an independent, or quasi-independent, subdiscipline within political economy and had its inception at the Thomas Jefferson Center in the early 1960s. What was to become the Public Choice Society was initially organized by Gordon Tullock and me at the Old Ivy Inn in Charlottesville in October 1963. When Tullock and I found ourselves relocated in the Commonwealth six years later, this time at VPI, we established the Center for Study of Public Choice.

This new Center had a somewhat narrower purpose than the Thomas Jefferson Center. Experience had shown us that an understanding of the market process was a necessary but not a sufficient condition to secure the intellectual-analytical foundations of a free society. This understanding is greatly strengthened in practice by a complementary understanding of the political process. And we found that public choice, which in summary terms is nothing more than the application and extension of economic tools to politics, opened up exciting new vistas for social scientists, some of whom could never have been affected by exposure to old-fashioned, hard-headed price theory alone. Public choice quickly gained prominence in intellectual circles more generally, both in and out of the academies. Our program in Blacksburg, supported initially by the exciting administrative leadership of T. Marshall Hahn, enjoyed a success quite different from that of the earlier program in Charlottesville. Graduate students came to VPI, and many of these now carry forward the public choice perspective in their research and teaching at many institutions. But perhaps the most dramatic impact of the VPI program is reflected in the internationalization of public choice over the decade of the 1970s. Public choice emerged as the "new political economy" in Europe, Japan, and elsewhere. Blacksburg, Virginia, of all places, became a mecca for economists, political scientists, philosophers, sociologists, and other scholars from all corners of the globe.

As was the case with the Charlottesville center a decade earlier, however, public choice research, like Virginia political economy, its parent, was too unorthodox, too different, indeed too successful, for the dreary bureaucrats that have come to command positions of influence in modern American academies. The year 1982 marked a turning point. The Public Choice Center at VPI, like the Thomas Jefferson Center before it, was a victim of its own successes. It was unable to defend itself from its adversaries within the University. So, in 1982, a new story commenced. We made a decision to start anew, to shift the Center's operations as a unit (faculty, staff, facilities) to what is currently the most dynamic institution in the Commonwealth, to George Mason University in Fairfax. So my narrative here becomes, in part, a celebration, one of renewal of the spirit of Virginia political economy in a more receptive and congenial academic environment. That which Warren Nutter and I launched in 1957 remains alive and well. As I tell everyone who will listen: "Yes, Virginia, there is a Virginia School."

The Orthodoxies of 1982

I repeat my apologies for too many lapses into autobiographical detail that will interest only selected members of my audience. But I have a larger purpose in detailing my own experiences. I want to compare and to contrast the challenges that Warren Nutter and I thought we faced in 1957 with those challenges that seem to face anyone who seeks to promote a research-educational program in political economy in the decade of the 1980s.

Recall that I said earlier that the 1957 mind-set of the academy's members was dirigiste or implicitly socialist. Among economists, market failure was all the rage, and a demonstration that markets could fail by comparison with a totally imaginary idealized construction was widely held to be evidence that political-governmental intervention was justified. The macroeconomic fluctuations in employment, output, and the price level were held to exist only because old-fogey politicians had not yet learned the Keynesian policy lessons. Recall how economists of that time laughed with scorn when President Eisenhower said that public debt imposed burdens on the generation's grandchildren.

It is easy to criticize the attitudes of the economists of the 1950s. But let us also give them due credit. They were wrong on so much; we are allowed to say this in hindsight. But they were interested in ideas, and they thought that ideas mattered. They were not frauds, and they were not conscious parasites on the community.

A quarter-century is a long time. But the shift in the mind-set of the economists who dominate the nation's academies has been such that we now seem a whole century away from that of the 1950s. Surely for the better, implicit socialism has almost disappeared. Even under the most inclusive definition that might be possible, the economists of 1982 who could be enrolled under socialist banners would make up a tiny minority of the profession, and they control almost no programs or funds. The dominant dirigisme of the 1950s has vanished, but it has not been replaced by any comparable offsetting ideological commitment.

Economics, as a discipline, became "scientific" over the quarter century, but I put the word in quotation marks and I deliberately use it pejoratively here. As it is practiced in 1983, economics is a science without ultimate purpose or meaning. It has allowed itself to become captive of the technical tools that it employs without keeping track of just what it is that the tools are to be used for. In a very real sense, the economists of the 1980s are illiterate in basic principles of their own discipline, even if in a quite different manner from those of the 1950s. Their motivation is not normative; they seem to be ideological eunuchs. Their interest lies in the purely intellectual properties of the models with which they work, and they seem to get their kicks from the discovery of proofs of propositions relevant only to their own fantasy lands.

Command of the tools of modern economics is a challenging intellectual achievement, and I do not question for a minute the brilliance of the modern scientists who call their discipline by the same name that I call my own. I do deplore the waste that such investment of human capital reflects. The intellectual achievement comes at major resource cost, and, as with any such commitment, the opportunity cost is measured in benefits that might be expected from the alternative that is sacrificed. In modern economics, that which is sacrificed is an understanding of the principles of market process, and of the relationship of this process to the institutional setting within which persons choose. In other words, learning to master the tools of modern economics, as exemplified in the educational programs of our major graduate schools today, does not leave time for the achievement of an understanding of political economy in the classical meaning of the term.

Our graduate schools are producing highly trained, highly intelligent technicians who are blissfully ignorant of the whole purpose of their alleged discipline. They feel no moral obligation to convey and to transmit to their students any understanding of the social process through which a society of free persons can be organized without overt conflict while at the same time using resources without tolerable efficiency.

The task faced by those of us who would restore political economy to its proper place as the central research program of our discipline is, then, quite different from that which we faced in the 1950s, and it is in many respects much more difficult. The socialist commitment was dislodged in part by the simple observation of the cumulative historical experience, which finally does affect human consciousness, even of those long immunized within the ivoried towers. The success of some of our earlier efforts in instilling an understanding of the elementary principles of market and political order was made possible only by the sweep of events over the three decades. To say that events overwhelmed the intellectual arguments is not, of course, to deny the relevance of the latter. Public choice theory did offer the intellectually sophisticated "government failure" analogue to the earlier "market failure" thrust of welfare economics. But general attitudes about governmental failures were much more directly affected by straightforward observation of those failures in action.

Our job in 1983 is, therefore, less one of ideological displacement and more one of methodological revolution in our parent discipline of economics itself. We find ourselves in the bizarre position where those of us who seek to define our central research program as it was defined for the first century and one-half of our discipline's history are now the methodological revolutionaries. At VPI, for example, we were told that basic price theory is not now part of "mainstream economics," that economic theory, as defined in 1982, is really a branch of higher mathematics, and that the applied economics that we seek to emphasize is simple chorework for the pedestrian minds.

Our task is made difficult because of the genuine awe that partially trained mathematicians feel for mathematics itself. It is useful to try to understand just why this awe arises, and why it tends to create such serious inferiority complexes in those economists who do not fully understand economic process. Why do the acknowledged masters in mathematics itself not feel some comparable awe at the understanding possessed by the genuine political economists? What is the ultimate source of the one-way awe?

I suggest that the asymmetry emerges because of the methodological revolution in economics that did take place, almost unnoticed, in the twentieth century, and notably since Alfred Marshall wrote his *Principles*. Once the "economic problem" becomes the research program of the discipline, and the search is on for maximizing or optimizing solutions within the constraints of specified wants, resources, and technology, we become unwittingly trapped in a mathematical perspective. In this perspective, we must defer to those among us who have superior command of the tools and techniques that only sophisticated modern mathematics can provide. In this perspective, those among us who cannot "border the Hessians" are ignoramuses, and we should be made to feel pedestrian and second rate, left behind by the mainstream scholars of the 1980s.

The basic commitment to the mathematical perspective in economics may be challenged, however, and, outside this perspective, we need feel no more awe for the mathematicians than we do for the logician, the linguist, or the fiddle player. In comparison with these specialists, we simply acknowledge that we are trained to do differing things. So it should be with the mathematicians. The methodological revolution that is required in political economy must remove the awe by shedding the mathematical perspective; unless this perspective is modified, we shall remain the slaves of the economist-cum-mathematician.

Let me be quite specific at this point, and let me try to illustrate my argument. It is necessary to be clear especially since many of our colleagues who are outstanding political economists, in the way that I should define the term, remain trapped in the mathematical perspective, even if they remain unconscious of its effect on so many lesser lights. It is their own ability to have become solid political economists while not having been awed by the mathematicians that distinguishes members of this group, but this very ability does tend to blind them to the genuine methodological trap that the mathematical perspective places upon the whole discipline.

I must be bold on this occasion of all others, and I must suggest that the mathematical perspective takes hold once we so much as define persons as utility or preference functions and implicitly presume that these functions exist independently of the processes within which persons make actual choices. The utility function apparatus can be properly employed as an ex post reconstruction of the choices that may have been made, but it becomes totally misleading to postulate the independent existence of such functions. By postulating such functions independently, and by imposing the resource constraints, it becomes possible to define, at least conceptually, the "efficient" allocation of resources, quite apart from any voluntary processes of agreement among trading parties. This formalization of the efficiency norm then allows the market to be conceptualized as merely a means, a mechanism, one among others, to be tested or evaluated in terms of its efficacy in attaining desired results in the utilization of resources.

It is indeed hard for almost anyone trained in economics almost anywhere in this part of our century to exorcise the false constructions and presuppositions that characterize the mathematical perspective. It is not easy to give up the notion that there does, indeed, exist an efficient resource allocation "out there," to be conceptually defined by the economist, and against which all institutional arrangements may be tested. Despite the emerging emphasis on process as opposed to end-state philosophizing, economists will only reluctantly give up major instruments of their kit of tools.

Prospects

In any short-term context, I am not at all optimistic that the required methodological revolution will take place. Academic programs almost everywhere are controlled by rent-recipients who simply try to ape the mainstream work of their peers in the discipline. These academic bureaucrats will not be easily displaced, and it is only in fortuitous circumstances that favorable academic settings will present themselves to those who would take the foundations of their discipline seriously.

I remain thoroughly convinced, however, in 1983 as in 1957, that those of us who do place a value on the transmission of the intellectual heritage of political economy face a moral imperative. We must exert every effort to ensure the survival of the ideas that were formative in generating what Hayek has properly called the great society.

Warren Nutter was fond of saying, in the sometimes bleak days of the 1950s and early 1960s, that one of our most important functions was to "save the books." Interpreted in the way that I know Warren meant that statement, our function remains basically unchanged. Classical liberalism—the ideas and the analysis that nurtured these ideals for a society that became a near reality—need not perish from the earth. As the saying on Fred Glahe's Colorado T-shirt puts it, "Adam Smith was right—pass it on."

Adversaries, Allies, and Foreign Economic Policy

Yuan-li Wu

November 28, 1983

YUAN-LI WU was a research economist at the Stanford Research Institute from 1951 to 1954 and a professor of economics at Marquette University from 1956 to 1959. From 1969 to 1970 he was deputy assistant secretary of defense of the United States. Since 1960 he has been a professor of economics at the University of San Francisco and a consultant at the Hoover Institution at Stanford University.

Introduction

Richard A. Ware

I am privileged to welcome to the Nutter Lecture Series Professor Yuan-li Wu, a one-time colleague of Warren's and of mine in the Office of International Security Affairs at the Pentagon.

My first contact with Mr. Wu was indirect and without his knowledge. Sometime in the 1950s I had occasion to be concerned with economic warfare and found a book by that title in the graduate library in Ann Arbor, Michigan. The book, published in 1952, carried as author, Yuan-li Wu. I was impressed with its content and with the fact that it was the only book-length treatment of the subject. I also noted Mr. Wu acknowledged the influence of Professor Friedrich von Hayek at the London School of Economics. This acknowledgment established his credentials for me.

In 1964, Mr. Wu and I assisted the Republican Platform Committee in San Francisco in a group known as "Rhodes Scholars," named after Congressman John Rhodes of Arizona.

In 1969 Secretary of Defense Melvin Laird appointed Mr. Wu deputy assistant secretary of defense for international security affairs (ISA) with responsibility for policy plans and National Security Council affairs. Under his direct supervision were strategic and nuclear planning, defense participation in the National Security Council system, and defense concerns with the People's Republic of China. These were matters of major importance. Mr. Wu functioned in his usual quiet, competent manner and earned a citation for responsibilities executed with distinction.

As an aside, I would like to cite a comment about ISA in the Nutter years, when Mr. Wu was aboard. In 1970 (on May 5 to be specific) Joseph Kraft observed that ISA had become "a corps of right-wing clowns." You may judge for yourselves as you share Professor Wu's thoughts today.

Born in China, Professor Wu earned his undergraduate degree and his doctorate at the London School of Economics after having been awarded the prestigious Tooke Scholarship and Leverhulme Research Grant. He has served with the United Nations staff, the Chinese Central Bank, and the Stanford Research Institute and has held faculty appointments at Hofstra College, LaTrobe University in Australia, Nanyang University in Singapore, and Marquette and Stanford universities. In 1960 he joined the University of San Francisco where he is now professor of economics. He is also a consultant at the Hoover Institution.

Professor Wu has published scores of books, monographs, research studies, and journal articles. They range over such subjects as international economics, arms control, the economy of China, economic development, economic warfare, linear programming, entrepreneurship, raw materials, and strategic problems in the Pacific basin.

An introduction has the purpose of providing the audience some "feel" for the speaker, for his abilities, qualifications, and character. My remarks thus far have related to the first three purposes. To complete my assignment I quote an entry in the *Congressional Record* of June 5, 1969:

> Mr. Goldwater: Mr. President, this morning it was my pleasure to attend the ceremonies in the Pentagon at which Dr. Yuan-li Wu was sworn in as Deputy Assistant Secretary of Defense. I have known Mr. Wu for a number of years. I hold him in high regard as a citizen, a statesman, a scientist and a man. After the swearing-in, Dr. Wu asked that he be heard for a few moments, and he read a statement which he had composed before the ceremonies. That this man, who now occupies the highest position any Chinese-born American has ever held, would ask to express his feelings about his adopted country touched me to the point that I asked permission from him to have the statement placed in the RECORD, so that more people can know the type of man who is now helping in our defense.
>
> I ask unanimous consent that the statement be printed in the RECORD.
>
> There being no objection, the statement was ordered to be printed in the RECORD, as follows:

Statement by Mr. Yuan-li Wu
I know of no other major country in the world that would

accord an immigrant citizen the honor the United States has just accorded me this morning. I will do everything I can to deserve it. My obligation to this country and to my fellow citizens goes, however, far beyond this. For my wife and I were twice refugees in our lifetime, from the Nazis in the '30's, from the Communists in the '40's. The United States has given us a haven of liberty and personal security; my fellow Americans, in their generosity of spirit, have accepted us among them. We are not citizens by birth right; we have become citizens by adoption. Believe me, when I say that we know how precious is the gift to be Americans. It is this gift that I must seek to repay over and above the honor granted me today that I must earn to deserve.

Under the leadership of my superiors and in cooperation with my colleagues I shall endeavor to serve our country well. I shall follow the spirit of the few lines which I hope you will permit me to quote, and which are my favorite, from Micah, Chapter Six, Verse Eight:

> It hath been told thee, O man,
> What is good and what the Lord doth require of thee:
> Only to do justly, and to love mercy,
> And to walk humbly with thy God.

The title of the lecture by our guest is Adversaries, Allies, and Foreign Economic Policy. I present to you a man of superior character and distinguished scholarship, Professor Yuan-li Wu.

Adversaries, Allies, and Foreign Economic Policy

Yuan-li Wu

It is a privilege to be invited to address this distinguished audience in the lecture series in memory of G. Warren Nutter, an esteemed colleague and friend. I am also deeply appreciative of Dick Ware's most gracious introduction.

My association with Warren was an invaluable education for me, particularly on the subjects of foreign policy and political realism. I need only to mention two events during this period to give you a hint of the flavor of our association and my learning process: the presidential campaign in 1964 and the beginning of the U.S. withdrawal from Vietnam in 1969. It is in this contemporary context of American policy debate that I have chosen for my topic this afternoon, "Adversaries, Allies, and Foreign Economic Policy."

National Security and Foreign Economic Policy: A Puzzle of Apparent Inconsistencies

I recall that the first assignment I was given in 1969, when Warren and Dick asked me to join them across the river, had to do with economic sanctions. As a matter of fact, the question whether U.S. machinery should be exported to equip the Soviet Union's Kama River truck plant then under construction figured prominently during the period when my task was to review such matters from time to time. Today, more than a decade later, we are debating the advisability of selling oil and gas equipment to the Soviet Union. Ten years ago we were busily engaged in strengthening and multiplying our economic ties with the Soviet Union to encourage Moscow to moderate its foreign political behavior as a matter of self-interest. Perhaps we did not persist long enough; perhaps we were mistaken in our expectations in the first place. Somewhere things have gone awry. Today we are busily engaged in strengthening economic ties with the People's Republic of China, an avowed enemy in the 1950s but now officially designated a friendly nation, not only to improve bilateral relations through the exchange of grain, technology, and even arms for Chinese resources and textiles—which incidentally some American manufacturers and workers really would rather not receive—but also to develop a strategic dialogue that is at least partially aimed at influencing Soviet behavior. It is plain that, as far as adversaries are concerned, we have not solved certain fundamental problems of linkage between national security policy and foreign economic policy.

As for allied trade, the past decade has witnessed the growth of disputes between the United States and some of our present and former allies and among these countries themselves. Textiles, automobiles, steel, electronics, citrus fruit, beef, and many other products have appeared on a crowded list of items in dispute between the United States on the one hand and Japan and some European Community members on the other. Charges of trade restriction through tariff and nontariff barriers have been thrown at one another on all sides. Allied nations have accused one another of "beggar-thy-neighbor" policies, which at varying times have included holding one's own currency at an artificially low exchange rate to promote exports, callously disregarding the external impact of unrestrained inflation, and setting unconscionably high interest rates that drain capital from other countries as an integral part of maintaining monetary restraints while running budget deficits. These issues are, of course, among the traditional sources of international economic dispute; they stem from problems of domestic employment and economic fluctuation, from specific industry and labor interests, and from the polemic that always surrounds the distribution of economic welfare and burden, both among nations and within each nation. These controversial issues are complicated by disagreements on how best to deal with third-world countries, including the Soviet Union. Because of the recent recession, the desire to expand exports to the Soviet Union, which presumably still is a common adversary, has increased in many allied countries just when, for the same reason, interallied economic disputes of the traditional type have worsened.

Lack of consistency between national security and foreign economic policies is a common problem, not one for the United States alone. Consider, for instance, the relation between the United States and Japan. Since the two countries regard each other as the linchpin of their respective security in the Pacific, as leaders in both countries have repeatedly averred, common sense suggests that both should try to minimize each other's economic difficulties while seeking prompt resolutions to economic disputes. If Japan is truly concerned about the increasing military strength of the Soviet Union, it behooves Japan not to help develop Soviet resources and improve Soviet transportation in Siberia or to bolster Soviet naval capability in the Pacific with supplies and repair service. By the same token, the United States should not threaten Japan with import restrictions that could increase Tokyo's incentive to export more to the Soviet Union. One can also question whether some of our European allies are wise to strengthen the Soviet Union's ability to earn hard currency through natural gas export or to refinance bad loans made in the past in pursuit of détente and *Ostpolitik* to some Warsaw Pact countries. Consistency has been a rare currency in the West as a whole.

Nor has the West been exemplary in meeting the economic challenge posed by some third-world countries, like those of OPEC, that are neither allies nor adversaries. The sharp oil price increases of 1973–1974 and of 1979, as well as the steady price rise during the years in between, have successfully brought about a radical redistribution of the world's wealth and foreign-exchange reserves and have decidedly enhanced the political and strategic importance of some oil-producing countries, notably those in the Middle East. This change has greatly affected the foreign policies of large oil-importing countries, such as Japan, some European Community members, and the United States (not to mention many third-world countries) by narrowing their policy options. The dispute between Western Europe and this country over the natural gas pipeline was partly a result of the Europeans' desire to shift away from oil and to diversify sources of energy supply. Japan's willingness to help develop Siberian (including Sakhalin) energy resources has been similarly motivated by a desire to shift energy supply away from the Middle East to geographically closer sources.

We need not dwell on the global economic impact of oil price–induced inflation and the subsequent world-wide recession. Nevertheless we should remind ourselves that the huge foreign indebtedness piled up by some developing countries during the period of rising oil prices and through petroleum dollar recycling daily threatens the health of more than a few financial institutions. Nor should we overlook that the refinancing of some of the imprudent loans

Western creditors have made to the less developed countries now in severe financial straits has been made doubly difficult by the existence of many equally improvident loans that the same Western countries have extended to Warsaw Pact countries. The latter loans also have had to be refinanced and will continue to require refinancing. One wonders how those Brazilian financiers who last month went around the world's financial centers looking for credit must feel about the manner in which Western bankers had earlier negotiated with Soviet bloc borrowers. The International Monetary Fund and Western commercial creditors have rightly urged borrowers in Brazil, Mexico, and Argentina to tighten their belts and to transfer resources to the external sector so that they will not default. Yet Western creditors would have significantly greater difficulty in urging Warsaw Pact countries to transfer to their external sectors resources they now devote to military spending and domestic repression or to restructure their economies in favor of more economic efficiency and debt-servicing.

In short, numerous examples from many countries can be cited to prove the existence of inconsistency between national security and foreign economic policies in the treatment of allies, adversaries, and third parties. This inconsistency demands an explanation.

Five Main Reasons for Policy Inconsistency

I submit that there are five main reasons why such inconsistency has existed so long and has been so widespread. The reasons interact with one another and create additional complications. Although I am speaking primarily from the U.S. perspective, the points I shall raise are really of wider application.

The Effectiveness of Economic Sanctions. First, whether or not economic sanctions should be applied, for example, by the United States against the Soviet Union, is a matter of controversy because there is disagreement on their effectiveness even when there is agreement on their desirability. Some argue that sanctions in the form of denials through export control over the sale of specific goods are ineffective because of the existence of other suppliers. As a corollary of this argument, efforts to extend national controls to suppliers located in other countries run into disputes over extraterritoriality. Typical examples are the 1982 pipeline dispute between the United States and Western Europe and the concern over the Kama River truck plant.

The effectiveness of economic sanctions also depends upon the timing of their intended impact. Some argue that the effect of sanctions is short-lived because in the long run the target country can make adjustments that could even lead to favorable developments, which would not have occurred in the absence of the special incentive to counteract the initial sanctions. Clearly the ability to make such adjustments varies according to the country, to the nature of the exports denied under the sanctions, and to the will of the affected country to make the necessary adjustments.

In contrast to the above, others argue that some economic sanctions can be effective only in the long run and only if they are consistently applied over many years, during which adjustments on the part of the target country are inadequate and costly. For instance, the denial of certain high-technology exports to the Soviet Union may have little immediate effect on that country's military strength, but it can retard the growth of Soviet capability and help maintain a U.S. technological lead if the Soviet Union fails to catch up or to find a sufficiently economical bypass. Some argue further that this U.S. lead has been narrowing progressively over an expanding area.

The effectiveness and desirability of sanctions are disputed, according to another argument, through the existence of many dual-use goods. This argument underlies some of the disagreements among allies in the Coordinating Committee (COCOM) in Paris. On one hand, those who dislike sanctions stress the civilian aspect of such goods and thus advocate their export to an adversary in the name of free commerce. Those who favor sanctions, on the other hand, stress the potential military use of such goods and warn against decontrol. Occasionally compromises are struck between the two sides by requiring guarantees that such items not be diverted to military use by the importer or that reexport be subject to control. Yet it is never quite clear how such promises can be effectively policed or what sanctions can be applied in the event of a breach of the promise.

The effectiveness of economic sanctions can be weakened either by limiting their scope to only a list of selected commodities or through eliminating parallel financial restrictions. Yet, from time to time, some countries will make loans to an adversary or to an adversary's ally while agonizing over the exportation of specific commodities to either. The inter-European differences on export credits in the case of the natural gas pipeline provide an illustration of this continuing issue.[1]

---

[1]See Axel Lebahn, "The Yamal Gas Pipeline from the USSR to Western Europe in the East-West Conflict," in *Aussenpolitik*, vol. 34 (March 1983), pp. 256–80.

Clearly some of the disagreements on the effectiveness and urgency of economic sanctions are based on honest differences in the reading of facts. Many of the disagreements, however, stem from differences on desirability and goals, which must then be explained by examining the remaining reasons.

The Disagreement of Allies. A second reason for inconsistency in foreign economic policy partly explains the many divergent national viewpoints on economic sanctions among allies. This has to do with the nature and purpose of defensive alliances and with the absence of certain specific arrangements and of accompanying positive goals. Since such alliances have the primary purpose of deterrence and defense, they do not call for winning by active, intentional, and all-out effort to weaken the economic and general capability of an adversary. The goal of victory is actively pursued only in a hot war and sometimes not even then (*vide* the U.S. experience in Vietnam). Accordingly, the goal of economic sanctions is subject to varying national assessments of threat and must compete with other national political and economic goals, which are by no means shared to the same degree by individual allied countries. International institutions such as the International Monetary Fund and the World Bank, organized for some of these other goals, pursue their separate objectives in the same self-justified manner.

More specifically, of America's major allies in Europe and Asia, both West Germany and Japan have national reasons for not antagonizing the Soviet Union unduly, even though they fear the Soviet Union most, probably more than does the United States. The sentimental longing for reunification has sustained Bonn's subsidization of East Berlin since the postwar division of Germany. The 1983 loan in which the conservative Franz Josef Strauss played a prominent intermediary's role is a recent good example. Through West Germany, the German Democratic Republic is able to earn more hard currency in the European Community; one can probably assume that East Germany at the same time is a gateway to the Soviet market for many Western goods. On the other side of the globe, Japan has always promoted exports to both the Soviet Union and the People's Republic of China, drawing on ample official and private credits. This export-promotion policy appears to be a long-term effort to rebuild the nation's external investments, going far beyond the mere replacement of the colonies Japan lost in defeat. Japan is applying this general policy equally to both the Soviet Union and China in order to maintain diplomatic equidistance from the two Communist powers and in the belief that no one in his right mind would kill a goose laying golden eggs. The willingness of both Germany and Japan, and this is equally true with respect to other alliance members, to accede to U.S. demands in controlling trade with the Soviet Union—the United States of course no longer requires such severe sanctions against Peking— is a function of their perception of Washington's ability to match the Soviet Union in strength and to provide alternative economic opportunities.

It would be a mistake to think that leaders in such allied countries as West Germany and Japan are unaware of the strategic benefits provided to the Soviet Union by their own exports and loans. The security cost of such trade and credit, however, is not expressly visible as long as there is no direct link between the present economic benefits received and the present and future incremental defense costs and taxes a stronger Soviet Union may necessitate. In short, one cannot expect an allied country to be too concerned about the consequences that expanding economic relations with an adversary could entail so long as taking a "free ride" in financing collective defense is possible. Apparently the mutual defense and alliance treaties of the United States have inadequate provisions to link defense cost–sharing among the allies with the magnitude and nature of their individual economic relations with the adversaries against whom the agreements were originally concluded. The concept of defense cost–sharing has been conceived too narrowly and has not allowed for the disproportionate distribution of gains from developing economic relations with a common adversary.

Furthermore, it would be much more persuasive as one demands more uniform economic sanctions and more equitable sharing of all direct and indirect collective defense costs if one could at the same time raise the prospect of greater economic benefits from further economic liberalization among the allies. The defense consensus in NATO in the past was no doubt strengthened by the positive vision of a better future in international relations.[2] Hence intra-alliance free trade, or better still, free trade in the free world is an objective that members of the defensive security pacts must be able to offer one another.

---

[2] For a review of these and related issues, see the IISS Annual Conference papers published in *Defense and Consensus: The Domestic Aspects of Western Security*, Adelphi Papers, nos. 182–84 (London: International Institute for Strategic Studies, Summer 1983), part 1, pp. 1–58; part 2, pp. 1–42; part 3, pp. 1–32.

Elections and Domestic Interests. The third main reason for inconsistency in external economic and security policies involves the nature of political democracies and the ways they operate. When popular elections are held at intervals of only a few years, short-term domestic business and political interests often receive greater attention than long-term national interests. Given the sometimes fixed schedules of elections and the uncontrollable, random occurrence of external events, such as the Soviet invasion of Afghanistan or the Polish imposition of martial law, to which immediate policy responses are required, the nature of the response will vary with respect both to the specific experience of the administration in power and to the lead or lag in time with reference to the next election. The further away the next election is, the less is the domestic political cost of restricting exports; the closer the next election, the greater the political cost of an export embargo, unless the embargo is deemed necessary to demonstrate decisiveness and leadership, which could offset the cost. Not only does an elected representative realize that citizens of foreign countries are not a part of his electorate, but experience convinces him that most of his real electorate have short memories.

Given the interplay of political calendars, sectional interests, and uncontrollable external events, it is not surprising that the official attitude toward economic sanctions could flip-flop. For the same reason it is entirely possible for economic disputes with military and political allies to flare up in a seemingly inexplicable manner until special domestic conditions are taken into account.[3]

Changes in National Interests. A fourth reason underlying policy inconsistency is that national interests are not always defined in the same way by the same country. As long as national interests are determined by absolute values, that is, in ideological terms, it is easy to identify adversaries as against allies; such categories tend to be stable. Accordingly, it is also relatively easy to assess the desirability of specific economic policies such as total sanctions against an adversary or totally free trade and capital flows among allies. Once absolute values are abandoned, however, in favor of relative positions of power in

---

[3]See, for instance, the most interesting discussion on some U.S.-Japanese trade issues in I. M. Destler, P. Clapp, H. Fukui, and H. Sato, *Managing an Alliance: The Politics of U.S.-Japanese Relations* (Washington: Brookings Institution, 1976), pp. 9–88 and 167–195; and I. M. Destler, "United States Trade Policymaking during the Tokyo Round" in Michael Blaker, ed., *The Politics of Trade: U.S. and Japanese Policymaking for the GATT Negotiations* (New York: Columbia University Press, 1978), pp. 13–64.

comparison with one or more other nations, the distinction between allies and adversaries becomes blurred in a dynamic context. One tends to see threat from countries that are potential rivals if their relative position in strength, military or economic or both, rises faster than one's own. One looks for allies among those countries that harbor similar sentiments toward one's actual adversary or potential rival. The direction or lines of development in this continuing process of jockeying for position are necessarily unclear. The relative strengths of the major powers of our time, as well as the numerous third-world countries of which the role of a few (for example, OPEC and the newly industrializing countries) has been increasing in importance in recent years, do not change at the same rate or in the same direction. A constant search for new partners to face existing and new rivals lends inevitably to policy instability in bilateral relations. Accordingly, those who expect a stable policy toward a historical adversary and equally stable policies toward historical allies are often perplexed. When those who are thus perplexed are themselves policy makers in other countries, they are likely to become less committed to past courses of action and to adopt positions of greater ambiguity. Is it surprising then that confusion becomes doubled?

The Carrot or the Stick. Fifth, policy makers do not agree on the best approach to foreign economic policy. Some people argue that the carrot is better than the stick. Instead of economic sanctions that are intended to reduce the ability of an adversary to do harm and his penchant to misbehave, one could try to induce an adversary to behave better with offers of economic advantages. Furthermore, an even more sophisticated argument is that these economic advantages are an opening wedge to enduring economic relations that would make the destruction of these relations in the future too painful for the present adversary to contemplate. This theory rests on specific assumptions about the nature of the economic systems of both sides and the respective policy responses when things fail to develop in the propitious manner desired.

If the adversary is predisposed to seeking accommodation with the country offering such enticements, it may indeed respond positively to them. This, however, is far from saying that any positive response will necessarily be sufficiently satisfactory to the other side or that it will be enduring and irreversible. Furthermore, unless the adversary is unusually trusting or naive, it will guard against becoming overdependent upon the opponent. The chance of unwittingly becoming economically dependent upon a foreign country is less for a planned economy or an authoritarian regime than for a market system in which pluralistic decision making by businesses and competition for economic benefits from abroad make individual firms and industries more vulnerable. Market economies are more likely to grow accustomed to these benefits and therefore to become susceptible to external pressure later on. How Soviet negotiators were able to best Western bankers and manufacturers in the pipeline case by adroitly exploiting the latter's competition with one another and Moscow's position as a monopsonist was recently told by a former representative of the Deutsche Bank.[4]

The country tempted with economic benefits may have a different goal from one's own. For instance, it may wish to achieve strategic superiority or it may wish, for the foreseeable future, only to broaden its options by taking advantage of every proffered opening. In either case, the "nice guy" approach would not lead to any real change in adversarial behavior on the other side. Our negotiations with the Soviet Union in the 1970s amply demonstrated that the assumptions underlying détente at that time were overoptimistic. Our present negotiations with the People's Republic of China could well meet with the same fate.

Yet at what point one should finally admit to oneself that previous policy assumptions were mistaken is a question that has never been squarely answered. In the absence of such an admission and of adequate institutional memory, new policy makers will from time to time return to the same old assumptions and be perhaps disappointed another time. Although there always is uncertainty (one can never be certain of what might have been if a different decision had been taken—the alternative outcome might even have been worse), one must nevertheless endeavor to avoid repeating the same mistakes. Failure to monitor closely and to report openly on how one's assumptions have worked out intensifies policy confusion. A mistake in judgment is bad enough; when the initial error is compounded by lack of information feedback and of policy correction, the result can be much worse.

If the above five reasons are correct, we can readily understand (1) why nations founded on ideologies hostile to our beliefs are nevertheless frequently courted with economic advantages; (2) why major allies, joined together in the past by shared beliefs and mutual de-

---

[4]See Lebahn, "The Yamal Gas Pipeline."

fense needs, are nevertheless often embroiled in bitter, continuing economic disputes both in dealing with each other and in regard to the best approach to their more or less common adversaries; (3) why policies of détente and confrontation tend to alternate in our dealing with nations that are more often adversaries than friends; (4) why short-term tactical and symbolic responses to external events, often unanticipated and caused by smaller third parties, take the place of deliberate and long-term policy; and (5) why the policy on economic sanctions has perplexed us. It is not at all that policy makers here and in other major Western countries behave irrationally; it is that when rational calculations of cost and benefit are made over the short run on the basis of a limited number of the many variables that should have been included, the decisions reached cannot yield an optimal, comprehensive external policy made up by mutually consistent economic and political parts.

What Is to Be Done? The Pothole Theory and the Second-Best Policy

The twists and turns that managers of U.S. foreign policy have had to make in both its security and its economic components can sometimes be compared to the maneuvers a car driver has to go through when faced with potholes on the road. He may have started from his home, heading for downtown. He finds himself unexpectedly coming upon a pothole, and he steers around it; he sees another and again successfully negotiates it. Inasmuch as the potholes are randomly distributed, there is no way to foretell where he would find himself headed after he has nimbly driven around a few, each time congratulating himself on his successful crisis management. Indeed he may no longer be headed downtown. But no matter. Perhaps he did not know where he was going in the first place and cared little.

In the continuum of foreign policy making, some of the potholes in the story are not truly randomly distributed. They may be of our own making. Some are look-alikes, which suggests that mistakes may have been repeated. When national resources have to be used to undo past mistakes, we have plainly failed to use them optimally.

Ideally—and I stress ideally—to create the conditions for an optimal external policy, we need to do the following:

- adopt or, as some might say, restore certain absolute values, such as the respect for individual liberty and the rule of law, as positive criteria in identifying allies, adversaries, and countries in between

- develop a national consensus on and an understanding of the effect of domestic and foreign economic policies on defense needs (whether quantifiable or not) and on the cost to meet such needs (that is, an understanding of the trade-offs between short- as well as long-term national or private economic interests and short- as well as long-term political and security interests)
- conclude arrangements with allies that would link defense cost-sharing with suitable indicators of the benefits all alliance members receive from their respective economic (including both trade and credit) relations with certain adversaries
- integrate the preceding arrangements with and expand the scope and frequency of the existing consultation processes among market economies (for instance, between the U.S. special trade representative and his foreign counterparts, but going far beyond the scope of current practice)
- develop a more effective system for regulating the trade of individual businesses in allied countries with nonmarket economies.[5]

In theoretical terms, the preceding proposal aims at (1) broadening the scope of foreign policy making by bringing in more key cost and benefit variables and relating benefits to accountability in their total real cost and (2) establishing mechanisms for qualitative if not quantitative assessments of these broadening categories of costs and benefits both in this country and among allies. Of course, like the general equilibrium approach in pure economics, such a state of affairs can hardly be expected in the real world. Yet, on one hand, one should not assume the defeatist attitude that none of the above conditions can ever be realized to the point that efforts to establish them will be treated as a waste of time. On the other hand, to expect that any of these conditions can be established quickly would be totally unrealistic. Hence the realist must look for the "second-best" policy and the minimum requirement as a stepping stone to the second best.

A principal component of such a second-best policy is to establish for all alliance members—for example, in NATO, the U.S.-Japan Security Treaty—an acknowledged link between the tax burden of defense

---

[5]In the United States, specifically, the need for domestic policies to develop a greater defense capability in the context of the existing alliance systems and a greater willingness to increase our own international competitiveness is here taken for granted. The first condition will increase our usefulness to allies; the second condition will reduce the call for protection by domestic interests, thus reducing interallied disputes. Together the conditions will be conducive to reaching agreement with allies on establishing uniform standards in economic sanctions against adversaries and to developing mutually supportive economic and security relations.

each country has to bear and the advantage each country derives from its economic relations with the adversary or adversaries, the defense against whose possible aggression is the raison d'être of these pacts. Clearly this may require revisions of existing agreements, which, if accomplished, would be a major step toward allied unity. One cannot expect a wholesale move in this direction in the short run, but the movement must begin somewhere. Introducing the subject in the continuing U.S.-Japan economic and security dialogues might be an appropriate starting point.[6]

If linking the benefits an ally derives from trading with an adversary to the defense cost his tax-paying public must shoulder is too ambitious a goal to set immediately, one can take a less ambitious step. One may offer to make alternative purchases from such an allied country, assuring the latter's businesses and workers of the benefits they might otherwise lose if they do not trade with the adversary.[7] If this measure succeeds in reducing the adversary's present or future ability to make mischief, the cost of such preemptive purchases could be readily offset by a slight reduction of defense spending. As a matter of fact, for the United States, there seems to be little reason not to extend such a policy to cover the sales from potential Soviet contracts that U.S. companies lose to European and Japanese competitors.[8]

As a minimum condition for developing an optimal economic and overall external policy, a deeper and broader public understanding of the cost-benefit links between international economic and political/security policies is needed. As a necessary step toward policy

---

[6]According to Lebahn, the subject of the pipeline was studiously avoided at the Economic Summit in Williamsburg in 1983. See Lebahn, "The Yamal Gas Pipeline."

[7]For a public accustomed to seeing producers (for instance, farmers) paid for not producing, the "illogic" or "logic" of such a measure is by no means too outrageous. I am grateful to Professor Herbert Stein for this idea.

[8]For illustration, the values of U.S. license applications for export to the Soviet Union, to Eastern Europe, and to the People's Republic of China in recent years were as follows:

Fiscal Years
(in million dollars)

	1980	1981	1982
Approved	736.4	647.6	535.3
Denied	44.0	1,900.0	90.4
Total	780.4	2,547.6	625.7

Even if these figures were multiplied several times by including selected European and Japanese sales, they could be easily offset numerically by a proportionately very small reduction of the allies' collective defense budgets. They might even justify a larger reduction in terms of defense equivalent units, however defined. See U.S. Department of Commerce, *Export Administration Annual Reports: 1980,* pp. 25-26; *1981,* pp. 27-28; *1982,* pp. 25-26.

consensus, we must think in bolder terms. We certainly must understand better how such nations as the Soviet Union, China, Japan, the Federal Republic of Germany, and some smaller powers coordinate their respective economic and noneconomic external policies in pursuing their own public and private interests, or in some cases how they too fail to do so effectively. We might then discover, as I believe we shall, that in more than a few cases their interests and their perceptions do not coincide with ours. Precisely because it is natural to indulge in mirror-imaging, we should guard ourselves against it. This task falls on the shoulders of scholars and publicists, of members in this distinguished audience, and of institutions like the hosts of this lecture series.

In conclusion, let me say in very general terms that there is a need for greater policy integration of many more factors than we are accustomed to deal with. Yet this is not just a matter of policy coordination or of establishing mechanisms for putting together lists of merits and drawbacks under different options for someone to choose. Analysts at various levels must be able to integrate an increasing number of considerations belonging conventionally to different disciplines. Certainly the practitioner/planner in tomorrow's international affairs, if not a complete renaissance person, needs to be as accomplished as possible in both economics and politics. In short, we need more people who take a long view and think in broad terms in order to bring about a better integrated foreign policy. This, Warren Nutter tried to do from the vantage point of the Office of International Security Affairs of the Department of Defense.

Thank you.

Warren Nutter: An Economist for All Time

Paul Craig Roberts

April 26, 1984

PAUL CRAIG ROBERTS holds the William E. Simon Chair in Political Economy, Center for Strategic and International Studies, Georgetown University. During 1981–1982 he was assistant Treasury secretary. He is credited by President Reagan and Treasury Secretary Regan with a major role in the Economic Recovery Tax Act of 1981 and was awarded the Treasury Department's Meritorious Service Award for "outstanding contributions to the formulation of United States economic policy."

Introduction

Stephen J. Entin

It is my very great pleasure today to introduce a friend and colleague, the Honorable Paul Craig Roberts, the William E. Simon Professor of Political Economy at the Center for Strategic and International Studies, Georgetown University.

It is particularly appropriate for Dr. Roberts to be presenting a lecture in the G. Warren Nutter lecture series. Craig Roberts has been inspired by Professor Nutter's many contributions in the areas of the Soviet economy, the economics of defense and foreign policy issues, and the application of price theory to public policy issues. Like Professor Nutter, he has been a leading figure in the field of political economy.

Dr. Roberts has a B.S. in industrial management from Georgia Tech and a Ph.D. in economics from the University of Virginia. It was at Virginia that Craig Roberts met and worked with Professor Nutter. In fact, Craig was the first Ph.D. candidate whose dissertation committee Professor Nutter chaired. Craig went on to do postgraduate work at the University of California, Berkeley, and at Oxford University, where he was a member of Merton College. He is a senior research fellow at the Hoover Institution, Stanford University, and has held academic appointments at Virginia Polytechnic Institute, Tulane, and other universities.

Dr. Roberts is the author of three books. His latest, *The Supply-Side Revolution: An Insider's Account of Policymaking in Washington*, has just been published by Harvard University Press. In December 1983 Praeger published a new edition of his classic study of Marxian economics first published in 1973. His first book, *Alienation and the Soviet Economy* (1971), is regarded as a seminal interpretation of Soviet economic experience. He has published many articles in journals of scholarship and the national media. He has held distinguished appointments in American journalism, including that of associate editor of the editorial page of the *Wall Street Journal*. Currently he writes the "Economic Watch" column for *Business Week*.

In the U.S. Congress, Craig Roberts served in the House of Representatives as economic counsel to Representative Jack Kemp, as staff associate with the Defense Appropriations Subcommittee, and as chief economist with the minority staff of the House Committee on the Budget. In the U.S. Senate he served as economic counsel to Senator Orrin Hatch. He drafted the original version of the Kemp-Roth bill. It is not an overstatement to say that he managed the tax-cut movement in the U.S. Congress during 1975–1978.

It was at this time that I first met Craig. We were both working on a project for Congressman John Rousselot, who was a member of the House Budget Committee and the Joint Economic Committee, where I was a staff economist. Mr. Rousselot and Congresswoman Marjorie Holt introduced a series of Republican alternative budget resolutions which made room for across-the-board tax rate reductions. During these semiannual exercises, during debate on the Kemp-Roth bill which followed, and during his sojourn at the *Wall Street Journal*, Craig was able to achieve a series of strategic objectives in the multiyear campaign for economic recovery:

- the discrediting of the economic models used to support big government, models that quite explicitly assumed that rising marginal tax rates would never retard economic growth so long as government spent the money and that assumed that the microeconomic incentive effects of tax changes could be completely ignored
- the shaking up of a complacent economic establishment and the Capitol Hill staff who relied heavily on these models—economists who had either forgotten their price theory or who favored the income-redistribution uses of fiscal policy that the models encouraged
- the advancement of a coherent neoclassical theory of the national economy based on sound microeconomic principles, an approach which could explain the economic expansion and low inflation of the 1960s and the economic stagnation and rising inflation of the 1970s
- the creation of a positive pro-growth economic program for conservative politicians to offer—a substitute for the negative austerity programs which had made conservatives a distinct minority

since the New Deal, a program which offered the benefits of tax reduction and economic freedom as a clear and attractive alternative to the liberal promises of more government handouts and the liberal price tag of economic subservience
* the presentation of this pro-growth program to the public, a presentation which was made with such remarkable journalistic talent and which so clearly squared with the real-world observations and common sense of the public that it became a true rarity—an economic theory that people could understand

By combining real-world economics and practical politics, Craig Roberts helped to form an intellectual and political coalition that put economic recovery and growth onto the national political agenda and finally into the law of the land.

In 1980, Governor Ronald Reagan ran for president on a platform of tax reduction and economic growth. In 1981, President Reagan appointed Craig Roberts assistant secretary for economic policy, U.S. Treasury, from which position he helped to secure passage of the landmark Economic Recovery Tax Act of 1981. In 1982 Secretary of the Treasury Donald T. Regan awarded Craig the Treasury's Meritorious Service Award for "outstanding contributions to the formulation of United States economic policy." Those few words cannot begin to express the contribution he has made to economic revival in the United States and to the reinvigoration of economic thinking here and abroad.

Compare where we were eight years ago with where we are today. In 1976, Congress watched complacently as inflation raised marginal tax rates across the board, and the big debate was whether to please constituents by increasing government spending programs or by using the revenues to narrow the tax base by granting special credits and exemptions. Today, the economic models are being overhauled, and the debate in Congress and in the economics profession is over how best to restore incentives to the private sector by cutting spending, broadening the tax base, and lowering marginal tax rates further.

Craig left Treasury in 1982 to become the first holder of the William E. Simon Chair in Political Economy at the Center for Strategic and International Studies. We at Treasury like to think that Craig's decision to leave was a difficult choice, but we recognize the great and well-deserved honor which this appointment represents. Treasury's loss has been Georgetown's gain. Nonetheless, we continue to benefit from his ongoing counsel and his insight.

In my work with Craig, I have always known him to stand for the defense of principle rather than the pursuit of power. He has striven to enhance economic understanding for the betterment of a free society, when the easier way was to conform comfortably to the prevailing wisdom and accept the status quo. Like Professor Nutter before him, he questions, he prods, and he gets results, while always conducting himself as a gentleman of moral and intellectual integrity. If there are two traits he shares above all with G. Warren Nutter, they are intelligence and courage.

It is my pleasure to present to you now Professor Paul Craig Roberts.

Warren Nutter:
An Economist For All Time

Paul Craig Roberts

It is an honor for me to address this audience. I can make no more appropriate use of this forum than to celebrate the work of the person in whose name we are assembled.

G. Warren Nutter was skilled at asking the right questions and finding the right answers. He had the courage, patience, and intellectual foresight not often found in the modern world, and he was not afraid to challenge the economics profession in the pursuit of truth. He was a master of his profession's tools and applied them widely to the central issues of his time.

The Soviet Economy

In the 1950s many academics stood in awe of Soviet economic growth. Nutter undertook a massive study to determine the actual nature and extent of that growth, putting it into its historical and comparative context. When *The Growth of Industrial Production in the Soviet Union*[1] appeared in 1962, this enormous body of research revealed that Soviet economic growth was to be neither feared nor admired.

The Growth of Industrial Production in the Soviet Union altered Western understanding of the Soviet economy. Prior to the appearance of this massive study, many people believed that Soviet economic growth was unprecedented and had no equal. Some hailed Soviet planning as the way of the future. Some were dismayed that the free

---

[1]G. Warren Nutter, *The Growth of Industrial Production in the Soviet Union* (Princeton: Princeton University Press for the National Bureau of Economic Research, 1962).

enterprise system would be overtaken by one that was not free, while still others were confused and did not know what to believe. Regardless of individual feelings, a majority of experts shared the perception that the Communist system was outperforming the free market system. It was Nutter who set the record straight.

In the context of Russia's own historical experience, he found that contemporary Soviet economic growth rates did not match those of the czarist period immediately preceding the Russian Revolution. In fact, the last fifty years of czarist Russia was a period of very rapid growth, which pointed to the possibility that the Communist revolution was riding a wave of economic transformation that had already been under way before Lenin took over the country.

Nor did the Communist economic model produce growth rates that were noticeably higher or more sustained than the capitalist model. Nutter found that Soviet growth rates did not stand up to the records of contemporary democracies such as Germany and Japan. Nutter also paired current Soviet growth rates with the years 1875–1917 in the United States—a comparable period. He found that even with the vast advantage in the level of technology at their disposal, the Soviets were doing no better than the United States had at the turn of the century.

The magnitude of Soviet economic growth, when compared with periods in Russian history or with the experiences of other countries, was wholly unremarkable. And there were other lessons to learn. Nutter told of the snags and pitfalls encountered by anyone using statistics generated by a Communist country. While, as he pointed out, statistics in general had to be used with caution, Soviet statistics are unique because their main function is not to serve as an indicator of actual conditions, but to fuel the propaganda machine. Without any mechanism for external review or criticism, Soviet statistics grossly exaggerate any positive characteristics of the economy and ignore the negative. The effect of poor statistical data, he determined, probably caused him to overestimate Soviet growth rates.

Perhaps the most important conclusion of *The Growth of Industrial Production in the Soviet Union* was that purely quantitative analysis leaves much to be desired. Aggregate measures of industrial production, as Nutter pointed out, disguise the real story of Soviet development. The Soviet Union, with its "command" economy, devotes a disproportionate share of its resources to the military/industrial complex at the expense of consumer goods and living standards.

Comparison with the United States is difficult for the simple reason that the pattern of growth adopted by the Soviet Union would never in a million years be imitated by a free economy. Traditionally important sectors of the economy—agriculture, construction, and consumer services—have taken a back seat to aggregate industrial expansion and weapons production. As the Soviet Union developed, leisure showed little or no tendency to augment. Worse still, certain periods in Soviet history witnessed masses of people who spent and lost their lives in forced labor camps for reasons hard to discern. Had they known more about it, people living in a free society might have wondered why those living under the Soviet system allowed themselves to be subjected to this kind of life. And they might have wondered about the apologies pouring out of Western universities for this system.

Nutter thought about it, and his answer was that people in the U.S.S.R. had no choice. In "The Soviet Citizen: Today's Forgotten Man," Nutter explained the situation of a characteristic Soviet citizen, Ivan Ivanov:

> We cannot blame Ivan if he is fatalistically resigned to his destiny. He is powerless to influence policies within his own country, and he is forbidden to leave—he is denied the right to vote with his feet. Even his movements within the country are strictly controlled by a rigid internal passport system, and he may not depart from the country without an external passport that he can receive only as a privilege and not as a right. He sees his country ringed by a frontier zone, constantly patrolled by troops, into which entrance is forbidden except by special permission. If he manages to receive permission to leave his country and, after doing so, defects, his renunciation of citizenship has no validity in the eyes of his government. Once a Soviet citizen, always a Soviet citizen.[2]

The Critique of Détente

Nutter's studies of the Soviet system also foretold that serious economic problems would not constrain the Communist leadership from building a military machine that was openly aggressive and a formidable threat to the rest of the world. This observation led him to question the validity of the new policy of détente at a time when the

---

[2]G. Warren Nutter, *Political Economy and Freedom* (Indianapolis: Liberty Press, 1983), p. 141.

conventional wisdom in the United States welcomed détente as a warming of cold war tensions.

Détente relied heavily on the twin strategies of arms control and interdependence. Deterrence, which was hitherto the foundation of U.S. defense policy toward the Soviet Union, would henceforth be pursued less as a direct goal, more as an indirect benefit of détente. Nutter examined the claims of détente and compared them with the past record of containment—the policy which détente was to replace. He found that, because of the flawed assumptions on which it was based, détente jeopardized its own stated objectives, which were to maintain security, peace, and stability in the world.

With characteristic ability to get to the heart of the matter, Nutter observed that the perceived benefit of arms control—fewer weapons in the world—masked serious dangers in the context of Soviet military policy. The relative defense efforts of competing forces such as the Soviet Union and the United States could not be expected to stand still but are forever changing, dynamic. There is therefore no way to achieve real arms control without on-site inspection of weapons facilities. The catch, which has virtually emasculated all arms control treaties between the United States and the Soviet Union, was that the Soviets refused to allow inspection of their military installments by outsiders. Under the circumstances, the Soviets could be expected to regard arms control not as an effort to reduce tensions but as a sign of weakness of resolve. Soviet perception of weakness on the part of the United States, Nutter logically determined, is likely to increase, not reduce, the risk of war.

Perhaps even more destructive was the jumbled perception of the nature and purpose of defense that arms control fostered in America itself. Nutter concluded that arms control and détente could lead to "a dangerous weakening of the will to resist, as a confused public tries to understand whether resistance is unnecessary or whether it is futile."[3]

The idea behind interdependency, the second branch of détente, is gradually to weave an aggressive power into a web of trade so that it would have no interest in starting a war. Nutter reminded proponents of this policy that an interdependent world had a poor historical record in averting conflict. In addition, he noted, any increase in trade with the Soviet bloc increases the Soviet advantage simply because the West has so much more to offer. Without some corresponding

---

[3]G. Warren Nutter, *Kissinger's Grand Design* (Washington, D.C.: American Enterprise Institute, 1975), p. 23.

political concessions, the increase in trade is likely to be regarded more as a further signal of weakness than as a sign of goodwill or enlightenment.

The Soviet economy often staggers under the strain of its military burden, and the Soviet people suffer for it. Problems are compounded by enormous inefficiencies in production, the absence of market pricing, and virtually nonexistent incentives. The real solution to the Soviet Union's economic woes lies in markets and private property, but that is not something the leadership is prepared to allow. The Soviets are periodically forced to turn to the West to be bailed out of their chronic agricultural shortages and technological backwardness. By accommodating the Soviet need for food and technology, the West is in effect subsidizing both the Communist domination of many nationalities and the Soviet military buildup that threatens the West.

Nutter thought it improbable that building stronger economic ties with the Soviet bloc would decrease the likelihood of war. It would more likely strengthen and encourage the Soviet leadership. Soviet leaders, Nutter argued, "will consequently be tempted to seek even greater gains through power politics and to treat the U.S. as a weakling deserving contempt."[4]

The Disillusionment with Communism

Despite the bleak terms he used to describe life under the Soviet system and the state of East-West relations, Warren Nutter was not a pessimist. He knew that history is not set in concrete—it can move toward freedom as well as toward despotism. Nutter viewed the Communist revolution as "one of the greatest reactionary events of all time," temporarily bringing to a halt centuries of movement toward Western-style liberalism in Russia. Sooner or later the Communist system would crumble. He concluded an essay, "Some Reflections on the Growth of the Soviet Economy," by noting that "the slow and tortuous movement toward liberalism continues to assert itself beneath all the turmoil, and we may perhaps expect reaction to be overcome eventually. As it is, the promise of revolution may gradually be realized."[5]

If Warren Nutter were alive today, he would be watching, with hope and skepticism, the continuing efforts to inject some capitalist vitality into the Communist economies. A recent article in the *Finan-*

---

[4]Ibid., p. 19.
[5]Nutter, *Political Economy and Freedom*, p. 196.

cial Times of London, for example, heralded the rebirth of private enterprise in Communist China. In 1978, two years after the Cultural Revolution, there were only 140,000 people engaged in private enterprise in a country whose population numbers more than a billion. The number of private businesses has been expanding rapidly since then and stands at last count around 7.5 million. Businesses are said to be free to hire and fire their own workers, to increase profit margins, and to struggle with their competitors to produce better and cheaper products to bid for potential customers. The report may be an exaggeration, but at least it suggests that the stamping out of private enterprise is no longer the sine qua non of success.

Many of the Eastern European countries in their own ways have been making progress toward liberalism under the disapproving gaze of the Soviet Union. Often there are setbacks, as was most recently the case in Poland, when the people appear to be gaining a voice in how they are ruled.

The Hungarians, who enthusiastically enjoyed a brief freedom in 1956, soon encountered Soviet tanks on the streets of their capital. Faced with overwhelming force, they adopted a different strategy and gradually gave more rein to markets while continuing to pay lip service to communism. Hungary has recently taken the bold step of bringing its underground private sector out into the open by making it legal. According to an article in the *New York Times* on November 10, 1983, private building companies have sprung up in response to a housing shortage, and private car owners are now allowed to operate their vehicles as taxis in Budapest to aid the city's transportation facilities.

As for the Soviet Union itself, today most experts acknowledge that the Soviet economy is heavily dependent on unofficial and illegal private activities. Within the official system, economic problems are aggravated by the difficulty of doing anything about them. Shortly before he died, Yuri Andropov added his voice to those that have noticed the economic shortcomings of communism: "It is intolerable that with the shortage of many products, high quality raw and primary materials are wasted on the manufacture of products that prove unmarketable, are stored in warehouses and eventually marked down."[6]

In his short tenure, Andropov did attempt to improve the Soviet economic system but, as a former KGB chief, went about it in the only

---

[6]*New York Times*, December 29, 1983.

way he knew how—by repression of illegal economic activity. According to an article by Professor Marshall Goldman in the *New York Times* on February 14, 1984, store managers caught diverting goods into the black market were executed or severely punished, and measures were taken to cut down on the complex system of bribery which lubricates the cumbersome Soviet system. There is some evidence that Andropov was becoming aware of the limits of repression and was starting to think about liberalizing the economy to boost growth. Western experts once saw the future in Soviet central planning; today they see the Soviet system as irredeemable. Goldman wrote:

> Mr. Andropov saw that before any significant improvements could be made, he would have to institute a new incentive system and reorganize the planning process, but his initial efforts were timid and tardy. The economic system is not easily restructured, partly because reforms threaten the vested interest of many in power.

A recent joke sums up the uneven movement toward capitalism in the Soviet bloc: a Hungarian dog, a Polish dog, and a Russian dog were running down the sidewalk one day when the Hungarian dog suddenly had a brainstorm. "Hey," he said, "let's stop on this street corner and bark for meat!" The Polish dog thought this an excellent idea but was puzzled. "What is meat?" he innocently asked. The Russian dog, however, was completely bewildered. Turning to his comrades, he queried, "How do you bark?"

The Growth of Government in the West

In contrast to the disillusionment with centralized planning within the Communist countries, Nutter perceived a disturbing trend in the opposite direction in the West. In his study *The Growth of Government in the West*,[7] he pinpointed the encroaching public sector as a serious threat to liberty. Over the twenty-five-year period from 1950 to 1975, the share of national income accounted for by government in the countries of the Organization for Economic Cooperation and Development rose from a third to more than a half. Nutter feared that the pace of government growth that had already taken place masked a potentially more rapid expansion to come.

For those people who saw nothing wrong with an economy dom-

---

[7]G. Warren Nutter, *The Growth of Government in the West* (Washington, D.C.: American Enterprise Institute, 1978).

inated by the public sector, Nutter spelled out his concern. The rapid pace of government growth was leading to the destruction of private property rights and the erosion of the ideas and values on which the West was built. In his essay "Liberty and the Growth of Government," Nutter wrote:

> A free society differs from a controlled one to the extent that the individual is protected against arbitrary seizure of his property by government. An individual owns property if he has acquired it legitimately, in accord with the principles of a free society. Taxes represent a claim that government asserts against private property, not a property *right* of government. Individuals alone have property rights in a free society.[8]

Recognizing that a problem exists is the first step to solving it, and many countries in the West are trying to arrest the growth of government. Here in the United States voters elected Ronald Reagan in 1980 on his platform of cutting taxes and government spending as a percent of GNP. The year before in Great Britain, Margaret Thatcher was swept into office with a similar program. This year has seen Prime Minister Pierre Trudeau of Canada announce plans to step down as public support for his Socialist policies evaporates. Even in France, the once-ambitious Socialist government of François Mitterrand is toying with Jack Kemp's idea of tax-free enterprise zones to revitalize old industrial areas and is attempting to hold government spending in check.

Despite the Reagan administration's commitment to spending control, instead of declining to 19.3 percent of GNP in 1984 as intended, the federal budget rose to 25 percent of GNP in 1983. Even conservatives find that the political temptation to boast of spending *for* the people overwhelms their principles. The London *Daily Mail* quoted Britain's "Iron Lady," Margaret Thatcher, when she launched her reelection campaign:

> They said we would cut pensions. Instead we have raised them by two-thirds—well ahead of prices. They said we would dismantle the National Health Service. Instead we have nearly doubled spending on the Health Service. They said we would cripple education. Instead expenditure per child is at an all-time record.[9]

---

[8]Nutter, *Political Economy and Freedom*, p. 105.
[9]London *Daily Mail*, May 14, 1983.

In the United States the recent explosion of spending as a percent of GNP has resulted in large deficits that have traumatized conservative economists, politicians, and journalists. Today George Will says that Americans are undertaxed, and many conservative voices join in. In three short years the effort to control the size of government has been turned into a push to raise taxes to balance the budget, regardless of the size of government. In the face of this failure, it is unrealistic to expect that the Soviet government would voluntarily change its ways.

The Defense of Free Enterprise

In addition to the preference of most politicians for more spending, the growth of government has been aided by the many attacks on the free enterprise system. One of these attacks came indirectly from a group of economists who argued that competition was being eclipsed by monopoly and that free enterprise was nothing more than an unrealistic textbook theory. Competition and free enterprise could no longer be supported, they declared, because such things no longer really existed. While Americans slept, monopolies had gradually been overtaking competition as the primary source of the national product, and it was the responsibility of the government to step in and make sure there was no excessive concentration of economic power in the hands of a few industrial barons. The argument appeared seductive to many, even to some proponents of competition, since the government was portrayed not as a hindrance to the free market, but as its defender.

Nutter observed that the extent of monopoly in the economy had never been satisfactorily determined. This was particularly strange since the assumption that monopolies were taking over the country was the foundation of government intervention into the economy. He resolved to look into the matter, and his conclusions, published in his book *The Extent of Enterprise Monopoly in the United States, 1899–1939*,[10] were startling to more than a few experts on the subject.

He found that over the period studied the share of the economy produced by competitive industry had actually risen slightly. Monopoly, depending on the industry studied, had either remained level or declined. Contrary to the established wisdom, monopoly had grown

---

[10]G. Warren Nutter, *The Extent of Enterprise Monopoly in the United States, 1899–1939* (Chicago: University of Chicago Press, 1951).

only where government was involved:

> There is a significant amount of governmental restriction of competitive behavior in certain sectors of the economy. If this intervention is taken into account, it becomes more and more likely that competition is decreasing. But in this case governmental action is the cause, not the result, of less competition.[11]

Following publication of *The Extent of Enterprise Monopoly in the United States*, the argument that monopoly was taking over the country lost much of its credibility and could no longer be employed as a reason to expand the government. But not even Nutter could stop the government's handmaidens from finding new reasons.

Other views, equally incompatible with the free enterprise system, are quickly drafted to take the place of defeated arguments. One view which has had considerable staying power is that the government is better able than the market to look ahead and allocate investment resources. Nutter remarked on the attraction of planning in his essay "Central Economic Planning: The Visible Hand." He wrote:

> It is hardly surprising that large segments of the public should get the idea that the way to solve a perceived problem is to turn it over to somebody and give him the power to get the job done. Nor is it surprising that many people should feel that such problems arise in the first place because nobody was given the responsibility of preventing them.[12]

Government has been quick to assume the responsibility to solve every "problem" perceived by the public and has eagerly found others that it was equally willing to try to solve. Industrial policy—the systematic intervention of government in the economy—is the latest in-vogue solution to problems created by previous government interventions. It is, in one form or another, being championed by many people, including Democratic presidential candidates, academics, big businessmen, and labor leaders.

Nutter would have been quick to note that industrial policy is the wrong answer to the wrong question. Proponents assume in framing their argument that markets and private property can no longer cope with foreign competition and that the government must become more involved to prevent the United States from being deindustrialized.

---

[11]Nutter, *Political Economy and Freedom*, p. 72.
[12]Ibid., p. 113.

The deterioration in U.S. economic performance tracks a persistent and growing presence of government in the economy. And yet, somehow, we are supposed to believe that more government is the necessary prescription to recapture past levels of achievement. It is tiresome that the burden of proof never seems to rest on those who argue for more government.

Industrial policy proponents claim that if only government, business, and labor could be brought together and equipped with adequate power to determine the allocation of resources, the economy's optimal growth path could be identified and pursued without further ado. One fundamental mistake of the planners is to believe that the optimal growth path of an economy can be perceived in advance, let alone manipulated.

The process of government planning is a futile exercise, but it is by no means a harmless one. Nutter pointed out that efforts to predetermine growth forestall growth in the most important sense of the word. He wrote:

> The best path of growth is the one that unfolds as the economy cuts its way through a jungle of ignorance, coming here and there and now and then onto places where the cutting is easier. These discoveries enable the economy to move more swiftly through the jungle if it is adventurous enough to explore for them in the first place and supple enough to exploit them when they are found. All the while, we remain in the jungle, seeing only a few feet ahead. We cannot know in advance the 'optimum' way out or what lies on the other side. We grope our way forward.[13]

Economic progress results from millions of independent business decisions being tested daily in markets. It occurs without central direction, and the market test has a better long-run record than any other system. The market is a source of infinite frustration to meddlers, but that is no reason to forsake the market.

A Warning to Economists

Warren Nutter saved one of his most important messages for his fellow economists, warning them to quit "hiding their heads in the sand of pseudoscientism" before they woke up one day and found their

---

[13]Ibid., p. 46.

profession discredited. He urged them to honor process and to "seek more after policies which will make conditions better and less after policies which will make them best."[14] In short, let economists focus on maximizing the use of voluntary agreement and not on the achievement of ideal ends. "Results," Nutter wrote, "are no more ideal than the process through which they are achieved."[15]

It may be dawning on economists that they have not been serving public-spirited men but have been used by power-hungry men, and that their piecemeal justifications of interventions have built a government juggernaut that serves its own interests. Freedom, Nutter would say, is imperiled; but the outcome is not inevitable. Those who learn the lessons he taught can carry on the fight.

---

[14]Ibid., p. 48.
[15]Ibid., p. 261.

Aspects of Current International Debt Problems:
Is the Problem Insolvency or Illiquidity?

Roger E. Shields

October 24, 1984

Roger E. Shields is vice president and head of the International Economic Research Unit of the Chemical Bank, which he joined in 1977. From 1973 to 1976, he was deputy assistant secretary for international economic affairs at the U.S. Department of Defense and twice received the department's Distinguished Civilian Service Award. In 1976-1977, he was deputy assistant secretary for international economic policy at the U.S. Department of the Treasury. Before entering government service, he served on the faculties of the University of Texas at Austin and the University of Virginia.

Introduction

Robert J. Pranger

In his role as assistant secretary of defense, Warren Nutter brought to the Office of International Security Affairs (ISA) in the period 1969 to 1973 a brilliant academic record and political contacts of some importance within the Republican party, as well as an economist's bias toward problem solving, which he described in his small book, *Kissinger's Grand Design*, published by the American Enterprise Institute in 1975. (One must add here that Warren was not only a superb economist, but also a master with the English language: he often read ISA policy papers as a freshman English teacher might, and he usually was as much distressed.) In criticism, Warren noted that Kissinger had a "tendency to put concepts into pigeonholes and to pose choices in terms of mutually exclusive alternatives." Perhaps, Warren added, this cast of mind is explained by his limited knowledge of economics. "The economist thinks in terms of scarce means, competing uses (values), substitutability and complementarity of goods, comparative advantage, optimal mixes of goods—all quantitative concepts involving more or less of things, not all or nothing. He also reasons stochastically and defines concepts through frequency distributions. Above all, he attributes the unfolding state of affairs more to the operation of impersonal forces than to the activities of specific individuals."[1]

Although Warren Nutter had his share of personal likes and dislikes, he wanted to have people around him in ISA—his really trusted assistants and deputies—who could reason as he did, people who could think conceptually, reason in terms of the national interest, and appreciate issues in terms of the "more or less of things, not all or

[1] G. Warren Nutter, *Kissinger's Grand Design* (Washington, D.C.: American Enterprise Institute, 1975), p. 17.

nothing." For those of us who spent considerable time with Warren in ISA, nothing was more disturbing than certain public impressions, often generated by those unsympathetic to his political philosophy, that his ISA was a hard-line, ideological place. Close colleagues remember Warren as a very principled person dedicated to the life of mind and reason in its most cosmopolitan sense: he was frequently critical of the bureaucracy precisely because it had lost contact with the wider world outside its narrow organizational confines and had settled into its own provincial understanding of "all or nothing" rather than "more or less."

Warren Nutter recruited some of us to ISA from outside the economics profession and we liked to think we lived up to his demanding ideal of reason in all things. Warren also recruited some, such as Roger Shields, from the discipline of economics, with the somewhat revolutionary idea—for ISA—that economics might actually have some relevance to national defense.

It is a great pleasure, therefore, to introduce our speaker for this Nutter Lecture, Roger E. Shields, vice president and head of the International Economic Research Unit of Chemical Bank, who will speak on aspects of current international debt problems. Prior to joining the Chemical Bank in 1977, Roger served as deputy assistant secretary for international economic policy in the U.S. Treasury Department. Before his service at the Treasury Department he served at the Department of Defense, in ISA, as deputy assistant secretary for international economic affairs.

Roger, who was twice awarded the Department of Defense Distinguished Civilian Service Award, has a record that speaks for itself: as an economist in ISA he became heavily involved with economic issues as they affected defense, and with defense as it made claims on national economic policy. He also was swept up in the Vietnam War's trying final days, in his case as chairman of the Prisoner of War and Missing in Action Policy Committee, where he directed the return of the prisoners of war from Southeast Asia in 1973. This latter task was more political than economic, as he worked to retrieve the POWs from captors who proclaimed the virtues of the rules of war as it suited their purpose, but who felt themselves exempt from codes of civilized conduct when these rules interfered with their special view of reality.

Roger Shields has been a member of the faculties of the University of Texas at Austin and the University of Virginia, as well as visiting lecturer at Brigham Young University. He received his Ph.D. in economics from the University of Virginia in 1969. His publications include one book and numerous articles that have appeared in professional journals.

It is a great pleasure to introduce our speaker for this Nutter Lecture, Mr. Roger E. Shields.

Aspects of Current International Debt Problems: Is the Problem Insolvency or Illiquidity?

Roger E. Shields

The international financial system has been subjected to severe strains over the past three years. These strains have threatened not only the well-being of the commercial financial institutions which form the core of this system, but the economic and political well-being of the major developing nation debtors as well. Because of the extensive involvement of the large commercial banks in the United States, Western Europe, and Japan in lending to the Eastern European and developing countries, failure to contain and ultimately resolve the problems currently facing the international financial system would inevitably have serious repercussions for the economies of the West as well.

The Beginnings of the Crisis

It was only a little more than two years ago that Jesus Silva Herzog, the Mexican finance minister, announced that Mexico would not be able to service its external debt without extraordinary assistance. This announcement is regarded by many as the start of the international debt crisis; it was followed in rapid succession by similar announcements from debtor nations around the world. Although in retrospect there were many indications that debt service burdens were becoming excessively heavy, Mexico's announcement and those that followed caught much of the international financial system unawares.

What has happened over the intervening two years is well

known. The initial response of the international financial system consisted primarily of what can best be described as first-aid measures. While virtually all of the international commercial banks ceased their business-as-usual lending approach to the financially troubled borrowers and the rate of new lending by the banks to these countries dropped sharply, the major lending banks joined with many of the central banks of the industrial countries and the official international financial institutions, primarily the International Monetary Fund, to provide short-term emergency liquidity to the hardest pressed countries. At the same time, the borrowing countries implemented austerity programs, in part but not altogether at the urging of the IMF, which sharply reduced their need for additional loans.

Those measures generally succeeded in relieving the immediate pressures on the borrowing countries and were followed quickly by preliminary agreements between the commercial banks and many of the borrowing countries, providing for the restructuring of amortization and interest payments that clearly could not have been made on the schedule called for in the original loan agreements. Aided in no small part by the global economic recovery now almost two years old, these actions have thus far forestalled major loan defaults and have succeeded, at least for the time being, in removing the crisis aspect from the international debt situation.

This defusing of the more immediate dangers of the international debt problems effectively marks the end of what may be called phase one of the program, which must continue if ultimately it is to restore the troubled debtor nations to financial health. It is difficult to deny the success of phase one in terms of its accomplishment of what is admittedly a very limited objective. But there is a great deal of doubt and skepticism about the ability of a phase two, or even a succeeding set of phases, to restore health and order to the international financial system as it is constituted today. Unquestionably, there are many differences between those who believe that the system can survive essentially as we know it now and those who do not, but in my view the fundamental difference depends on whether the difficulties of the developing nation debtors today are seen as problems of liquidity or problems of solvency.

Insolvency or Illiquidity?

If the majority of the financially troubled developing nations are insolvent today, then I view it as extremely unlikely that far worse problems than we have seen thus far, of a political as well as an economic nature, can be avoided. If, on the other hand, the difficulties of these nations are more closely related to problems of liquidity, or cash flow, then measures of adjustment designed to enhance liquidity over time should be capable of restoring fundamental financial soundness to the international financial system.

Admitting that thus far the measures taken to relieve the strains on the international financial system have served only to buy time, I believe we are at this point still dealing largely with a liquidity issue as we consider the problem of the external debt burden of the developing nations. To be sure, the problem is no less serious, and it will surely develop into a problem of basic insolvency if we fail to stay within a fairly narrowly defined path of action over the next several years. But a restoration of health to the international financial system seems not only possible at this time, but even likely, provided certain conditions are met.

Solving the Debt Problem

Before considering the prospects for a resolution of the external debt problem of the developing countries, it is essential, I believe, to understand what a resolution consists of. It does not require, as a lot of current comment seems to believe, that these countries be able to pay off all their debt. That view implies either that borrowing across international boundaries is altogether bad, or that borrowing, while appropriate at a particular time, should not be used as a fundamental source of financing of economic development. Economic theory rejects both of those propositions. The mutually agreed upon transfer of financial resources from savers to borrowers can enhance the economic wellbeing of both sides, and that is true whether the loans are purely domestic or are international. But the mutual benefit of the creditor-borrower pact obviously does not hold if the loans in force cannot be serviced—if the amortization and interest payments cannot be made. The criterion for measuring the success of the recovery of the borrowing nations is, therefore, not whether they achieve the capability of retiring their external debt, but whether they are able to resume service of their external debt without the need for prolonged extreme adjustment measures on their own part or on the part of their creditors.

An implicit assumption of many, if not all, of those who believe that a resumption of a capacity to make normal debt service payments is unlikely, is that this capacity in many instances never existed in the first place—that many of the international loans now in question were made to fundamentally uncreditworthy borrowers. According to this view, the commercial banks either ignored the usual standards for gauging creditworthiness or used inappropriate criteria in evaluating their international loan customers.

In my opinion, this view reflects in the main a fundamental lack of understanding of the nature of the problem we are dealing with today. This is not to say that the banks did not make some errors of judgment with regard to individual lending decisions. It would be remarkable, in fact, if they had not. Nor do I believe that there were no indications considerably before the Mexican announcement in 1982 that would have forewarned not only the banks, but other elements of the international financial system as well, of the developments that have occurred since. And as I will note in more detail in a moment, it is of the utmost importance that these indications be read and interpreted correctly in the future.

But it is also important to recognize that what we have witnessed over the past several years with respect to the international financial system is nothing less than a massive systemic disturbance. The international economic and financial systems are not delicate and fragile mechanisms. To the contrary, these systems are durable and tough. And the systems are remarkably tolerant of poor management decisions or honest and understandable mistakes made by some of their individual components, although those components themselves may not be so tolerant and durable. The loans which have already been, are being now, or will shortly be rescheduled, were not made by just one bank or a few banks. In the case of Mexico, for example, more than five hundred commercial banks were involved in the loans that have been rescheduled. This includes banks from the United States, the United Kingdom, West Germany, France, Switzerland, Japan, and other countries. Neither do we need to be reminded that Mexico is not the only country that has experienced extreme financial difficulties. A large number of Latin American countries, including all of the major international borrowers, with the exception thus far of Colombia, have been involved in debt restructuring negotiations.

It should be noted as well that Mexico was not the first prominent borrower country to acknowledge publicly its problems in servicing its external debt. That distinction belongs to Poland, which declared its inability to service its debt in 1981. In Eastern Europe, Poland's debt problems were followed by major problems in Romania and somewhat lesser, but still severe, financial difficulties in Hungary and East Germany.

Nor have such African countries as Morocco, Tunisia, Nigeria, or the Ivory Coast been spared. And in the Pacific Basin area, the Philippines is now in the midst of debt restructuring negotiations, while Indonesia has had to curtail its development programs sharply because of external debt considerations.

From a somewhat different perspective, external debt problems not only have been widespread geographically, but also have been no respecter of economic structure. In Latin America, for example, oil exporters like Venezuela and Mexico have arrived at an international financial position similar to that of oil importers like Brazil.

This systemic nature of international debt problems suggests to me a common thread with regard to cause, and in turn offers some important indications about what elements any feasible cure must have. I must stress again that I am speaking of the international financial system in general. Individual countries obviously have their own economic and financial characteristics, which will cause them to respond to an improvement in general economic conditions in different ways. It hardly needs to be said that a restoration of good health to the international financial system will not guarantee the same for all of its individual components. But in a healthy system, the inevitable losses on individual loans will be contained without threatening the system itself.

As I see it, by far the most important global economic developments over the past decade were the oil shocks of 1973–1974 and 1979–1980. Much, although by no means all, of the worldwide economic chaos of the past ten years—high inflation, generally poor real economic growth, highly volatile foreign exchange rates, and soaring developing country external debt—has its origin either directly in these oil shocks or in the policy responses of countries to them.

We do not have the time here to explore all of these areas, interesting though they are, nor is that necessary to make the link between many of the debt problems of the developing countries and the two oil shocks.

The Growth of External Debt in Developing Nations

During the 1960s, long-term loans to the non-oil-exporting developing countries increased at the rapid rate of 16 percent per year. But because of its low initial base, the outstanding long-term debt of these countries at year-end 1973 stood at just under $100 billion. About one-half of that debt was held by official creditors and only a little over one-third by the commercial banks. The long-term debt of the non-oil-exporting developing countries grew over the next nine years at an average annual rate of 19 percent, and by the end of 1982 totaled about $480 billion. Not only did the rate of growth of external debt accelerate—it averaged an even higher 23 percent between 1973 and 1978—but there was a shift in the importance of the lending institutions holding that debt as well. The relative share of official creditors in the debt of non-oil-exporting developing countries had fallen to just under 40 percent by the end of 1982, while the share of the commercial banks had risen to a little more than 50 percent.

Much of this rapid accumulation of external debt was associated with the financing of oil-inflated external deficits. The initial reaction of the oil-importing countries to the quadrupling of oil prices in 1973–1974 was that the increases were based not on a free-market response to supply and demand conditions, but on the pricing decisions of a cartel; and since cartel organizations had been historically unstable, the price increases were probably transitory. So with understandable reluctance the industrial and non-oil-exporting developing countries chose not to undertake fundamental structural adjustments in response to what they saw as a temporary situation, and instead made a fundamental decision to accommodate the oil-price increases—as it turned out, by trying to lower the real price of oil by inflating other world prices. As a result, the attention of the international financial system quickly focused on the problem of recycling petrodollars.

The surplus in the aggregate current account of the oil-exporting developing countries increased by a factor of more than ten in 1974. The counterpart to this development was an almost fourfold increase in the current account deficit of the non-oil-exporting developing countries in the same year. The international commercial banks stepped forward and financed the major part of this and subsequent external deficits, in the process becoming the major link in the petro-dollar recycling mechanism and accumulating rapidly growing external debt exposure in developing countries.

The commercial banks were not without experience in lending to developing countries when their rapid buildup of loans to these countries began in 1973. My own bank, for example, began its international lending activity in the 1890s with loans to Latin America. But there were no precedents for the scope of developing country lending activity which the international commercial banks undertook in 1973 either in terms of the number of countries involved or total volume of lending.

There was a great deal of apprehension on the part of the commercial banks as well as governments and the official international lending institutions about the economic prospects of the developing nation economies and the corresponding soundness of loans to these countries in the first year or two of petrodollar recycling. The failure in 1974 of the Franklin National Bank in the United States and the Herstatt Bank in West Germany did nothing to build the confidence of the banks in their growing exposure to the developing countries. These two failures, however, involved foreign exchange trading activities and were not related to lending to the developing countries. While these failures increased the cost of borrowing for the developing countries, they did not cause the banks to draw back from their international lending activities.

The strategy of financing current account deficits while lowering the real price of oil through global inflation of non-oil prices seemed to work well for a time. The growth of output in the major non-oil-exporting developing nations slowed along with the rest of the world economy in 1975, but buoyed by strong commodity prices and rapid growth in world trade, accelerated again in 1976 and remained strong through 1978—considerably stronger, in fact, than growth in the industrial countries. Just as impressive for these countries was the fact that their external deficits stabilized after 1975 and even came down a little through 1978.

Brazil, the largest developing nation debtor, illustrates these developments very well. In 1972 oil accounted for only about 12 percent of Brazil's imports. By 1974 that figure had almost doubled to 23 percent. By 1978, it had risen even further to 31 percent. Brazil's current account reflected the sharp increases in oil prices, moving from a deficit of $1.7 billion in 1972 to a deficit of more than $7.5 billion two years later. The need to finance these deficits resulted in large increases in Brazil's external debt. But facilitated by foreign loans, Brazil's economy grew from 1973 through 1980 in real terms at an average annual rate of about 7 percent, down from the rate of almost 9 percent it maintained from 1963 through 1972, but still high by any standards.

Whether this kind of progress could have been maintained and a soft landing achieved by the non-oil-producing developing countries if there had been no second oil shock in 1979–1980 is debatable. Like growth in the developing countries, growth in the industrial countries accelerated after the 1975 world recession, and although it did not return to the growth rates of the 1960s, average growth from 1976 through 1978 was higher than its 1971–1975 level. Much of this growth throughout the 1970s, though, was stimulated by huge increases in public spending. It is nevertheless significant that after 1976 the relative importance of government expenditure in the United States, West Germany, and the United Kingdom was beginning to decline.

In any case, the second oil shock did occur as a result of the start of the Iranian-Iraqi war and raised oil prices in absolute terms far more than had the price increases of 1973–1974. Some of the effects of this second round of oil-price increases were similar to those of the first round. Once again, the current account deficits of the non-oil-producing developing countries rose sharply.

A Change of Policy in Creditor Nations

There was a profound difference this time, though, in the policy response of the industrial countries. This time, a decision was made to follow structural adjustment policies which implicitly assumed the prolonged, if not permanent, presence of sharply higher relative energy prices. In Western Europe, policies designed to reduce the relative size of fiscal deficits produced three years of economic stagnation accompanied by unprecedented increases in unemployment to levels which still persist. In the United States, adjustment policies aimed at lowering inflation, reducing dependence on energy imports, and strengthening a weak and declining dollar drove up interest rates to totally unprecedented levels. These policies also initiated a period of dollar appreciation that continues today and that, as it did in Europe, resulted in three years of economic stagnation. Together, the adjustment policies of the industrial countries produced the world recession of 1980–1982, the deepest and most prolonged recession in the postwar period. They also produced three consecutive years of decline in world trade in 1981–1983, the first declines in more than twenty years.

It is hard to imagine a more difficult set of circumstances for developing nations and their creditors. The initiation of hostilities between Iran and Iraq which disrupted oil markets was not foreseen, and the same is true of its impact on oil prices. The willingness of the Western European countries to accept prolonged low growth and unemployment rates far in excess of anything they had experienced in the postwar years in order to pare down public sector deficits signified a profound shift in the economic priorities of these countries. In my view, this shift represents a welcome recognition of the need to pursue economic policies which will produce sustainable noninflationary growth, but it is not a development which was inherently predictable.

Similarly, there was no basis for forecasting the extent of the run-up in U.S. interest rates to record levels in 1981 which far exceeded previous highs. The external debt of the developing countries is overwhelmingly dollar denominated, and the interest rates these countries pay is determined largely by U.S. interest rate movements. Today, for example, a change of one percentage point in U.S. interest rates costs or saves Brazil about $750 million. The increase in U.S. interest rates in 1980–1981 resulted in increases in debt service payments for the developing countries far in excess of anything which could have been anticipated.

At the same time that their interest payments were increasing, the declines in world trade reduced the foreign exchange earnings of the developing nations—oil exporters and importers alike. The difficulties for these countries caused by falling world trade were magnified by the strengthening of the dollar in foreign exchange markets. The steady appreciation of the dollar continues today to maintain downward pressure on the mostly dollar-denominated prices of the commodity exports of the developing nations by raising the foreign currency prices of these goods.

With the primary and significant exception of Brazil, where adjustment policies began in 1980, the developing country debtors and their creditor banks reacted to these developments with a lag. Uncertainty about how extensive and long-lasting industrial country adjustment policies would be, coupled with perhaps too much confidence in their ability to bridge the second oil shock as they had the first, resulted in delays by the developing countries in implementing their own adjustment policies until reserve levels had been lowered sharply and problems in the servicing of external debt were already severe.

Economic Adjustments in Developing Countries

Nevertheless, adjustment policies were finally put into place and are in force at this time. One inevitable component of these adjustment programs has been economic austerity. The main goal of the adjustment programs as they were implemented was to reduce and to eliminate, where possible, the need for additional borrowed funds by depressing import demand. These programs have been successful in achieving that goal. Economists at the Chemical Bank indicated in a detailed study of twenty-six major developing and Eastern European country debtors that by the end of this year these countries will have reduced their borrowing requirements for the third year in a row. The increase in the external debt of these countries this year will be 5 percent, in sharp contrast with the average annual increase of 22 percent from 1973 through 1983. This reduction in the need for additional loans has been made possible because a recovery in world trade this year has combined with domestic austerity in these countries to produce an aggregate trade surplus that should total about $40 billion. In 1981, before the austerity programs had been adopted, these countries had an aggregate trade balance that was in deficit by $16 billion. Those numbers correspond to a reduction in the current deficit from $69 billion in 1981 to around $26 billion this year.

Equally impressive in my view, and critical to the future prospects of these countries, has been the reform of economic policies. This aspect of the adjustment programs now in place has been considerably less publicized than the austerity programs. The IMF has played an especially important role in this process. Many of the economic policies of the developing countries can be justly criticized. In many cases subsidies have served only to distort economic structures and to skew incentives counterproductively. In many developing countries, failure to allow exchange rates to reflect market forces has distorted trade patterns, increased borrowing needs by artificially stimulating imports and depressing exports, and resulted in massive loss of reserves through capital flight. Bloated public sector deficits have diverted badly needed resources from private sectors where they would have been more productive and in the process have caused persistent high inflation. The list could go on. I note here in passing that the industrial countries, too, have hardly distinguished themselves over the past decade by the quality of their economic policies.

In any case, IMF economic advice accepted and implemented by the borrowing countries as a condition for the granting of IMF credit has resulted, at least in some cases, in improved economic policies, which will result in stronger economic performance in the future. The private commercial banks do not have the same latitude for proffering advice on public policy that an official international institution like the IMF has, nor do countries have the same latitude politically for accepting counsel from the international commercial banks. The fact that many borrowing countries have accepted tough IMF programs, and generally have made good-faith efforts to implement them, to me is a sign of increasing political and economic responsibility on the part of the borrowing countries.

But if austerity and economic reforms by these countries are necessary conditions for a return to financial health, they certainly are not sufficient. The sharp reduction in 1982 and 1983 in the external deficits that I referred to a moment ago, which allowed these countries to reduce their borrowing requirements, was achieved almost entirely through a reduction in imports and at the cost of sharp declines in total output. At the same time, there has been a massive net outflow of capital, in the neighborhood of $40 billion this year, from the debtor countries to creditor countries. This is no basis for forecasting an amelioration in world debt problems, and if these conditions had no prospects of change, it would be impossible to come to any conclusion other than that the debtor countries are indeed insolvent.

I believe, though, that there are already indications of change in that situation and good indications that the change will continue and gather momentum. First and most important, global economic conditions have changed. The situation which I believe precipitated the international debt problems no longer exists. There seems to be little likelihood of another oil-price shock, at least in an upward direction, any time soon. The world recession of 1980–1982 has given way to an expansion now almost two years old. World trade will be up this year about 8 percent, reversing the three straight years of decline which devastated the foreign exchange earnings of the debtor countries. Interest rates in the United States are at high levels today, but at $12\frac{1}{2}$ percent the prime rate is far below its 1981 peak of $21\frac{1}{2}$ percent. Inflation in the industrial countries has come down as well, and at this time gives every indication that its peak in this cycle will be far below its peak in the previous cycle.

Economic developments in many of the debtor nations are beginning to reflect the benefits of these improvements. In Latin America, where debt burdens have been heavier and austerity programs more severe, real output will rise this year by about 1.5 percent. This represents a sharp and much-needed reversal of the decline of almost 4 percent that occurred last year. The recovery in growth in Latin America will also be widespread. Last year, of the major countries in this region, only Argentina and Colombia were able to increase output; this year, no country should see output fall. For the twenty-six major borrowing countries covered in the Chemical Bank study, aggregate real growth this year will be about 2.5 percent, after flat or even slightly negative growth last year. Perhaps of even greater significance, total imports for this group will be up for the first time in three years, and the trade balance will continue to improve.

The critical question now is whether this improving trend can be sustained. The Chemical Bank study indicates that it can if several key conditions are met. First and most obviously, the industrial countries must avoid a repetition of the prolonged 1980–1982 recession. That means, as well, an avoidance of the conditions of 1973–1980 which gave rise to that recession. As I have noted, those events seem extraordinary to me, and I do not expect them to be repeated in the near future. Finally, the borrowing countries cannot abandon their adjustment programs in an effort to return to their growth rates of the mid-1970s. At this time, I see no indications that these countries intend to do anything other than maintain their present policies, although I do expect some easing in import restrictions to facilitate a return to moderate growth.

But given these conditions, the study indicates that in the industrial countries a growth rate of around 3 percent will generate sufficient export opportunities for the borrowing countries to allow debt service burdens to decline slowly from their present high levels, provided there is no change in the present rate of new lending to these countries of 4–5 percent. The foreign exchange availability that this will provide will also accommodate slow-to-moderate growth in the debtor nations, a development I consider essential to the long-term resolution of international debt problems. But the study also shows a continuing transfer of resources from the debtor nations to the creditor nations for the next several years under these circumstances. That transfer seems unavoidable and a necessary cost of achieving a reduction in debt burdens.

The Future of Economic Assistance to Developing Countries

If I seem too optimistic, given the magnitude of present debt burdens and in light of the political and economic turbulence of the past decade, let me add a few caveats to my analysis. The developments of the past decade have impressed on the banks the difficulty of making accurate economic forecasts during a period of especially heavy political disturbances and rapid structural change in the world economy. What might be called a rule of prudence has led the international commercial banks to reduce sharply their lending to the developing countries. There is no reason to believe at this time that the banks will not continue to increase their exposure to the financially troubled nations at a rate—in the neighborhood of 4 percent, I believe—sufficient to accommodate modest growth in these countries. Unexpected political or economic shocks, however, could alter this picture considerably. Any substantial reduction in the growth of the external debt of these countries would severely jeopardize their ability to service their external debt.

Finally, the improvement in the world economy has been fueled to a considerable extent by the growth of the U.S. economy, and more specifically, by the growth of U.S. imports. In Germany, export growth has been an important contributor to overall economic growth this year. Germany's exports to its main trading partners, the countries of the European Economic Community (EEC), increased by about 8 percent during the first half of this year. In contrast, German exports to the U.S. grew by almost 50 percent during that period. U.S. demand for EEC exports in general increased by 33 percent in the first half of this year. Given the stimulus the Western European countries have received from U.S. import demand, it is surprising that growth in that area has not been stronger. Similarly, high growth of exports this year has played a leading role in a strong overall economic performance in Japan. Here again, the increase in exports has been due primarily to strong U.S. demand. The developing countries have also benefited directly from strong U.S. import growth. Latin American developing nations, for example, increased their exports to the United States by almost 20 percent in the first six months of the year. For the world as a whole, the increase in U.S. import demand this year will account for more than half of the increase in total imports.

Clearly, U.S. economic performance over the next several years will be crucial to the performance of the world economy. The forecast for the U.S. economy over that period must be considered generally good. But if we have learned any lesson from our experiences over the past ten years, it is that adjustment to disequilibrium cannot be delayed too long without serious adverse consequences. The U.S. trade deficit this year will total $125 billion, and the current account deficit will be $100 billion. Even larger deficits are likely next year. This is hardly equilibrium. Neither is a budget deficit of $175 billion. Reductions in these deficits will occur sooner or later, and how they are achieved will certainly have a profound impact, for better or worse, on the world economy.

Developments in the U.S. economy over the next few years will thus be a major determinant of prospects for the international financial system and the developing country debtors. The United States should not attempt to achieve balance in its budget or external accounts overnight. That would bring about a massive disruption in world trade patterns and cut off abruptly the export growth which the borrowing nations need so badly to service their external debt. But the

United States should move quickly to adopt measures which will pare its fiscal and external deficits down to manageable proportions over the next several years. If that is done, and if the structural adjustment measures taken by the borrowing countries remain in place, then there is every reason to believe that the present threat to the international financial system will recede and that the international economy will be restored to a state of good health.

High Technology
and
American
Foreign Policy

Lawrence S. Eagleburger

April 18, 1985

LAWRENCE S. EAGLEBURGER is president of Kissinger Associates, Inc., which he joined in 1984 after serving for twenty-seven years in various positions at the Department of State. From 1982 to 1984 he was under secretary of state for political affairs, the third highest position in the department. Previously he served as assistant secretary of state for European affairs, ambassador to Yugoslavia, deputy under secretary of state for management, executive assistant to Secretary of State Kissinger, deputy assistant secretary of defense, and deputy assistant to the president for national security affairs. Mr. Eagleburger has received the Distinguished Civilian Service Medal from the Department of Defense, the President's Award for Distinguished Federal Civilian Service, and the Department of State Distinguished Honor Award. He is a member of the board of directors of the ITT Corporation, Sedco, and Ljubljanska Banka.

Introduction

William J. Baroody
President
American Enterprise Institute

G. Warren Nutter was one of the great conservative intellectuals of his time. He was a scholar and statesman who understood better than most the importance of ideas in the development of public policy. He worked closely with my father, the late William J. Baroody, Sr., to foster new ideas and to create an environment in which the American Enterprise Institute and other public policy research organizations are able to flourish.

Warren taught for many years at the University of Virginia and was chairman of its economics department in the late 1960s. He took leave from 1969 to 1973 to serve as assistant secretary of defense for international security affairs. He was awarded the Defense Department's Distinguished Public Service Medal for his service there. He was a specialist in several aspects of economics: the economics of defense, industrial organization, the Soviet economy, and general microeconomic theory.

I had the privilege of knowing Warren beginning when I was very young, when he would join my father and other scholars at our home for dinner and discussion. Many times in recent years I have looked at the turns public policy has taken and thought back to what Warren Nutter said about the role of government in free societies. He advocated a greater balance between the public and private sectors.

"The question at issue," he wrote, "is not whether Americans should believe in either individualism or collectivism. Neither is adequate to serve by itself as the philosophic foundation of a viable democratic republic. The underlying philosophy must be a mixture of both. But it is critically important which dominates."[1]

---

1. G. Warren Nutter, *Political Economy and Freedom: A Collection of Essays,* edited by Jane Couch Nutter (Indianapolis: Liberty Press, 1983), p. 57.

He believed individualism was essential to individual liberty, and his life and his teachings were testaments to this idea.

The American Enterprise Institute, together with thinking Americans everywhere, owes a lasting debt to Warren Nutter. His integrity and his scholarship serve as a guiding light to those who carry on his life's mission. We are proud to present these memorial lectures as a tribute to him and as a forum for the continued competition of ideas that he treasured. Today's speaker, Lawrence Sidney Eagleburger, is an outstanding American statesman who is also an old friend.

There are many of us working around Washington—both in government and in the private sector—who will be forever grateful for the guidance and leadership we received from the likes of Warren Nutter and Melvin Laird. Larry Eagleburger and I are clearly in that category.

Larry today joins a distinguished group of scholars and statesmen who have given the Nutter Lectures at AEI. The lecturers are selected in cooperation with the trustees of the Thomas Jefferson Foundation—which was founded by Warren Nutter and James Buchanan in 1957—and they fall generally into three categories: former academic colleagues of Professor Nutter, including S. Herbert Frankel, Milton Friedman, R.H. Coase, and George J. Stigler; former students of his, such as Paul Craig Roberts; and former government colleagues, such as Admiral Thomas H. Moorer, Yuan-li Wu, and our most recent lecturer, Roger E. Shields.

Larry worked with Warren Nutter at the Pentagon in the first Nixon administration. He had one of those long titles that make life at the Department of Defense so much fun: deputy assistant secretary of defense for policy plans and National Security Council affairs.

He worked with Warren on a wide range of issues, including the negotiations in Vienna for a mutual balanced force reduction. He went from there to become principal aide to Henry Kissinger at the White House, then at the State Department. As many of you know, the relationship between Larry Eagleburger and Henry Kissinger has been a long and fruitful one that continues to this day—Larry is president of Kissinger Associates, a "somewhat successful" consulting firm formed by the former secretary of state.

I was a special assistant to Mel Laird while Larry was the key aide to Henry Kissinger, and I must say we had some interesting exchanges in those days. You may be assured that the turf battles among the State Department, the Defense Department, and the National Security Council predate Cap Weinberger and George Shultz.

I never worried about Larry, however. He may have spent a career at the State Department—he served there twenty-seven years in all—but his heart was in Wisconsin, his and Mel Laird's home state. In fact, I believe his mother was very active in Mel's first congressional campaign.

Larry Eagleburger worked his way up in the State Department and became one of this nation's foremost experts on European affairs and one of its most influential foreign policy makers. He served as a distinguished ambassador to Yugoslavia, chief of the political mission to NATO, assistant secretary of state for European affairs, and under secretary of state for political affairs. In all these roles, he has been a vital force in keeping the Western Alliance strong and in protecting U.S. interests in that region and in other parts of the world.

I am pleased to introduce our tenth Nutter lecturer, Mr. Lawrence Eagleburger.

High Technology and
American Foreign Policy

Lawrence S. Eagleburger

I first met Warren Nutter in 1971 when he was assistant secretary of defense for international security affairs, and I had been recalled from an overseas assignment to be interviewed for a job as one of his deputies. It was an interesting meeting. Although he never quite said so, I suspect that from Warren's point of view he had been asked to consider hiring a cookie-pushing, soft, wrong-thinking, vaguely leftist Foreign Service officer. His lack of enthusiasm for the exercise was readily apparent to the sensitive, perspicacious fellow I then was.

From my perspective, I had been invited, like Daniel, into the lion's den. ISA had never been popular in the State Department for reasons not hard to fathom. For the Foreign Service it is a self-evident proposition that amateurs should never be permitted near the intricacies of foreign affairs. Yet, there were all those professors, politicians, and GS civilians substituting their judgments for those of the Foreign Service. Worse, they were in the Defense Department, which everyone knew was populated by pushy, hard-nosed, wrong-thinking, right-wing nuts.

The interview, somewhat akin to a meeting between a cobra and a mongoose, led soon thereafter—and somewhat to my surprise—to a job offer. I returned to Washington and ISA, and Warren immediately went on an extended vacation. I have no doubt that had my mother not been a long-time admirer and supporter of the then secretary of defense when he represented Wisconsin's Seventh Congressional District, I would never have been interviewed—much less employed—by the Defense Department.

From that less than auspicious beginning, I grew to have great affection, respect, and admiration for Warren. I rapidly came to appreciate his superb mind, which moved so quickly through problems that confounded the rest of us; I just as rapidly learned that here was a man who better than most understood the greatness of his country and the challenges, foreign and domestic, that threatened that greatness. Last but by no means least, I came to know a warm and decent human being who proved to be a kind teacher and a good friend.

It was therefore with real pleasure that I accepted the invitation to speak today in memory of, and in honor of, a man who has been rightly described by William Baroody, Jr., as "one of the great conservative intellectuals of his time."

I have for some time been fascinated by the potential impact on our foreign policy of the revolution in technology we now see gaining momentum around us. Last year, shortly before I left the State Department, I suggested in a speech that not only was America's attention turning away from Europe toward the Pacific Basin, but that the worrisome evidence that our European friends and partners were falling behind in the high-technology race could further strain the transatlantic relationship in the years ahead. The reaction to that speech, particularly in Europe, was less than laudatory. *Le Monde*, in questioning my wisdom and paternity, remarked that I did not even have the excuse of being from California.

In the course of the past year, since I left government and, as a consequence, am permitted to think, I have become ever more convinced that, despite *Le Monde*, the changes taking place, and yet to occur, in high technology—particularly changes in information systems technology—will have profound domestic and international consequences. The foreign policy ramifications of the explosion of high technology in information systems are what I propose to examine with you today. Let me begin by stating the three propositions that form the outline of my approach.

- First, we are entering an era of revolutionary change occasioned by technological breakthroughs in the way we develop, store, process, transfer, and use information.
- Second, the United States will be uniquely able to sustain and exploit this "revolution."
- Third, as the United States moves more deeply into what future historians may well describe as another Industrial Revolution, we will find ourselves facing an international environment that is inevitably more complex—but an environment made even more complex be-

cause we are coping so much better than others with the challenges of a new era. Our very success could, instead of enhancing international stability and security, adversely affect our relations with friends and allies, adversaries, and the developing world alike.

If my own research and conversations with businessmen and academics are any indication, there is substantial consensus that the developed world, with the United States and Japan in the lead, will undergo, between now and the end of the century, revolutionary changes in the efficiency with which we store, process, transfer, and use information. There is, as well, general acceptance of the proposition that this "revolution" will profoundly affect our social and economic environment, creating opportunities that are today unimaginable.

Here are some relevant facts and predictions:

• The manufacture of information technology today produces yearly revenues for U.S. companies of some $110 billion, which is some 3.3 percent of our gross national product, and about equal to the yearly activity of the automobile industry. By 1994 the information industry's yearly revenues will be $330 billion, or 6 percent of U.S. GNP.

• Before 1990, information technology will be the world's largest manufacturing industry.

• Given expected improvements in existing technology, plus predictable developments in new technology, computers will provide at least 100 times more power within ten years, at costs roughly comparable to those of today. An improvement of 1,000 times over today's computers cannot be more than two decades away.

• There are now more than 6 million computers in the United States, and some estimate that one-half of all U.S. households will have a computer-based system by 1990.

These are but a few examples of what is already under way around us. Microprocessor chips the size of a fingernail can already be combined in machines the size of a dining room table that would hold all of the information contained in the Library of Congress. Optical disks the size of a long-playing record are now being developed that will be capable of storing on one disk all the information now contained in all the world's telephone books.

I do not pretend to know what our lives will be like as we enter the twenty-first century, but that they will be substantially different seems inevitable. No one can easily predict how individual countries will react to, or take advantage of, the information revolution. Nevertheless, the competition for leadership in the development and exploitation of information systems technology will be intense. What can we say about the future of this competition? Which nations are likely to be most successful? Which less so?

The United States, I believe, enjoys such substantial advantages that it would take monumental government ineptitude and an industrial mind set akin to that of the U.S. automobile industry of the 1960s and 1970s to keep us from leading the way into this new era. Japan, almost certainly, will be close behind; Western Europe is much more uncertain; and the Soviet Union is likely to be condemned to second-class status in the absence of fundamental systemic changes. I come to these conclusions because of three factors that will be critical in determining how the protagonists will perform: the size of the market, the society's orientation toward "engineering," and the existence of an entrepreneurial culture.

Market Size

Whatever else one can say about the development of the new information technology, it is brutally obvious that it will be expensive. High-technology research costs, plus the costs of translating those research findings into products for sale, tax many of our largest companies and have already driven many others—foreign and domestic—out of business. Those costs, as competition becomes more fierce, will grow rapidly. A major factor in the ability to remain in the game will thus be the size of the market available to support the industry.

The American market is now, and is likely to continue to be for some time, the largest single consumer of computer hardware and software and other information systems products. It is, as well, still the freest market, as names such as Fujitsu, Toshiba, and Mitsubishi demonstrate. U.S. firms, through a series of interlocking agreements with Japanese and European firms, are also moving to strengthen their access to foreign markets and to cooperative R & D schemes. IBM, for example, has entered into one agreement that includes relationships with twelve semiconductor makers, two computer manufacturers, and two telecommunications companies, all of which involve five countries.

Even at this relatively early stage we see a whole range of information-related industrial giants working hard to ensure access to as wide a market as possible. Yet there are countertrends as well. Japan remains unprepared to permit meaningful access to its domestic information market, as it does with so many other industries. I am told, however, that such firms as IBM have been able to beat the Japanese on their home ground more than once and remain confident they can continue to do so, particularly in software.

The Western European market—or more aptly, the various national markets in Western Europe—remain open to foreign firms, particularly if the foreign companies have working relationships with companies located within the various European countries. Yet evidence of growing European concern over the state of its information industry could engender protectionist pressures. The Esprit program of the European Economic Community (EEC), an effort to develop a Common Market information technology, envisages EEC Commission, member government, and private industry cooperation aimed at overtaking the U.S. and Japanese lead in information systems in ten years. Imaginative as this program may prove to be, it is avowedly aimed at taking the European market away from U.S. and Japanese firms, though even here one must wonder if it can be truly successful with so many U.S. companies already present in Europe through subsidiaries or cooperative agreements of one kind or another.

In sum, then, market size is critical—and increasingly so—to the ability of information technology industries to recoup their R & D costs. Both the United States and Japan have access to large markets— the United States to its own and the fragmented European market, the Japanese to those markets and its own as well. Whether that will continue to be the case for the Japanese remains to be seen. They seem well on their way to awakening the sleeping giant for the second time in this century; should the United States move to shut out or restrict severely Japanese computer or electronics exports, Japan's market would shrink overnight, with serious consequences to Japanese competitive abilities.

Western Europe's problem is of a different character; no common Western European market exists for the products of its various high-technology industries. As *The Economist* (London) for November 24–30, 1984, said in a superb article on Europe's technology gap:

> Young, innovative European firms labour under crippling burdens that their American and Japanese counterparts do not have. One—the uncommon market—is well known, though the extent of the damage it does is not. Testing and

certification requirements, differing standards, border delays and restraints on trade in services all take their toll on trade between EEC countries. These obstacles add as much as 20% to the cost of goods in intracommunity trade. . . . And the effects of Europe's market fragmentation are getting worse all the time: as development costs rise and product lives contract, it becomes even harder to recoup investment in a single national market.

In 1983 the EEC accounted for 30 percent of the world market for information technology. Yet the community was able to capture only some 10 percent of that world market; its share of the European market was only 30 percent. These facts seem to prove fairly conclusively that Western European technology—or at least its practical application—is not up to American or Japanese standards. The Esprit program previously referred to may do something to improve this situation, but we are nonetheless left to wonder how much can really be accomplished until and unless the Common Market countries get back to the business of building Europe. Arguing over milk quotas, corn gluten, or even budgets may keep bureaucrats and politicians off the streets, but it is unproductive work compared with the truly crucial task of building a market sufficient to support the R & D costs that must form the base of a healthy and competitive information industry in the last decade and a half of the century.

Orientation toward Engineering

Harder to define, but equally critical to exploiting successfully the new information technologies, is the degree to which a society is oriented toward engineering in its broadest sense—a society that is comfortable with new technologies and knows how to use them. American GIs during World War II were unique among combatants in their familiarity with things mechanical. When the engine on the truck gave up, someone was inevitably able to fix it because he had grown up tinkering with the family car or tractor.

America is now in the process of building a nation that is comfortable with the computer—comfortable with our movement toward an information culture. My eleven-year-old son already speaks a language full of "modems," "mouse," "RAMs," etc.—a language I only pretend to understand. His generation certainly will be as comfortable with, and as dependent upon, the computer and its ancillary equipment as we are the automobile or the telephone. These are the people who will transform the information revolution from the new and mysterious to the commonplace and essential.

The United States is perhaps the world's only truly revolutionary society. We are a people who are comfortable with change; we often seek change for its own sake. New inventions intrigue us; new gimmicks bring us to the stores in droves. We are also a people who will not rest until we have found new uses for the devices our technology creates. So the information revolution in this country will fall on fertile ground—not just as something that scientists, businessmen, bureaucrats, and educators can use, but as something that the most average among us will sooner or later find to be an intimate part of everyday life.

As in so many things, Japan is hard to classify in this respect. Certainly it is a nation of great technological imagination and ingenuity, a nation that must, therefore, be classified as an "engineering-oriented" society. Yet, it is as well a nation profoundly conservative in its traditions and culture, with a homogenous population that has known little of the daily turmoil and change that are the everyday fare of an America of varying religions, racial makeup, and global responsibilities.

It may be that Japan will be able to contend with the revolutionary impact of the information explosion on its society and culture. Given the record, one would have to argue so. Nevertheless, the strains on the system may prove to be intense. In any event, I suspect that the United States will be better able to cope with the inevitable changes than will Japan.

At first blush most Western European nations appear to be societies comfortable with technological change. Further examination leads to a more qualified view. Try as I have to find authorities in any of the current literature who would argue that Europeans—or some European nations—are at the forefront of technological development over a broad spectrum, I could find none. Certain industries in certain countries do well. The general consensus remains, however, that Europe is falling further behind in the high-technology race. Let me quote again from the same *Economist* article:

> Few doubt that Europe is in real trouble. There are two reasons, one specific, the other much broader. The specific worry is Europe's poor performance in the information industries. . . . The general worry is Europe's inability to inno-

vate: its sluggishness in creating the new businesses, high-tech and low, which alone can generate growth and jobs.

There are many reasons for this phenomenon, not least of which is the "little Europe" thinking that has led to the "uncommon market" already discussed. Another, I believe, is that throughout the postwar years Europeans have opted for security over innovation. There has been a steady trend in every important Western European country toward the kinds of social legislation that inevitably make industry less able to adjust to changing times and market demands. I intend no social commentary here: certainly one could argue—though I would not—that European labor legislation, for example, is more humane than ours. Even if that were true, however, a cost has been exacted, not only in the dollars and cents terms that economists can quantify but in psychological terms as well. To generalize excessively to make my point, Europe has chosen the stability of predictability, and in the process lost the taste for change and challenge that was probably never as strong as it was and is in the United States.

The Entrepreneurial Culture

Of the three factors critical to the development of the new information society, the importance of an entrepreneurial culture should require the least discussion. The willingness—both personal and corporate—to take a chance is highly developed in the United States. And despite the concerns voiced by many that we are losing our entrepreneurial spirit, the facts seem to prove otherwise:

• In 1983 approximately 600,000 new corporations were established in the United States.
• Over 7 million *net* new jobs have been generated in the United States over the past two years, with much of this increase coming from companies with fewer than 200 workers.

Silicon Valley has rightly become famous as the outward manifestation of what risk taking in the field of information systems high technology can produce—the failures as well as the successes. It is a uniquely American institution, based on the concept of risk, but reinforced by other highly developed support mechanisms.

Our venture capital system, for example, provides an efficient means of assisting small firms to get their start. In 1983, $2.8 billion was committed to start-ups in the United States. Our tax system, at least until now, has tended to favor risk takers; our share option system rewards risk takers handsomely. In short, America's entrepreneurial spirit remains strong, and is supported by institutions, public and private, that raise the risk taker's odds of success appreciably.

It is certain that as the information revolution proceeds over the next decades many more companies seeking to be a part of that process will fail than will succeed. If history is any precedent, however, the successes will be noteworthy, with the probability that the end of the century will see new industrial giants that today can only be imagined. What is hard to see is how the information revolution could take place without these risk takers. The computer industry could not have advanced as it has were it not for the intense competition that developed to produce ever more efficient microchips and semiconductors. The same will remain true in the years ahead; the pace of change will be affected by the development of new industries finding new ways to use the new technologies, and thereby creating demand for newer technologies, newer applications of those technologies, and so on, ad infinitum.

Can Japan do as well? While the United States is a nation that prides itself on its individual entrepreneurs, Japan is a nation of collective risk takers. Japanese industry, often encouraged by government, finances and provides the personnel for new ventures. The system has certainly, thus far, proved successful and imaginative. But in an ever more complex environment one can at least be permitted to wonder whether this structured system can be as productive as the semichaotic but probably much more broadly based system we enjoy.

One must, again, be pessimistic about Western Europe. Individual entrepreneurs exist, to be sure. But the habit and concept of risk taking as we know it is by no means so deeply engrained in the European psyche. Nor are the institutions necessary to support risk takers particularly well developed. The *Economist* article mentioned previously notes, for example, that risk capital, except in Britain, is in short supply throughout Europe, with investment running at only some 10 to 20 percent of U.S. levels. The *International Herald Tribune* just yesterday carried an article on venture capital in Europe; while arguing that more effort is being made to support high-technology industries than in the past, it also admitted that the amount of risk capital available was minuscule when compared with the United States. Under such circumstances, one can but wonder if the question of whether there are any entrepreneurs in Europe is particularly relevant, since the means to finance them, in any event, are so insubstantial.

I have deliberately left the Soviet Union out of the discussion until now because its circumstances are so very different. Of the three factors I have discussed, the Soviets possess *only* the market, for whatever that may be worth. It could, in the abstract, be a vast market over the coming years, but I doubt that it will become so in any time frame relevant to this discussion. The Soviets certainly cannot be accused of having a society oriented toward engineering, nor are they well known for their entrepreneurial culture.

Foreign Policy Consequences

It is, therefore, hard to see how the Soviets can ever be a major player in the information revolution. Its computer industry is hardly in the first rank and is not likely under the best of circumstances to become so. Thus, it is probably condemned, no matter how much technology it can steal, to be several generations behind its Western betters at any given moment. But what of it? The Soviets have always lagged far behind the West in most areas of high technology and have nonetheless been able to build and maintain their superpower status.

The past may not, however, be wholly relevant this time. While I do not believe that the Soviet Union is on the verge of sinking into insignificance, I do suggest that the transition into the twenty-first century presents the nation with some extremely difficult problems that probably cannot be solved by old methods.

The information revolution, by its very nature, will have ramifications far beyond the new information systems themselves. The importance of the new technology is that it generates *knowledge*—knowledge that will open up new opportunities for technical advance across a broad spectrum. Industries of all kinds will benefit, and these in turn will generate new advances and new breakthroughs. The consequences will be, in the truest sense of the word, synergistic.

For this to happen one thing will be essential: information will have to flow freely. The new information technology will prove so productive in the United States because the impediments to information flow are minimal. Proprietary rights will, of course, have to be protected, as will national security data, but these limitations will not fundamentally restrict information flow and use.

Can the Soviet system tolerate such a free flow of information? To ask the question is to answer it. Aside from the normal Russian paranoia and historical penchant for secrecy, other more fundamental factors are at work. The most obvious is that in a dictatorship any instrument that facilitates information flow outside the control of the ruling oligarchy strikes, over time, at the very fundamentals of the system. Yet if the information is kept in the hands of the few it loses the creative aspect that graces it with such promise.

Mr. Gorbachev may put a computer at every school desk. He may even succeed, though I doubt it, in training the bureaucracy to use the computer as a management tool. Can he, however, permit computers in homes or individual offices, with open access to data banks and the ability to cross-talk freely? Not unless he is prepared fundamentally to change the nature of the system that promoted him to his current position.

This, then, is the Soviet conundrum: make whatever use you can of new information system technologies, but always under firm state control, thereby forgoing the advantages of a free flow of information, or loosen the control network, free your citizens' inventive capacities, and run the risk that you will not long be in power. I have no doubt which path the Soviet leadership would choose if it even thought in such terms—which it does not.

Under these circumstances I find it hard to conceive of a way out of the box for the Soviets. They will certainly develop a computer capacity substantially better than they now possess and will use it to good effect for military purposes. Nevertheless, the development of a broad new information technology that transforms the nature of the society is, I believe, almost certainly beyond their capacities. Thus, as we close out the twentieth century and enter the twenty-first, we are likely to see increasingly clear evidence of the fundamental inefficiency of totalitarianism. The Soviet Union will come ever more to resemble the dinosaur, incapable of adjusting to the surrounding environment.

This is not an unalloyed message of hope. The dinosaurs died slowly, and were dangerous in the interim. The Soviet military machine will, for many years to come, remain the awesome instrument it now is (though I would add, parenthetically, that even here I believe the information revolution will, over time, provide those who know how to use it with great advances in weapons technology). Given the strains I believe we will see with allies and the developing world in the years ahead—in part caused by the information revolution—the Soviets will have fertile ground for mischief making at our expense. In other words, the Soviet Union will remain our principal foreign threat for decades to come, and as its relative position vis-à-vis the United States diminishes, it may well become more rather than less dangerous.

What that will mean for the United States is what it has always meant—a steady commitment to the maintenance of a defense establishment that even the most frustrated Soviet leadership would fear to challenge. It should mean, as well, that we resolve *not* to make the "transition" for the Soviets more palatable by finding ways to reduce the pressure on them. It should also mean major efforts at rebuilding our transatlantic and Pacific coalitions along new lines more appropriate to the twenty-first century, and substantial attention to finding ways to ensure that the developing world has some hope that it, too, will benefit from the new information age.

The thing I find most disturbing about the analysis I have presented today is the conclusion that Western Europe is falling further behind in the information technology race. This disease is not limited solely to information systems, but infects other high-technology areas as well.

Europe's difficulties should be no cause for rejoicing but rather a source of grave concern. I have for some time believed that the transatlantic relationship, despite the contemporary calm, is in for rough sailing as the century closes. The relationship is strained by generational changes on both sides of the Atlantic, the global nature of America's role versus the regional nature of European interests, increasing differences in how the security threat is perceived and dealt with, and increasing though seldom-stated European disquiet with American unpredictability and naivete. American frustration with Europe's unwillingness to accept its "responsibilities," trade differences of growing asperity, and increasing American interest in the Pacific also bode less than well over the longer term for a constructive transatlantic relationship.

Add to these strains the tensions that would be created by a Western Europe left behind in the information technology race and the resulting brew could be dangerous. An increasingly uncompetitive European partner would be an increasingly uncertain and protectionist Europe that would inevitably be drawn toward a closer relationship—at least economic—with the Soviet bloc. America, at least as much as Europe, would be the loser.

It would behoove us, then, to examine what we can do to encourage Europe to strengthen its high-tech capacities. We cannot, of course, force the EEC to return to the dream of Monnet and get about building Europe again—which would be the single most important step that could be taken. We can, however, *encourage* Europe in that direction and be critical when it falters. We can support and indeed encourage U.S. industry to make cooperative R & D arrangements with European firms, and we can give European industry a fair chance to capture U.S. defense contracts when their bids are competitive. We can resist with all our strength the rising demand in this country and abroad for protectionism, for nothing could more quickly destroy all hope of cooperation in dealing with the challenges of the new era we are entering than for the democracies to engage in economic warfare among themselves.

Our future relationship with Japan is an equally pressing issue, and one that may well get out of hand before we are able to do much about it. It may be, as the Japanese claim, that our trade deficit is no one's fault but our own. Nevertheless, the Japanese give us little opportunity to test the claim; their stubborn refusal to grant meaningful concessions—made worse by constantly conciliatory rhetoric—provides the protectionists with substantial ammunition.

Yet, as we examine the future, particularly in such specific areas as information systems technology, it becomes quickly evident that the United States is in a potentially predominant position that could only be adversely affected by any protectionist steps we might take. We can only hope, therefore, that the Japanese will soon realize how dangerous the game they are playing is and come to grips with reality. If they do not, and if pressures for protectionism become irresistible, then we should take steps explicitly aimed at Japan alone; we should resist at all costs the temptation to fashion measures that have a wider sweep. We should also be ready, as soon as the Japanese make adequate compromises, to return to the *status quo ante*.

The tragedy of the current trade dispute with Japan is that it diverts our attention from the truly important: the future of our relationship with Japan and the countries of the Pacific Basin. I find it hard to believe that our traditional postwar relationship with Japan can last the century. The anachronism of a continuing substantial commitment of American forces to the defense of the North Pacific rim while Japan spends less than 1 percent of its GNP on defense will find ever less enthusiastic adherents here, with growing U.S. pressure for Japan to share more of the military burden. Such messages from Washington now fall on less than receptive ears in Tokyo, but this may change. To expect a nation as economically powerful as Japan to eschew forever a military establishment of some significance may be rational but lacks historical precedent.

These considerations may appear far removed from issues of high technology and the information revolution, but they are not. Our relationships across the Atlantic and the Pacific are going to become increasingly strained over the rest of this century under the best of circumstances; too many things are in flux and transition to believe otherwise. Add the potentially destabilizing revolution in information systems and you have a prognosis that deserves serious high-level concern on both sides of both oceans, beginning now. I am no great lover of international conferences, having sat through too many of them. I nevertheless believe that we and our Pacific and Atlantic friends need—and soon—to fashion some method for collective examination of the challenges of the next several decades, and what steps might be taken, jointly and severally, to make the century we are entering a better and safer one than the century we will soon be leaving behind.

One final word about the foreign policy consequences of the information revolution. The developed world has for too long failed to take seriously the growing gulf between ourselves and the developing world; that disparity can only get worse in the years ahead. The information revolution can increase the rate at which we grow apart, or, if wisely used, help to reduce it. Just as we and our Western European and Japanese allies need to concentrate on our common future, so should we jointly examine how we can begin the common task of reversing a trend that if permitted to continue can only lead to an explosion that will threaten the security of us all.

America is on the edge of a great experience that will change the world in which we live. We will benefit as a nation no matter what we do. Whether we are more secure as a result, or simply an island of growing technological excellence and economic prosperity in a sea of turmoil and poverty, remains to be seen. If we have the imagination and wit to manage wisely the riches that will come to us, then we will have achieved that greatest of accomplishments: to pass on to future generations a world better than the one we inherited.

The Public Policy
Roots of
Recent Thrift Crises

William F. Ford

October 23, 1985

William F. Ford is the president and chief operating officer of First Nationwide Savings and First Nationwide Financial Corporation, which he joined in 1983. From 1980 to 1983 he was president of the Atlanta Federal Reserve Bank and served on the Federal Open Market Committee. He has also served as vice-president, senior vice-president, director of strategic planning and chief economist of the Wells Fargo Bank, as director of research and executive director of the American Bankers Association, and on the faculties of the Universities of Michigan and Virginia.

Introduction

John H. Moore

All of us here this afternoon have come because of our friendship and respect for Warren Nutter. All of our lives have been touched in some way—as student, as colleague, or as friend—by the remarkable man to whose memory these lectures are dedicated. For some, the contact with Warren was brief, perhaps casual. For others, it was deep and powerful, affecting ways of thinking and careers.

Whatever the extent of our contact with Warren, we all know that he was a man of great abilities, fierce loyalties, and profound dedication to principle and to country. This series of lectures has demonstrated well the esteem in which he is held; and the wide range of subjects, all within the scope of Warren's interests and knowledge, is testimony to the breadth of his abilities. It is a privilege to be associated with the series and with the Thomas Jefferson Foundation, founded by Warren in Charlottesville more than fifteen years ago and the principal sponsor of the series.

Almost six years ago, I had the privilege of introducing the first lecturer in the series, my good friend Professor S. Herbert Frankel. It is my privilege today to introduce another good friend, Dr. William F. Ford. I first met Bill at Warren's home in Charlottesville when he arrived at the University of Virginia as an assistant professor of economics almost twenty years ago. Bill had recently completed his Ph.D. at the University of Michigan. That immediately gave us something in common, since I had also been a student in Ann Arbor.

I remember talking to Bill that evening about his years in the Navy submarine service, which he entered in 1954. After a tour of active duty, Bill entered the University of Texas at Austin. In 1961, he graduated from Texas with numerous honors and distinctions. A year later he also graduated from the Navy, having completed four years of reserve duty in addition to his active duty.

Bill had the good fortune, as did I, of being at Virginia in the great days of its economics department. He and I even wrote an article together, on a subject that reflects the tenor of those days in the nation—the social and economic characteristics of the cities in which riots had occurred. There were enough riots in those days that it was possible to do some cross-section regression analysis on the data, a real testimony to the violence of the late 1960s. Bill left Virginia soon after the publication of that article to become the dean of a business school. His career since then reflects a diversity of interests and a range of talents that make his appearance in this series especially appropriate. It spans academics, business, and public service, with success and high achievement marking every step.

After his service as dean, he moved to Washington, D.C., to become director of research for the American Bankers Association. While at the ABA, he created its electronic funds transfer unit and its high performance banking analysis program, in the process rising to become executive director. After four years at the ABA, his record of accomplishments led to his being lured away by the Wells Fargo Bank in San Francisco, where he initially became vice-president, and later senior vice-president.

At Wells Fargo, Bill was director of strategic planning and chief economist. He developed the bank's strategic plan for 1975–1980, which was the blueprint for doubling the company's profits in the late 1970s. As chief economist, he supported the bank's line operations and represented the bank in industry and government affairs, a responsibility for which his years in Washington no doubt provided good background.

At that time, I was at the Law and Economics Center at the University of Miami. I remember picking up the *Wall Street Journal* one day and seeing that the new president of the Atlanta Federal Reserve Bank was none other than my old friend Bill Ford. Bill moved to the Atlanta Fed in August 1980, and served with great distinction as its president for the next three years. His managerial skills were tested and proved at the bank, which at that time had the largest check-clearing volume in the twelve-bank Federal Reserve system. Instituting economies in operations, he made the bank the most cost effective in the system. He also served on the Federal Open Market Committee, where he put monetarist principles to work in the most practical of ways. You will recall that it was during the early 1980s, when Bill served on the Open Market Committee, that inflation was brought to heel.

While in Atlanta, Bill engaged in another form of public service. He created a magnet school to train inner-city youths for entry-level positions in the city's banks and thrift institutions. The school was supported by the major banks in Atlanta and has been highly successful in placing its graduates in professional positions.

Atlanta and the Federal Reserve System were not enough to hold Bill for long, however. His outstanding record and national reputation led to another irresistible offer. In October 1983, he became president and chief operating officer of First Nationwide Savings (one of the largest savings and loans in the nation) and of its parent company, First Nationwide Financial Corporation in San Francisco, which is the position he holds today. As in everything else he has done, he has posted an outstanding performance in this demanding position. I will not dwell on all of his accomplishments, but the bottom line is that net income has tripled in the two years he has been president. Naturally, this record has attracted attention, and as a result the corporation was recently sold to the Ford Motor Company for a figure more than thirty percent over book value. And at First Nationwide, he can't print his own money!

Bill has seen the financial industry at the highest levels from both the public and private sides of the fence. This afternoon he will bring this experience to bear on a problem of grave potential for our nation, the crisis in our thrift institutions. I am very pleased to present to you the eleventh Nutter lecturer, my old friend and former colleague at the University of Virginia, William F. Ford.

The Public Policy Roots of Recent Thrift Crises

William F. Ford

It is a pleasure for me to join the outstanding speakers who have preceded me in the G. Warren Nutter Memorial Lecture series sponsored by the Thomas Jefferson Center Foundation and presented by the American Enterprise Institute. Like all of the earlier speakers, I knew Warren for many years, admired him for his intellectual abilities, and considered him a warm personal friend and adviser.

Although he was known to the public primarily for his outstanding work in the international economic and public policy arena, Warren also had a deep and abiding interest in domestic policy issues. Very early in his professional career, for example, he wrote on the subject of industrial organization with particular reference to the role of antitrust policy in promoting economic welfare. Also, toward the end of his life he wrote an outstanding AEI manuscript entitled "Growth of Government in the West." In those and his other works in the same vein, Warren often expressed a profound skepticism about the role of government in western economies, including ours. My talk, as the title suggests, deals with an aspect of public policy that would surely interest Warren if he could be with us today. Specifically, I will share some thoughts with you about the public policy roots of the financial crises that have swept over the industry in which I have been working—the thrift industry.

To Regulate or Not to Regulate?

Unfortunately, hardly a day goes by when one does not read about some lingering or emerging crisis in our industry, in Ohio, Maryland, California, or some other part of our nation. And the pundits of our financial press are constantly raising the specter of financial instability—speculating about whether the thrift industry, as we have known it, will survive at all. Curiously, this happens at a time when my company and other well-managed thrifts are shattering their previous earning records by wide margins. In fact, it is now estimated that the industry will earn over $5 billion in 1985, even after writing off the huge losses of the sick institutions that have not been able to turn themselves around despite today's relatively favorable interest rate environment.

Nevertheless, the media and the regulators continue to focus, understandably, on the remaining bad news about our industry. When they turn to what should be done about the lingering problems, they invariably advocate greater regulation of our business. And they have little trouble finding people—both within and outside the industry—who are willing to support extensive *re*regulation of thrifts and other financial institutions.

I think it would be more useful, however—particularly in this case—to reverse the media's agenda by stepping back from today's headlines to look into the history of regulation of the financial industry. The object of this exercise, of course, is to see what we can learn about how public policy has served us in the past, *before* we move to further encumber it with additional rules and regulations.

Those of you who have read a book on economic history are no doubt aware that the idea of regulating the activities of financial institutions goes back to Biblical times, at least. In fact, Jesus himself served as a part-time regulator of the financial industry when he drove the money changers from Herod's temple. To be specific—and this will be the only footnoted quotation in my talk—in Matthew 21:12–13 we read that:

> Jesus entered the temple area and drove out all who were buying and selling there. He overturned the tables of the money changers and the benches of those selling doves. It is written, he said to them: "My house will be called a house of prayer but you are making it a den of robbers."

Since then, there have been very few places or times in history in which money changers or lenders (read usurers) have been popular. In fact, today, in major areas of the Islamic world it is a serious crime to charge *any* interest for the use of money. And orthodox Marxists, of course, also consider interest a form of "unearned" income. It may be appropriate, therefore, to begin our review of the public policy roots of the thrift industry's crisis by analyzing the role that usury laws have played in bringing it about.

In modern times, in this country, the application of usury laws has been uneven, both geographically and over time. Without going into a detailed review of the checkered history of America's usury laws, let me just note that during most of this century over half of our states have from time to time applied some meaningful (read submarket) limits on the amount of interest that lenders can charge for one or more types of loans. Economists, of course, have consistently argued that while the objective of usury laws may be noble, the actual effects of such laws are usually the opposite of those intended. Specifically, if lenders are limited to charging a submarket rate of interest for a particular type of loan, they will normally find it in their interest to make such loans—if at all—only to those who are most certainly able to repay their debts. That criterion usually rules out loans to the poorest and most marginal borrowers—precisely the group legislators hope to favor when voting for a usury law.

In the housing finance industry, until recently, the most relevant forms of usury laws were the limits some states placed on the amount of interest thrifts could charge on home loans. New York state, for example, until 1980 applied mortgage usury laws that did enable some lucky New Yorkers to obtain submarket fixed-rate thirty-year mortgages. Incidentally, when federal preemption finally overrode the New York law, New York thrifts were limited to charging 8½ percent on mortgages when inflation was reaching historic peaks of over 15 percent—or about minus 6½ percent in real terms. Against that backdrop, I think it is reasonable to argue that the major New York thrift institutions that have failed in the past few years can legitimately attribute their demise *partly* to the impact of submarket rate mortgage loans made while operating under New York's usury laws. The failure of these institutions is, of course, also a major public policy failure, the blame for which rests squarely on the shoulders of usury law advocates.

A second form of price control that has been a cornerstone of public policy in the thrift and banking industries is the regulation of deposit interest rates. Again, the intention of the regulations was noble. But the effects were quite the opposite. During the Great Depression it was widely but incorrectly perceived that one of the main causes of bank and thrift failures was "unbridled competition" for deposits among financial institutions. To make sure that such foolishness would not recur in the future, the Rooseveltian Congress passed a series of anticompetitive banking laws that, among other things, made it illegal for financial institutions to pay interest on demand deposits.

Because thrift institutions were not allowed to be in the business of taking demand deposits at that time, this form of price control did not become significant to our industry until the Interest Rate Control Act of 1966 was passed, when the original "Regulation Q" idea was extended to cover the rates that thrifts and banks could offer on passbook and time deposits. Because thrifts were judged to be furthering the public interest by making home loans (rather than commercial or international loans), the rates they were allowed to pay their savers were set slightly higher than those granted to banks (initially one-half percent higher).

These rate regulations caused the "small saver"—the alleged object of congressional affection—to be the *only* one unable to obtain a market rate of interest for his savings. Typically, the so-called Reg. Q ceilings were set below the yields that large investors could earn on Treasury bills or other market instruments. The U.S. Treasury, however, made sure that such market rate instruments were *not* available to the small saver by requiring that T-bills be purchased in minimum amounts of $10,000—well beyond the reach of most savers at that time.

Curiously, from the perspective of thrift executives in the 1960s and early 1970s, the combination of state usury laws and deposit interest ceilings was generally *not* particularly burdensome. In fact, for a number of years the thrifts were limited to paying not more than 5 or 6 percent interest to their saving customers; at the same time they were usually able to charge 2 to 3 percent higher rates of interest to their mortgage borrowers—even with usury laws in place. In the parlance of financial executives, this meant that they enjoyed a "locked-in spread" or gross profit margin. Because thrift taxes, loss provisions, and operating costs were generally smaller than the spread income they earned, a predictable *net* profit fell to the bottom line of most savings and loans every year.

That pleasant situation lasted until the mid-1970s, when our economy was subjected to the ravages of a generally rising and increasingly volatile rate of inflation, which continued until after the turn of this decade. It is not my purpose this evening to discuss how this might have been averted by better economic policy making. Other speakers here at AEI have eloquently addressed that subject. What is of interest though, is the impact spiraling inflation had on the operations of the thrift industry.

The Effect of Inflation on the Thrift Industry

First, on the asset side of the balance sheet, inflation sharply eroded the *real* value of the interest payments that millions of American families were making on their mortgages. This would not have necessarily destroyed the profitability of the thrift industry if savers had continued accepting submarket rates of interest in an increasingly inflationary environment. Unfortunately for thrift executives, the public did not long tolerate such a situation.

At the height of the inflationary spiral of 1973–1974, for several quarters, the consumer price index rose at an annual rate in excess of 10 percent. At the same time, banks and thrifts were permitted to pay savers only 5 to 5½ percent on their passbook savings, leaving the traditional saver with a *negative* real rate of interest of 5 percent (or less) as his or her reward for being thrifty. Then, to add insult to injury, savers were required to report this *negative* real interest to the IRS and to pay taxes on it at their marginal rate, producing an even more negative real yield after inflation and taxes.

As one might expect, the money markets began to react to the incentives in this situation by intensifying the search for ways to pay a positive rate of return to savers. It did not take long for some as-yet-uncrowned genius to invent what has come to be known as the money market fund (MMF). In research I conducted about eleven years ago while serving as the chief economist of the American Bankers Association, I demonstrated that the growth of balances in unregulated MMFs was directly proportional to the difference between the market rate of interest they offered to savers and the regulated levels of interest dictated by the financial industry regulators. In other words, the higher the free-market rates of interest vis-à-vis the Reg. Q ceilings, the more money one could expect to see flowing into these funds. When inflation temporarily abated in the late 1970s, and market rates of interest fell back toward the Reg. Q ceilings, the growth of the funds predictably slowed. But then, in the early 1980s, when inflation came back in its full fury, these unregulated funds grew like Topsy, reaching a peak level of almost one-quarter trillion dollars in 1982—equal to over one-third of the total savings in the thrift industry at that time.

The Response of Policy Makers

After finally noticing this historic change in saving market shares, the well-intentioned but slow-thinking regulators were faced with a Catch 22 situation. They could either persist in defending the Reg. Q interest rate ceilings—and thus watch the thrift industry's source of funds disappear—or they could move toward abolishing the rate ceilings and thereby cause the thrift industry's profits to disappear. They chose the latter, which precipitated the thrift industry's first serious crisis of the postwar era, the so-called spread crisis. Here is a thumbnail sketch of what happened.

The first significant development that precipitated the spread crisis was the resurgence of inflation coupled with an abrupt tightening of monetary policy that produced a prime rate in excess of 20 percent during 1981. Against that monetary backdrop, the thrifts found themselves relying increasingly on sources of funds that were more responsive to market pressures than ever before in the industry's history. Although passbook savings rates were still pegged at the 5½ percent level, a variety of other instruments became available to consumers, which featured rates that were much more sensitive to market conditions. In addition, the thrifts increased their borrowing from the Home Loan Bank System, whose advances to members were priced in relation to the cost of funds to the Federal Home Loan Banks (FHLBs). The FHLBs, of course, have to pay somewhat higher rates on their paper than the U.S. Treasury does because they do not have the full faith and credit of the government behind them. Thus, the cost to thrifts of both their consumer savings and borrowed funds rose very rapidly. The net effect of all this, on the liability side of thrift balance sheets, was to raise the cost and reduce the availability of funds to the industry.

Meanwhile, on the asset side of the industry's balance sheet, housing starts were also plunging as interest rates rose, producing a low volume of new mortgages at the higher rates that would help to offset the higher cost of savings flowing into thrifts. Taken together, the two foregoing trends actually generated, for a while, a negative net interest margin for the entire industry. And in the worst year of the crisis, 1981, after deducting operating costs, the industry realized a net loss of almost $5 billion. That loss eliminated almost one-sixth of the capital that had been painfully accumulated by thrifts in over one hundred years of operations. Nineteen eighty-two, while slightly less onerous, also produced a significant loss of over $4 billion and a sharp reduction in the number of thrifts as a result of failures and forced mergers.

Then, just as interest rates began to trend downward, the regulators added a new element to the game, which laid the groundwork for yet another aspect of the thrift crisis. Specifically, in March of 1980, Congress arbitrarily increased the level of deposit insurance for both bank and thrift depositors from $40,000 to $100,000 per account. Ironically, this 150 percent increase in the level of deposit insurance coverage was totally out of proportion to the inflation of prices, since the level of insurance was raised to $40,000 in 1974. And it was unaccompanied by *any* increase in the insurance premiums that fed the fund on which the deposit insurance was based.

To make matters worse, various state regulators then proceeded to grant the thrift institutions a wide variety of new asset powers. In fact, in California and a few other states, state-chartered institutions were permitted to invest in just about anything their managements cared to gamble on. With virtually unlimited access to government-insured funds from the money brokers, a "new breed" of expansion-minded S&L managers began to invest in businesses they knew too little about. This included investing in such diverse activities as operating fleets of airplanes, Wendy's hamburger chains, ski lodges in remote areas of the country, and—most ominously—redundant residential condominiums, as well as large commercial office projects and shopping centers in overbuilt areas.

A Case Study

As an ardent advocate of free markets, I have no objection to the deregulation of asset powers for financial institutions. In fact, I favor it. What does seem totally irrational to me, however, is the idea of granting unlimited investment powers to aggressive managers while they have essentially unlimited access to government-insured funds. I am sure I need not belabor the significance of this explosive combination of regulatory events to those of you who are familiar with our industry. But a brief exposition may be helpful to those of you who do not spend your idle hours studying thrift institutions. I will illustrate my point with a brief stylized case study, without naming the real institution on which it is based. The name of the institution is not nearly as important as its pattern of behavior. Why? Because it set the stage for the second thrift crisis of the 1980s—one that is still unfolding and that came about not through interest rate spread problems but, rather, through excessive investment in areas of the economy thrift managers knew little about. A flood of credit losses and another wave of forced mergers and failures ensued.

During the early 1980s, the prototype institution I have in mind grew from a totally insignificant S&L in a small California city to become the largest in the industry, in about five years. The captain of the enterprise in question quickly emerged as the quintessential example of the new breed of S&L leader who set out to demonstrate a new way of running the business to the slow thinkers who traditionally dominated the industry. A dashing figure, he spent much of his time zipping around the country—and Europe as well—in his fleet of corporate jets and limousines. Almost everyone who did business with his institution was dazzled by the speed of its jets—which could be dispatched in any direction to pick up a client or prospective employee—and by the speed of its decision making on multimillion dollar deals. These deals, incidentally, were not confined to every major type of real estate venture in California and dozens of other states. They included taking significant positions in the stock of major NYSE corporations totally unrelated to the S&L business.

In 1983, after consummating a merger that roughly doubled the size of the institution, this new breed S&L generated net income of over $170 million—about twice as much as any other S&L had ever earned on a continuing basis. The assets of the company soared to over $20 billion. The stock's price climbed to intoxicating levels. And the analysts and financial press—with a few significant exceptions—were truly dazzled. There were a few negative thinkers over at the SEC, however, who were not impressed by all this. But that was only because they were not properly schooled in understanding the virtues of the "creative accounting techniques" that were becoming popular in some quarters of our industry.

All of that was just a prelude to what unfolded at the new breed S&L in the first half of 1984. Its first quarter 1984 earnings of over $75 million again dazzled everyone. And, in exactly six months, the balance sheet of the institution grew by $10 billion, making it, by far, America's largest thrift. To put that growth record in perspective, it took our company about one hundred years of hard work to build a $10 billion company, and that included some significant mergers. The company of the new breed team grew by that amount in just 181 days! No one in the industry except the other new breed managers believed that kind of growth could be managed safely, particularly on the asset accumulation side of the business.

Then, the SEC stepped in in August of 1984 and asked for a major restatement of earnings because of accounting practices they considered questionable. The press and the financial analysts then began to perceive the institution's problems. There was a $6.8 billion run on the institution spread over a few weeks, and the new breed leader resigned. When the dust finally settled, losses for 1984 mounted to almost $600 million—more than all the operating income previously earned by the new breed institution. Only the magic of goodwill accounting prevented its equity from disappearing entirely. Today, the company's new and competent management team is still struggling, valiantly, to turn the institution around.

Unfortunately, a growing list of other new breed institutions—which were smaller but proportionately even more venturesome than the one I just reviewed—have actually failed. Most of them are now being managed, under a consignment program, by the "slow-thinking" institutions that resisted the new breed's siren song. In fact, my company is managing one such institution, in Beverly Hills.

And the industry, along with its regulators, is struggling to find a way to clean up billions of dollars of losses in overvalued real estate and other subpar investments left behind by the new breed as its legacy to the industry.

New Directions for Public Policy in the Thrift Industry

My conclusion is that the recent thrift crises have been caused, in large measure, by ill-conceived public policies directed toward the industry. Specifically, usury laws, government price fixing through interest-rate regulations, and excessive reliance on deposit insurance laid the groundwork for the crises we have endured. Then, poor macroeconomic policies—which produced historically high and volatile levels of inflation—drove our industry's net interest margin into the red. That, in turn, set off the first landslide of earnings and capital losses, which brought our industry to its knees in 1981 and 1982.

In the past two or three years, the explosive combination of broad new assets powers and the irrational expansion of deposit insurance levels have permitted opportunistic new breed executives to place huge bets on the unlikely combination of falling interest rates and rising commercial real estate values. Had they been speculating with their own money, their appearance on the scene might not have been a problem. Why? Because a truly free financial market would *never* have given such people instant access to the massive volume of funds they tapped through the deadly combination of high-level deposit insurance amplified by the explosive growth of brokered funds networks.

For a while, the new breed S&L executives were the toast of our industry as they basked in the applause of some of the stock analysts and of many financial reporters who should have known better. Then, as disinflation swept over the real estate markets, billions of dollars of underwriting losses began to appear on the books of the new breed institutions. One after another, those institutions went down in flames, burning up the real reserves of the industry-backed insurance fund as they fell. And the question before the House today (and the Senate as well) is: What to do next? If you accept the foregoing interpretation of the problem, the following public policy "dos and don'ts" seem appropriate to me.

Decrease the Level of Deposit Insurance. The single most important measure on my "do" list concerns deposit insurance. It was originally enacted in the 1930s as a way of protecting the small and financially unsophisticated depositors who kept their life savings in banks and thrift institutions. The FDIC and FSLIC insurance programs, it was hoped, would prevent a replay of the losses millions of depositors suffered during the rash of bank and thrift failures in the 1930s.

The original level of deposit insurance was $2,500 per account in 1934. No one ever dreamed or intended, then, that today's elaborate money brokerage networks would emerge to enable wealthy and sophisticated individuals to invest very large sums of money in risk-free accounts. Since the mid-1930s, the level of prices in the United States has risen approximately eightfold. That would suggest an insured deposit ceiling today of, say, $20,000—*not* $100,000 augmented by essentially unlimited multiple account leverage through the medium of computerized funds markets.

My first suggestion, therefore, is that we begin a gradual rollback of the level of deposit insurance, in $10,000 increments, every six months, until we get back to a reasonable level of insurance that protects only relatively small and unsophisticated savers. To be specific, I would gradually roll the level back to, say, $50,000. That move should be augmented by strict limits on *multiple* insured accounts in any form whatsoever. Also, to make these lower insurance limits credible, the regulators would at least occasionally have to liquidate a failing institution so that uninsured depositors would know the insurance limits mean something.

The purpose of all this, of course, is to place *large* investors at risk again—rather than the taxpayers who really back the FDIC's and FSLIC's solvency. If that were done, the next flock of new breed managers in their corporate jets would stand a good chance of getting their wings clipped earlier, before they could undermine public confidence in the insurance funds.

There would be some added costs involved as investors moved their accounts around to get their uninsured funds out of shaky institutions. I believe, however, these measures would enhance market discipline over financial institutions by forcing informed investors at least to consider the question of *whom* they are trusting to invest and protect their money. Right now, the riskiest and most poorly managed institutions tend to set the rate that depositors receive in the savings markets. That makes no sense to me, as an economist, particularly when in many cases such institutions are also permitted to operate without any real capital.

Implement Risk-Related Deposit Insurance. A second measure I support is moving toward some form of risk-related deposit insurance. This move, to be sure, is far easier to advocate than implement. Nevertheless, the pure logic of the case for relating insurance payments to the vastly different risks that competing institutions present to the insurance funds cries out for a serious effort to separate the Boy Scouts from the firebugs in the forest of financial institutions.

Increase Disclosure Requirements. The third reform measure I advocate is a significant upgrading of the accounting and disclosure standards that are applied to financial institutions. I wish I had time to regale you with the examples I have seen of absurd accounting practices in our industry. Let me just assert, without proof, that if baseball or football were played with scorekeeping systems like ours, no one would ever know for sure who was really winning or losing the game. America's financial institutions need to be subjected to better external auditing, coupled with more disclosure of audit findings, in order to apply more market discipline to their activities.

Do Not Reregulate. Turning to the "don'ts" in my policy prescription, number one on the list is *don't reregulate* the financial industries. I have argued that the recent thrift crises flowed from two sources: inflation-driven negative interest margins followed and compounded by bad underwriting of loans and investments by a new breed of opportunists who invaded the industry. The negative interest margin problem would never have emerged to cripple the thrift industry if the erratic macroeconomic policies of the 1970s and early 1980s had not produced high inflation and double-digit short-term interest rates. And if the new breed managers in our industry had had to rely on the free (read uninsured) funds markets, rather than on excessively insured deposit channels, to raise the money they spread around America as they invested in everything from hamburger joints to ski resorts, the severe asset quality problems we now face also would not have arisen.

So my conclusion is that we should first acknowledge the role that bad public policies have played in creating the recent crises in our industry. If Congress and the regulators really want to help prevent future crises in the financial sector, their first priority should be to find a way to avoid another outburst of uncontrolled inflation and abnormally high interest rates. Then, rather than reducing the competitive powers of the industry through a maze of new regulations, we should be paying more attention to reducing access to risk-free (that is, insured) funds and to improving the scorekeeping system we use to play the banking game.

The Pentagon's Office of International Security Affairs, 1969-1973 or Two Citizens Go to Washington

Richard A. Ware

January 22, 1986

Richard Anderson Ware has been associated with Earhart Foundation (and also Relm Foundation, 1951-1973), Ann Arbor, Michigan, since 1951. He currently is president emeritus and a trustee. In 1969-1970 he served as principal deputy secretary of defense (international security affairs) and then as consultant to assistant secretary Nutter through 1972. Prior to his career as a foundation manager Mr. Ware was engaged in research and administrative survey work on Michigan state and local government. He is a member of the Board of Foreign Scholarships by appointment of President Reagan and of Phi Beta Kappa (Lehigh University 1941).

Introduction

John F. Lehman, Jr.
Secretary of the Navy

In introducing me, Bill Baroody, the president of AEI, made a reference to the Navy's "Qaddafi watch." Actually, I came from more perilous waters, dealing with *more* of a threat. I bring you greetings from Senator Phil Gramm, which is why I was a little late.

This is an opportunity I have been looking forward to for a long time because I go way back with Dick Ware. Our relationship started in early 1963 when I, at the recommendation of Vic Milione of the Intercollegiate Studies Institute, took a trip to Detroit to interest Dick in helping us put together a conference at the University of Pennsylvania. At the time it was called the Philadelphia Collegiate Disarmament Conference. When I first presented the idea to Dick, he reacted in a, shall we say, less than enthusiastic fashion until I explained that we wanted to organize a forum to attempt to stem the tide that was running for unilateral disarmament and unilateral initiative in the test ban treaty of 1963. It was only then that he began to listen; and after I had talked a long time, for the first time I heard the wisdom of Richard Ware, which I have been listening to ever since.

Dick is one of those special people who, as those of you who are "Washington junkies" know, exert the really important and beneficial influences over time. They have a sense of history and a feel for the important, as opposed to the unimportant, ripples on the surface. They stay out of the limelight and out of the press, yet they have an influence far beyond their public image. Dick is one such man.

I worked with him for two years on several conferences and published two books as a result, and throughout Dick was my guide. He introduced me to such little-known persons as Ed Feulner and Richard Allen and helped bring us to work together and to write and "do good works" for the cause of a more sensible view of national security policy. He has always been a tremendous catalyst for bringing good people together in a way that facilitates their helping each other. This has been a hallmark of every stage of his service.

During those two years I was in a bit of a quandary: Dick was quietly questioning why I was headed to law school intent on becoming a Philadelphia lawyer. He would get going on how much more the country needed people in public service than it needed those merely chasing lucre. His arguments had the fermentative effect intended, and I ended up going to graduate school, first at the University of Pennsylvania and then at Cambridge University on a Weaver Fellowship and an Earhart Fellowship, which Dick had a major hand in bringing together.

Then, when I came to Washington for the first time, moving in with Ed Feulner thanks to Dick's earlier introduction, whom did I find at the first meeting I attended in the interdepartmental group at the White House but Dick Ware! I watched his performance carefully because I had never viewed him as a government wallah, and I was unsure of how he would operate.

Well, operate he did. For two years I think I saw Dick in the White House basement more than almost anyone else—at the interdepartment group meetings and the Staff Interagency Group meetings, and so forth. One of his hallmarks was the unique way he had of blending differing civilian and military perspectives. He worked as a tremendous catalyst for keeping the uniformed and civilian sides of the Pentagon from becoming polarized. His successful endeavors have since been mentioned to me a number of times, by people in the Navy at the time, many of whom were junior officers then, and by more senior leaders such as Tom Moorer and others who were major beneficiaries of that inestimable catalytic talent that Dick had.

Another of his qualities worth emulating was that he didn't speak very often. But when he did everybody listened attentively, a lesson that I didn't fully grasp at first. Only in the later part of Dick's tenure at Defense and in my current incarnation have I come to understand fully the value of such a strategy.

Of course, since that time, Dick has remained active, again behind the scenes where it counts most—keeping the right people communicating with each other, keeping the issues that are really important on the agenda of people who count, and quietly introducing new ideas and thoughts.

Dick has had a remarkable career. I am sure you all know his educational background—Phi Beta Kappa from Lehigh, a master's degree from Wayne State—so when he was luring people like Ed and me into government service it was not without some considerable experience. If you look at his record of public service—in the Air Force, in the civilian side of the government during World War II, in state government, as a member of boards of directors and advisory boards for Tufts, the Fletcher School, the University of Chicago, charities, and civic groups—you find that all of these groups are major molders of the ethical direction of this country.

So I feel it a great honor to be able to precede him on this podium. I hope I'm not sounding too much like a funeral eulogist, Dick, but I don't get a chance very often to speak your praises. I have, as I have indicated, a personal debt to Dick that continues to this day. He is a source of continuing inspiration to me and to all of us. If it weren't for you, Dick, I would today, instead of being a poor public servant, be a rich Philadelphia lawyer, so I want to thank you very much.

I recall, Dick, shortly after I got back from Cambridge, your saying, "I remember, John, when I first met you, you were a modest, good-humored boy, and now Cambridge has made you insufferable." I hope that was meant in jest, and I would like to ask all of you to join me in welcoming Dick Ware to this distinguished podium.

The Pentagon's Office of International Security Affairs, 1969–1973 or Two Citizens Go to Washington

Richard A. Ware

Warren Nutter was a unique combination of scholar, teacher, citizen soldier, and public servant. Aside from pride in his family and students, I believe he treasured most his combat infantryman's badge and his doctorate from the University of Chicago, where Frank Knight was his mentor. His qualities also included a quiet sense of humor. At the Edinburgh Festival, just after a stunning performance of a selection from a Verdi opera by a military band of a country not to be identified, he remarked: "If only they had an army to go with it."

I met this man in 1956 or 1957, and our friendship began over a mutual interest in political economy. It ripened when we served together in 1964 on a presidential campaign staff. In 1969 I was one of several who encouraged Warren to accept the Defense Department appointment to the position of assistant secretary of defense for international security affairs. He turned about and nailed me as his principal deputy.

My service in this role proved that a friendship could survive long hours under much stress and strain. Our thoughts and reactions were such that I was comfortable with his instructions, and he never overruled a decision of mine. Our relationship continued through his long illness, including overseas travel to Europe and the Orient. My wife and I share with Jane many treasured memories.

Until now I have not discussed the Pentagon experience of Messrs. Nutter and Ware. I have preferred to honor the combined Yankee humor and advice of Senator Muskie: "Don't speak unless you can improve upon silence." But, in the Spring 1983 issue of *Political Science Quarterly*, an article assigned a low rating to the Office of International Security Affairs (ISA) of the Nixon-Ford years, with special reference to the Laird-Nutter period. The article was developed without contact with me. So I break my Yankee silence to place in this lecture series a modest and partial record of a major interlude in Nutter's professional life. To put it more colorfully, as Frank Knight did, using the words of a Chicago politician: "The time has come to take the bull by the tail and look the situation square in the face."

My text is culled from a valedictory that Mr. Nutter and I prepared upon his departure from E-Ring of the Pentagon. I also drew upon a scattering of notes I recorded at the time. I shall not "modernize" the context to reflect later events.

Permit me first to mention some of the stagecraft and props useful for senior officials beginning a political appointment in Defense. A discussion of a few of the substantive issues that crossed Secretary Nutter's desk will follow. Then I will conclude with observations founded upon a learning experience in public management in a defense environment.

Power and influence in a bureaucracy are determined by the perceptions of others as much as by one's own ability and activity. There are some conditions and symbols of office that furnish a Pentagon newcomer with a headstart in the daily struggle.

Physical facilities create the first impression. An E-Ring office regularly "swept" or "debugged" is a must. Furnishings should include an oversize desk, conference table, sofa, stuffed leather armchairs, coffee table, flags, and one wall covered with a world map. Do not underestimate the power of a safe of closet size and a private latrine, especially one with a shower. Outside it is best to have an assigned car and driver or at least an assigned parking slot at the foot of the steps to a main entrance.

Support personnel are indispensable. Minimum requirements are a military assistant, sometimes known as a "horse holder," and two personal secretaries, one of whom should be a noncareer political appointee. These three assistants create inaccessibility and wire you to meaningful back channels.

A side table display of telephone buttons to be certain every visitor knows you have direct communication upward and downward is a must. Be sure the one from SECDEF (the Secretary of Defense) rings during the first hour you occupy your office. Another telephone, a white one, must be on display to signify inclusion on the White House switchboard. If it ever rings, you have it made. Be sure to be on the switch of the National Military Command Center, both at the office and at your residence, and have a paging device and a car radio.

Valuable miscellaneous items include both a regular White House pass and one from the Joint Chiefs, the latter providing authority to commandeer a helicopter in event of an attack; clearance for the daily intelligence pouch that goes to about two hundred in the government; "open" travel orders; and membership in SECDEF's mess.

With these "badges of office" and assuming a high degree of self-importance, how can one fail? Well, it is easy, but that's an essay for another day.

I recall SECDEF remarking that about one-third of the policy issues crossing his desk daily originated in Nutter's shop. Some had to do with the newly integrated program of military assistance and sales, a program of in excess of $5 billion that took on greater importance under the Nixon Doctrine. This is a complex and seperate subject.

Another such subject is SALT, but ISA did not have principal responsibility. Early in 1969 the deputy secretary decided to treat SALT as a technical rather than a political problem. ISA participated but did not drive the staff work.

I have selected some geographic areas and issues to illustrate ISA's activities during Nutter's stewardship.

East Asia and the Pacific

Leaving aside such policy issues as Korea, the Republic of China and the PRC, and the trust territories of the Pacific, I will take up Vietnam and Japan.

In virtually every significant respect it was necessary to start almost from scratch in working out the program for extricating the United States from Vietnam and for improving and modernizing South Vietnamese forces. Until 1969 there was no focal point within Defense for supervising the effort. The services were devoting their efforts to military operations. They were not preparing the Vietnamese to take over. Secretary of Defense Melvin Laird assigned to ISA the task of overseeing the Vietnamization effort, and he participated through daily meetings with Mr. Nutter and his staff.

ISA proceeded first through a loosely formed coordinating group and then with a Vietnam task force created in November 1969 with Brigadier General George S. Blanchard as director. Manned by selected personnel on temporary duty, its counterpart elements emerged throughout Defense and other agencies. Time-phased planning was undertaken covering all aspects of turning the war over to South Vietnam. As one-half million American forces were withdrawn from active combat, Vietnamese forces were recruited, trained, and equipped.

In large measure this effort was successful, but we did not anticipate withdrawal in 1973 of American logistic support. Those of us involved with the Vietnamization activities always have had concern with what was to follow under the communist "program of reeducation."

There was an economic dimension to Vietnamization that was of special interest to Nutter. Until 1969 little had been done to develop a self-sustaining economy in South Vietnam. The fiscal policy followed was one in which low taxes and high government spending were rewarded with U.S. economic assistance. The policy generated a growing deficit in the balance of payments and a built-in incentive for corruption.

Secretary Laird and Mr. Nutter visited Vietnam in early 1970. In his report to the president SECDEF emphasized that the economic situation was the weakest link and stressed revision of the program of economic assistance in preparing for self-generating growth and stability. This aroused little enthusiasm elsewhere in the government. ISA took the initiative in sponsoring a study by William Ford setting forth an economic strategy for South Vietnam; another by Stephen Enke proposed a course of action to implement that strategy.

To stimulate the U.S. mission a section for economic affairs was established in Military Assistance Command, Vietnam, staffed by military officers who were trained economists. An economic counselor was introduced into the mission, a section of the National Security Council (NSC) staff was charged with reviewing the economic program, and a National Security Decision Memorandum was issued setting forth a new course of action. The South Vietnamese government responded on its own part and succeeded in 1971 in cutting the inflation rate in half. The importance of the economic reforms became evident in the ability of the economy to absorb the shock of the North Vietnamese invasion in 1972 to the extent that less assistance was required in the economic than in the military area.

A tragic problem of the Vietnam War revolved around the treatment of U.S. POWs and the accounting for the missing-in-action. The policy until 1969 had been one of silence on the ground that publicity might worsen the prisoners' conditions. Early in the Nixon presidency SECDEF decided to make the issue public despite strong opposition within the government. A token release of three prisoners assisted in securing the attention of the world. These men were permitted to describe their mistreatment, and from that point on Defense pressed the POW/MIA issue as a humanitarian one. Mr. Nutter chaired the policy committee on the issue and had a special assistant charged with coordinating all action implementing Defense POW policy. These efforts were rewarded when the prisoners were returned home. Questions remain about many, and the issue is not closed. Mr. Nutter and I regretted we could not do more for these men and their families.

Another significant issue in the region had to do with the evolving relationship between the United States and Japan. The accepted government position assumed a special Japanese-American relationship that followed the surrender on the USS *Missouri*. This relationship derived from two fundamentals that disappeared in the late 1960s. First, there was the physical and psychological fact that the United States had been the overwhelming victor. Second, there was the unhindered military presence of the U.S. military on Okinawa. As time passed, the American victory diminished in significance, particularly as the Pacific countries grew in strength. The turning point came with the reversion of Okinawa to Japanese control. This act, for which Japan received a cash supplement, removed a foundation of prime power for the United States and placed a burden on bases in the Philippines and possibly in the trust territories.

There were those who argued that Japan would adhere to the mutual defense treaty and forgo a military effort of any significance; that it would content itself with wielding its power through economic and diplomatic force, all the while supporting and following U.S. leadership in world affairs. The reversion of Okinawa removed a burr in the relationship between the two countries. This relationship will remain stable as long as the United States continues to reassure Japan that it will provide both a nuclear shield and a conventional military presence adequate to safeguard Japanese interests.

Mr. Nutter and a few close associates disagreed with the foregoing rationale. Japan as a sovereign state is bound ultimately to base its policies on its national interests as the Japanese perceive them. The Japanese, sooner or later, will realize or draw the appropriate conclusion on how much dependence they can place on being protected by U.S. military forces. Japanese foreign and military policy (not to mention economic policy) will take on an increasingly independent character. The challenge will be to find means of influencing emerging Japanese power in a direction consistent with U.S. security. The U.S. relationship with Japan must be built upon mutual self-interest within the context of the realities of military and economic power. It cannot be built upon a misconceived sense of friendship and affection.

Europe and NATO

Although I cannot discuss all the problems confronted in this directorate (that is, those associated with Iceland, France, Greece, Turkey,
Norway's North Cape, and the Dutch desire for a submarine), NATO
should not be overlooked as an alliance that has preserved a general
European peace for two generations.

One of the consequences of the Vietnam War was a deterioration
of U.S. relations with Europe and particularly with the alliance. By
1969 Vietnam had consumed our military resources as well as the
attention of those charged with the conduct of foreign relations. We
had degraded our military capabilities in Europe and the Mediterranean to fight in Southeast Asia. We had engaged in other reductions
of forces under pressure of the "balance of payments" problems created by the war and inadequate fiscal and financial arrangements to
prosecute it. Our attention had been shifted from that part of the
world most vital to the defense of the United States.

The degradation and neglect were compounded by a domineer-
ing attitude toward our allies. It was slight wonder that there was little
enthusiasm among them for any concerted effort at mending fences
and building a sounder partnership. The foregoing was reflected in
ISA. In addition Defense had ridden roughshod over State in setting
some of this policy.

Major staff changes were accomplished to achieve a more cooperative stance with State. SECDEF brought military problems out in the
open and then discussed them with candor. Proceeding step by step,
it was possible to promote a sense of cooperation and partnership, to
expand NATO activities, and to improve the structure of forces. Successful negotiations were held with the French, and groundwork was
laid for the eventual membership of Spain in the alliance. The member nations developed a more sophisticated attitude with special reference to the changes necessary because of the parity in strategic nuclear forces attained between the United States and the USSR. The
Secretary of Defense cultivated close personal relations with his counterparts of the NATO countries. This was a considerable shift from the
prior administration.

For a few moments I want to describe some of the problems in the
NATO directorate below the policy level that occasionally enlivened
and complicated one's day.

Late one afternoon State delivered to ISA a policy paper setting
forth the basis for Spanish base negotiations, including a fallback
position for the use of some military assistance funds. Our staff
worked until 11:00 that night preparing comments for the deputy
secretary and the chairman of the Joint Chiefs to use at a National

Security Council group meeting. This paper was presented to me at 10:10 the next morning for signature and delivery to the deputy secretary by 10:30. Too frequently, neither Secretary Nutter nor I was able to give much thoughtful consideration to a major policy before recommending it to our superiors.

At another time State dispatched a cable to U.S. embassies in Europe having to do with a 10 percent reduction in forces. The principal deputy had approved the contents for Defense, but after his approval someone in State deleted a paragraph, but left in place the deputy's initials. It took several hours to restore calm within the Joint Chiefs and to prepare a follow-up cable.

Sometimes the error of a clerk in records and control has major consequences. Certain information about the storage of nuclear arms was sent to NATO ministers of defense by SECDEF. As sensitive documents, they should have gone by courier. One day they were placed in the wrong outbox and were transmitted by registered mail. The minister of defense of the Federal Republic of Germany reported the lapse to ISA. Life immediately became hectic. We knew that registered mail to at least one NATO capital went through a Warsaw Pact country.

Within an hour after the situation had been reported to the principal deputy he had consulted the security services, created a task force to manage any special problems and recommend corrective procedures, developed a report to SECDEF after having notified his executive officer, reported to Atomic Energy Commission authorities, and briefed the U.S. ambassador to NATO by secure telephone. We had to make sure the registered mail had been delivered in all destination countries and that the material was got back into regular channels without being compromised. The latter required a careful political watch with tight security on knowledge of the incident. The file was successfully closed six months later.

Southwest Asia

This region usually is described as the Middle East and South Asia. In ISA Africa was thrown in for good measure. At the outset of our watch Africa was a part of the Directorate for Inter-American Affairs, and the Indian Ocean was divided among three regions. We believed this did not accord with strategic reality since this ocean is an entity for the control of sea lanes and is used by the Soviet Union to establish a presence.

Insofar as the Indian Ocean is concerned, the single significant accomplishment was support for the establishment of the U.S. communication facility on Diego Garcia. It is not necessary over a decade later to say more.

The Arab-Israeli conflict dominated staff activity, although it was not given a high priority by the White House in the early months of the Nixon administration. Secretary Nutter's considerations of it were guided by three principles. First, the tail should not wag the dog, which is to say that the United States should not permit a condition to arise wherein actions taken by either Israel or its enemies would automatically determine U.S. policy. The United States should maintain sufficient independence to ensure that its foreign policy flows from an American appreciation of its own national interests. Early on we discovered this concept was violated at the working level within our own shop. Israeli intelligence officers could contact ISA personnel directly and independent of the policies governing activities of military attachés. Further, we learned that intelligence elements of one U.S. service had established special relations with counterparts in the Israeli armed forces, entering into agreements and arranging exchanges of information without reference to other components of Defense. This practice was eliminated by the deputy secretary in a special directive.

Second, every effort was to be made to prevent a serious confrontation in the region between the United States and the USSR. Such a confrontation, particularly if it should imply a nuclear showdown, could result in a Cuba in reverse. A careful reading of the realities of the American scene makes it reasonably clear that U.S. military support of Israel is likely to be greatest when least needed and least when most needed.

Third, avoid creating a powder keg likely to lead to a wider conflict. The United States had (in 1969) no enemies among the countries and peoples of the region; Nutter believed it was in our national interest to maintain friendly relations with all states to prevent any oil-rich territory from falling into the hands of another major world power, and that it was also in our interest to maintain a climate sufficiently peaceful to remove the basis for steady Soviet infiltration.

Last, it seemed to us that the Mediterranean should be considered somewhere within the Pentagon as an entity with its own economic, political, cultural, and strategic concerns. We never succeeded in mounting even a study based on such a notion.

Inter-American Affairs

In 1969 individuals in State were allied with some in ISA in an almost messianic mission of social reform in Latin American countries. Essentially, this meant removing the military from positions of authority, with the resultant ascendancy of left-wing forces. Contacts with the military were minimized, and Defense was substantially removed from any role in the formulation of U.S. policy. It was as if there were no national security interests south of the border.

These views also dominated the policy in the Caribbean area where there was an emphasis on promoting independence for all colonial islands, no matter how sparsely populated or how strategically located with respect to the U.S. mainland. Among the efforts to rectify the situation were the visits to Latin America made by Secretary Nutter in late 1971, the first made by an assistant secretary of defense for international security affairs. From then on, trips by senior military and defense officials were scheduled to some part of Latin America.

The case of Chile loomed large during our watch. Many thought this unusual because it is about as distant from Washington as Moscow is. Some urged that if Chile chose communism then the United States should abide by that choice. ISA consistently took the position that it is important to recognize a potentially aggressive totalitarian state as it develops.

We were concerned about the danger to stability in the Western Hemisphere should Chile and Cuba become partners in communism. Chile also is of strategic importance because of (1) its long border with Argentina and other countries, (2) its long coastline with the only three deep-water ports on the west coast, (3) its control of both shores of the Straits of Magellan, and (4) its control of Easter Island in the South Pacific. Fortunately, Chile stepped back from the brink.

ISA managed to hold a strong position on the Panama Canal issue and gave attention to Guantanamo as an outpost. I visited the base to demonstrate the importance we attached to it and to "show the flag" to the 5,000 U.S. military then stationed there.

One should remember that during this time the Soviet Union made its first move toward establishing a naval presence in Cuba, a presence that has continued with far-reaching consequences for the defense of the continental United States, along our South Atlantic perimeter. Even so, a draft paper prepared for the National Security Council gave no attention to a visit of Soviet warships, underplayed the export of revolution from Cuba, and placed the retention of a U.S. base in Cuba in the lowest category.

Strategic Trade and Foreign Military Rights

Among the miscellaneous functions of ISA were those having to do with controls governing trade and technical disclosure with potential adversaries, and the politics in the host countries of overseas military facilities and forces. I will discuss only the former. Under directives from Secretary Laird, ISA formed a rear guard and opposed almost every action that was sought by other departments or allied nations. It made no sense to provide economic and technological information to the Soviet Union without receiving something commensurately valuable in return. In New England this is known as "dickering."

Our staff stood fast in the face of mounting pressure from every quarter of the government. Defense sometimes was overruled, sometimes after a controversy's escalation to the highest level. Important examples included sale of machine tools for the Soviet Kama River truck factory, of French and UK integrated circuit-making machinery to Poland, and of communication equipment to Warsaw Pact nations. "Diplomatic gain" was the usual reason given.

Bureaucratic games were played. In one case an American firm applied for an export license to sell $21 million worth of machine tools to the Soviet Union to produce truck gears. State and Commerce told NSC staff that Defense would agree, and NSC staff told Defense staff people that the White House wanted approval. ISA staff went along but were overruled despite pleas from Commerce. Secretary Laird agreed, and Defense voted "no," forcing the decision to the president. By the close of business on February 6, 1970, word was received that the president had upheld the Secretary of Defense. On March 27, 1970, State cabled the U.S. Embassy in Moscow that the "cases remain under review."

In a recent book by Ambassador U. Alexis Johnson there is a reference to such problems.[1] After commenting that Warren Nutter had none of a predecessor's "flair for making decisions and getting things done," Ambassador Johnson went on to say that he was forced "to take up an unusually heavy volume of business between State and Defense with the Deputy Secretary of Defense." He explains that "Though many of those issues on which we collaborated were insignificant and should have been settled at lower levels, such as minor export licensing matters . . ." Translated, this suggests that ISA was an obstructionist to sound national policy on strategic trade matters. I respectfully disagree.

The French newspaper Le Monde has been quoted as saying a KGB document shows the USSR gets 61.5 percent of its industrial secrets from the United States, 10.5 percent from West Germany, and 7.5 percent from the United Kingdom.[2]

The assistant secretary and his principal deputy were subjected to a clinical learning experience in public management. The office they headed is most easily described as the Pentagon's "little State Department." As might be expected Foggy Bottom did not relish a rival activity, especially one run by "amateurs" in a military setting.

Upon assuming office Mr. Nutter was given a twofold charge by Secretary Laird: conduct ISA's affairs with the lowest possible profile within and outside the arena of government, and do all possible to prevent a wedge from being driven between State and Defense. I suggest that the first part of this charge hardly was a prescription for being perceived as an effective bureaucrat.

ISA had principal responsibility for coordinating all activities in DOD concerned with the international aspects of defense, and for being the principal contact on these matters with other government agencies. This meant ISA coordinated with the Joint Chiefs of Staff in developing the position of the Secretary of Defense in the formal NSC structure and process initiated by the Nixon administration. This included the responsibilities of the Washington Special Actions Group for the policies in a variety of crisis or sensitive situations.

In 1969 it was reasonably clear that our immediate predecessors had assumed a personal control over many activities. Such details in Vietnam as bombing targets consumed attention to the neglect of guidance and leadership in other areas of political-military affairs. There was more concern with the influence they could be seen wielding on policy formulation than with providing staff support to the Secretary of Defense and contributing to an overall executive branch policy. Their style was freewheeling and flamboyant.

We found relations between the Office of the Secretary and the Joint Chiefs to have deteriorated to the point that cooperative effort was the exception. The basic cause was a presumption that the military was misguided, ill informed, and most of the time wrong. Each side considered the other an adversary. Trench lines were everywhere, and there was almost constant cannonading in the corridors. It was not an atmosphere in which knowledge and judgment could be brought to bear properly on serious defense issues.

The management problem was one of shaping an organization independent of the day-to-day decisions of a single individual and recasting it into an important element of support for the president and the secretary. This task required a change in style with a focus on getting the job done instead of getting credit for it, on cooperating with other parts of the executive branch, and on forming a relation with the military based on mutual respect.

The NSC process facilitated good working relations within the department, particularly between the Office of the Secretary and the Joint Chiefs. There was teamwork in preparing coordinated defense positions, and this carried over into other activities. NSC demands on the department during 1969–1970, however, were so overburdening that staff was tied up in producing papers of low quality at best.

Perhaps this was by design to free the White House to take on and decide issues of its choice.

The foregoing experience produced some suggestions useful for assuming control of a policy shop in Defense in a new administration differing sharply from its predecessor. First, and no later than when sworn into office, be sure all positions held by political or noncareer appointees are vacant. Fill the vacancies quickly. Meanwhile continuity will be assured by career military and civilian personnel. Second, identify those who have moved from noncareer slots back to permanent grades in the classified service in order to better understand their policy concerns and interests.

Third, by reclassifying positions or establishing new ones, move out of the direct line of responsibility and command those who determined policy under the previous administration. Fourth, have at least one person in the front office with knowledge of the bureaucracy and its functioning. Equally important, have someone with political know-how.

Fifth, identify all those who control the flow of information, making sure of their loyalty to the new administration. The president, cabinet, and subcabinet officers learn only from information filtered by staff. Sixth, the front office should control budget and personnel matters. Mr. Nutter changed the relationship of the assistant secretary and his principal deputy so the latter could act for the former or be his alternate at any time. As a part of this arrangement the principal deputy controlled those functions necessary to maintain a responsive staff, including recruitment and assignment of personnel, travel and leave, security violations, etc.

I turn now to some illustrations and special problems.

Personnel records were a mess. It took from mid-March to mid-July 1969 to determine the number of slots in ISA, the number of employees aboard, and who was assigned to do what. Only a threat to have a "dress right dress" lineup in the corridor of everyone—general to clerk—produced the requisite information. We found ISA personnel at the White House and elsewhere on informal assignments who were charged to Defense. Contracts with "think tanks" provided staff persons at costs frequently double a government salary. Military personnel were selected and assigned by subordinate offices without regard to overall requirements.

Throughout such trying experiences the military personnel assigned to ISA facilitated efforts for change and improvement. They are accustomed to a new skipper coming aboard and they responded. Furthermore, the 1969 change in command was welcomed by most career officers and by some dedicated civilians. These career staff proved to be strongly motivated, competent, and willing to work long hours.

Secretaries Laird and Packard always moved for the reduction of administrative costs, and ISA cooperated by cutting staff at least 10 percent. Such reductions in force have a price, however. Those with seniority are retained, making it impossible to keep newer employees of superior competence or to bring in new people more responsive to policy.

It seemed sensible to develop an all-inclusive list of consultants. The process got under way in May 1969 with the selection of forty-six. Fourteen months later six had been cleared. By April 1971, forty specialists were available, with an additional three by 1973. This frustrating experience did not end there. We then found that senior policy people in our own shop, and who were our own appointees, did not call on this talent bank. Special efforts were made to set up seminars, staff conferences, and "A" and "B" teams, but they were not taken seriously unless the assistant secretary or the principal deputy participated. There was the notion that those on the "inside" have a monopoly of information and wisdom.

ISA must relate to a variety of other departments and agencies of which the Department of State is the most important. Even though instructed to work cooperatively with our colleagues there, differences in respective approaches led inevitably to institutional differences in policies, thus underscoring why the president needs the advice of both departments to project foreign policy.

State, for example, is most comfortable when policy is loosely defined, thereby providing the greatest flexibility for diplomacy. Defense is most comfortable when policy is strictly defined, thereby providing a firm base for military plans and operations. State is inclined to postpone every possible decision because circumstances may change or the problem may go away. In military affairs decisions cannot be deferred; if an army or fleet is to be provisioned and moved, precise logistical decisions must be made. Last, State sometimes is inclined to use defense assets, although Defense finds the means and also better appreciates the limitations.

Fundamental to all national security decisions is the quality of intelligence. ISA was one of the largest consumers and had little to say about levying requirements on the community. The staff suprisingly had few comments on the adequacy of the intelligence received. In the front office, we were concerned after listening to a briefing on the burden of military spending on the Soviet Union that implied some of the same conclusions and theories extant in 1950–1955. We were informed on the same occasion both that the Soviets had no intention of more than maintaining a balance with U.S. strategic power and that the United States had no precise knowledge of Soviet weapon technology.

We made three generalizations about the U.S. intelligence function in 1973 that may remain valid. First, it is based on a "mirror image"; that is, we assume another power or adversary will react to the United States as we react to that power,[3] and inadequate attention was given to the unpredictable or to the acts of irrational leaders. Pearl Harbor and the Cuban missile crisis are examples. Second, analysis and evaluation of events tilted toward support of policies already decided. Third, post-mortems seldom were held to evaluate intelligence performance.

There had been hope that a series of special research studies could be produced using intelligence sources and our consulting panel. Already mentioned was consideration of the Mediterranean as an economic and strategic unit. Another could have dealt with Soviet intentions in the world's "hot spots" or with Soviet basing plans as the Soviets saw them.

This recitation of an assortment of administrative trials and tribulations cannot be complete, but perhaps I have conveyed some of the flavor for the challenges two citizens found after reporting for duty on the fourth floor of the Pentagon's E-Ring.

Conclusion

Most important of all was the dedication and know-how we encountered among a large percentage of our civilian and military comrades. The Republic is fortunate to have a corps of loyal servants.

From relationships established with employees in policy and substantive positions, I observed that all "doves" were not civilians, and all "hawks" were not in the military. Neither were all "politicians" found only among the political appointees.

The last, the political appointees, play an essential role in bringing new perspectives and policies to policy determination and implementation plus a degree of independence of judgment, especially if they are on leave from a nonfederal position. Those whose economic well-being depends upon political acceptance of their decisions, or who wish to ascend the ladder to more power, do not have this independence of judgment or do not choose to use it. This is a "glitch" not to be minimized.

Long-range planning—the lack thereof—was a disappointment. It should have been a major ISA function, but it was poorly performed before 1969 and was no better upon our departure in 1973. ISA was tagged with the longest and shortest fuses in Defense. Operational and urgent problems preempted resources.

General Andrew Goodpaster once described to Secretary Nutter and me a small strategic planning group. Working under General Marshall and consisting of Colonels Bonisteel, Goodpaster, and Rusk, the group was given free rein to think about the future. We were not successful in replicating such an effort.

There were a few successes, if I may be excused for mentioning them.

ISA had a role in putting the Vietnamization program on track so that 550,000 American military personnel could be withdrawn without major losses. It is unfortunate that future decisions in Washington canceled what might otherwise have prevented death and misery for millions and handed over to the Soviet Union some excellent military bases.

The ISA role in securing the return of the POWs furnished satisfaction, and the key island outpost of Diego Garcia has proven itself. Some fine officers and civilians were trained for greater responsibility. Many rose to high rank in their services or in the State Department. The principal deputy was totally immersed in public affairs and national security matters that strengthened his work as a foundation manager over subsequent years.

Secretary Nutter, with his logical and perceptive mind, retentive memory, and sense of the Republic's well-being, experienced a four-year postdoctoral program of training for responsibility at a higher level. The citizens of this nation are the poorer for the too early loss of Warren Nutter's capabilities and his loyalty to country.

I thank the Thomas Jefferson Center Foundation, the American Enterprise Institute, and you patient listeners for indulging my desire to enter these remarks in the record.

Notes

1. U. Alexis Johnson, *The Right Hand of Power* (Englewood Cliffs, N.J.: Prentice Hall, Inc., 1984), p. 523.

2. *U.S. News & World Report*, Sept. 30, 1985, p. 32.

3. In commenting on the Cuban missile crisis this is phrased more elegantly by Walter Laqueur in *A World of Secrets* (New York: Basic Books, 1985), p. 169: "The primary reason seems to be that the estimators were inclined to foist American constructs about nuclear strategy on Soviet policy and to attribute American conceptions of rationality in policy making to the Soviet leadership."

Science
and
Public Policy

John H. Moore

April 16, 1986

John H. Moore has been associate director and senior fellow of the Hoover Institution, Stanford University, since 1981 and has been on leave of absence since 1985 to serve as deputy director of the National Science Foundation. Before going to the Hoover Institution, he was an economics professor and associate director of the Law and Economics Center at Emory University. From 1966 to 1980 he served on the faculties of the University of Miami and the University of Virginia.

Introduction

Steve Pejovich

When Tom Johnson asked me to participate in the G. Warren Nutter Lectures in Political Economy series by introducing John Moore, I felt truly honored. Warren Nutter had a powerful and lasting effect on my life. John Moore is a highly respected friend. Speaking about Warren, John said: "All our lives have been touched in some way—as students, as colleagues, or as friends, by this remarkable man." This brief sentence captures the essence of what so many of us feel. My own life has surely been touched by Warren Nutter.

In 1964 I was a second-year assistant professor in a small college. Since I was trained in the conventional wisdom of the late 1950s and early 1960s I did not understand economic processes, my philosophical paradigms were not clear, and intellectually I felt empty. Fortunately, I met Warren Nutter. In the summer of that year, I was invited to attend the General Electric seminar at the University of Virginia. Those four weeks in Charlottesville turned out to have the most profound effect on my intellectual life. Warren enhanced my intellectual horizons, linked them to the appreciation of classical liberalism, and helped me *to understand* economic processes.

Warren asked me to read *University Economics*, and I was one of the first people outside the Chicago school to adopt it. The result was a long and most valuable friendship with Armen Alchian.

On my return from Charlottesville, I felt both confident and anxious to rewrite my Ph.D. dissertation on the Yugoslav economy and send it to a publisher. Several weeks later Warren called to tell me that he had refereed the manuscript and liked it very much. My article on "Liberman Reforms and Property Rights in Russia," published in the *Journal of Law and Economics*, was a direct consequence of my discussions with Warren Nutter, and so was my subsequent research on the relationship between property rights and economic life.

Warren Nutter's influence on my life has been too comprehensive to be cited in a few pages. It suffices to say that my intellectual debt to him is immense. Indeed I had every reason to feel deeply moved when Tom Johnson asked me to participate in this event.

At a Southern Economic Association meeting Warren Nutter introduced me to John Moore. Since we met, my respect for John has grown steadily from one year to another. I have always appreciated his intellectualism, the clarity of his writings, the intensity of his commitment to liberty, his personal integrity, and his impeccable manners.

John's professional, administrative, and academic accomplishments are many. I will highlight a few.

John Moore earned a bachelor of science degree in chemical engineering at the University of Michigan in 1958. The following year he earned a master of business administration degree at the same school. Upon graduation John worked as a research chemist for Procter & Gamble (1959–1963). Driven by the invisible hand, he went to the University of Virginia, where he was awarded a Ph.D. in economics in 1966. Dr. Moore stayed at the University of Virginia in various teaching and administrative capacities until 1977. In 1977 he joined the Center for Law and Economics at the University of Miami and later at Emory University. He was associate director at the Center for Law and Economics when he moved to the Hoover Institution in 1981. At Hoover he held several important positions, the last being associate director for research and administration. In June 1985 he moved to Washington, D.C., to become deputy director of the National Science Foundation.

During his career Dr. Moore has held a number of academic posts, including senior associate member of St. Antony's College, Oxford; research professor at the University of Miami; professor of economics at Emory University; and senior fellow at the Hoover Institution. He is also a member of the Board of Directors of the Thomas Jefferson Foundation and a member of the National Advisory Board of the Center for Free Enterprise at Texas A&M University.

Dr. Moore's publications include articles in the *Journal of Law and Economics*, the *American Economic Review, Revue de L'Est, Economic Inquiry, Economic Journal*, and *Management Science*. Hoover Institution Press published his important and frequently quoted book on the Yugoslav economy. Dr. Moore has also edited several books, including *To Promote Prosperity: U.S. Domestic Policy in the Mid 1980's*, published by the Hoover Institution Press.

We must keep in mind that Dr. Moore's true accomplishments exceed those that could be quantified. His academic standards, philosophical commitment to classical liberalism, deep understanding of economic processes, and warm feelings toward fellow human beings (with a few exceptions such as Mao, Stalin, and Tito) have been and will continue to be a major source of inspiration for a growing number of his personal friends and philosophical comrades in arms. Warren Nutter would have been truly proud of John Moore and his work.

It is my real pleasure to introduce Dr. John Moore, deputy director of the National Science Foundation.

Science and Public Policy

John H. Moore

Twice I have had the honor of introducing lecturers in this series, including the first, Professor S. Herbert Frankel. This afternoon I have the honor, and most challenging task, of presenting the lecture myself. As I review the list of lecturers, I must confess to some trepidation, for it is a most distinguished group. For me, one who has looked to giants like Coase, Friedman, Stigler, and, of course, my good friend Herbert Frankel for knowledge and understanding as student and academician, it is particularly daunting.

As I have remarked in my introductions of other lecturers, the distinction of the lecturers and the range of their topics stand as eloquent testimony to the abilities and character of the man these lectures honor and commemorate. I well remember my own first contact with Warren Nutter, in the spring of 1963. I was in a telephone booth in Cincinnati, and he was at the other end of a long-distance call, asking me whether I would reject "out of hand" a NASA graduate fellowship that required a dissertation on a topic related to the space program. It was a characteristic remark, reflecting his concerns about much deeper matters—specifically, academic freedom and the freedom of inquiry. As for me, I was innocent of understanding of such things and accepted the offer with scarcely a second thought.

Warren's question reflects, it seems to me, a good deal more than just his concern with academic freedom. That particular concern led him to support the institution of academic tenure even though tenure was and is less than fully consistent with free market principles. For Warren it was important above all else that professors be free to express themselves without fear of retribution. Without tenure, he believed, that freedom would be diminished—especially in the *real* academic world, where ideas are not always accepted for their truth but are frequently judged on how they fit with the conventional wisdom of the day.

I think that illustrates another facet of Warren's character—his recognition that within a universe of positive values, it is necessary to rank some higher than others. And certainly above all else he placed the independence of the individual. He recognized this not only as the wellspring of the great economic engine that made America the richest nation in the history of the world but also as the foundation of the good society. I believe that he infused in all his students this bedrock conviction; it was surely the greatest lesson he taught, far more important than the economics, important as they were.

Some of you will recall that Warren was asked at his confirmation hearing why he would be willing to take up such a difficult position. His response to that question is a memorable one:

> Mr. Chairman, that decision to accept the nomination of the Secretary of Defense was not an easy one to make, because I have deep roots in the academic community. I have been for many years at the University of Virginia. But after long reflection on the conditions as I see them in the world, the fact that I have exercised my rights as a private citizen to criticize from time to time what has been done in our Government, I felt I owed an obligation to serve when called upon to do so.

That statement is typical of Warren's integrity, his sense of duty, and his devotion to country. Together with his deep dedication to the principles of freedom, in which he saw the fundamental nature of this country and its best hope, that is not a bad summary of the character of the remarkable man to whom these lectures are devoted.

The Growing Importance of Science and Technology

My topic this afternoon is science and public policy, and I must begin by saying that what I have to say reflects my own thoughts and not any position of the National Science Foundation or the government.

My point of departure is Warren Nutter's lecture on the American bicentennial, "Freedom in a Revolutionary Economy," in which he refers to the noted coincidence of the invention of the steam engine by James Watt within the same decade as the publication of the Declaration of Independence and *The Wealth of Nations*. He points out that this constituted a "congenial triad: a novel concept of representative government, a science of economics, and an industrial technology, each revolutionary in its own right and exponentially so when combined together." We all know where the Declaration of Independence and *The Wealth of Nations* led.

The third element, the steam engine, led to a wave of industrialization unprecedented in economic history. Its direct impact was important, but its symbolic importance was even greater: it signified the turning of the forces of nature to the improvement of mankind through technology. Surely the realization that it was possible to control mankind's circumstances through design and technique was one of the most important forces that drove the great industrial revolution of the nineteenth century. Just as surely that same realization and understanding have persisted and remain central to economic development wherever it occurs.

In the decades following Watt's invention, technology continued to spur economic growth. It also became a driving force behind scientific development. The many contributions of science and technology to the effort during World War II led to official interest in science as a matter of public policy and, in a fairly direct way, to the establishment of the National Science Foundation in 1950. (Early formulations of the structure of the NSF included a department devoted to military research.)

Working at NSF, I have come to realize that science and science policy have taken on a new significance, necessarily becoming central to our policies, both domestic and international. As recently as twenty years ago, and maybe even ten years ago, it was possible to understand the great movements in the world economy and the international political order without taking scientific developments into account. Today that is not so. For the rest of this presentation, I want to describe some of the developments that are occurring and remind you of the position that the Reagan administration has taken on science and engineering policy. I begin with some examples.

Supercomputers and Export Controls

During the past two years the National Science Foundation has established five National Supercomputer Centers in association with universities across the nation. The primary purpose of the centers is to make available to university researchers the unprecedented computational power offered by these machines, such as the Cray XMP, the Cyber 205, and the IBM 3084. In this field as in perhaps no other, technology is sweeping ahead, with order-of-magnitude increases in speed occurring in cycles of less than two years. Not only can researchers tackle computational problems previously beyond the realm of possibility, but the supercomputer is opening an entirely new method of doing research, to be put alongside the classical approaches of theory and experiment. In fields ranging from the medical sciences to aircraft design to climate research and astrophysics, the supercomputers have opened new vistas of inquiry and discovery.

Because of their great power, they naturally attract controversy. Most obviously controversial for the National Science Foundation are decisions on where to locate the facilities. But another issue that has important foreign policy implications has been at center stage in recent months: access to these machines by foreign nationals, specifically those of the Soviet Union and its allies. This controversy finds the national security and university communities in disagreement, with the foundation, in a sense, caught in the middle.

The matter may seem obvious. My own instinctive reaction would be to deny access to all Soviet-bloc nationals, particularly in view of our knowledge about the use by Soviet intelligence organizations of Soviet scholars traveling abroad and the relatively primitive state of Soviet computers. As it has developed, a general denial of access to Soviet-bloc nationals is the starting point for the security regime that is emerging from many months of discussion. But there is more to the story.

A blanket denial of access affords clear security benefits. It is the national security equivalent of zero-risk environmentalism. But it also has costs. These include lost research opportunities; the collaboration of Soviet-bloc nationals on certain research projects that are of no security risk but may involve supercomputer use is valuable to American scientists.

There are also costs having to do with the universities themselves. That is important, because the bulk of our fundamental research is carried out at universities. One of the great strengths of our political system is its openness, and openness in the universities is essential to the scientific productivity of the society as a whole. The free flow of research results within our university community must, for that reason, be carefully protected. The Soviet system is fundamentally flawed in this respect. Indeed, this fact presents the Soviet leadership with one of its most difficult problems, and it is a major reason for optimism about the future as far as we are concerned.

To many people a blanket prohibition on access by Soviet-bloc nationals constitutes at least a symbolic erosion of our universities' openness. It is certainly viewed that way by many university scientists and engineers, some of whom see it as the opening wedge for further intrusions.

Of course, fears such as these are easily exaggerated. But in this situation perceptions are as important as reality; indeed it can be said that they constitute reality for practical purposes. Since World War II a kind of partnership has existed between government and academia, an occasionally uneasy but nevertheless very fruitful partnership. Universities protect their independence jealously; the proposed blanket prohibition is seen as a threat to their independence and, more important, to their openness. Would it weaken their effectiveness, either because of a real closure or because of their perceptions of its implications? If so, that is a cost to be reckoned in the balance.

So there is a calculation to be made. On the one hand, what security risks would there be in an access policy that admits exceptions, controlled by existing clearance mechanisms, which would allow access to these supercomputers by Soviet-bloc scientists working on approved projects in collaboration with American researchers? On the other hand, what benefits to U.S. research through these collaborations would be lost and what damage would be done to the American system of university-based fundamental research by a blanket prohibition? Without an understanding of the underlying scientific aspects of these problems, an informed conclusion is not possible.

That is one example of the importance of understanding science and science policy and their relation to foreign policy issues. Let me give another. A recent Defense Department study describes in detail the highly organized Soviet programs to obtain militarily significant technology from the West. According to the report, the Soviets saved at least 1.4 billion rubles during the Tenth Five Year Plan by these activities. Perhaps more important, the Soviets also saved time and reached technical levels that might otherwise have been unattainable.

The export control law, effected through COCOM, is part of the U.S. approach to denying such benefits to the Soviets. Throughout its history, questions have been raised about the efficacy of the law. Now another, more insidious question is developing: the effects of the law on U.S. exports of high-technology goods to our allies and the possible effects on our relations with Western Europe.

Many European multinational firms have subsidiaries in numerous countries, which may or may not be members of COCOM. Increasingly, they run into snarls of red tape in handling products that include American-made components on the export control list (which is not short—the Militarily Significant Technologies List is a book the size of the Washington phone book). This is particularly costly for them because the regulations apply not only to finished products that they might sell to customers worldwide, but also to the transshipment of intermediate products among their subsidiaries. The immediate result is that European firms are beginning to de-Americanize their products by producing their own components and substituting them for American-made parts. The aerospace industry has been particularly affected.

In addition to the purely economic considerations, however, foreign policy questions also hinge on this matter. Recently I heard a French academician mention a "West-West split" in this regard, as resentment over burdensome regulations spills over into the political arena. As business is swept into the problem, the long-run political consequences could be serious.

Twenty years ago we could have viewed the situation very differently. Then the United States unquestionably dominated the world in science and technology. We led the world in research and development (R&D), whether measured by investment in research or by numbers of scientific and engineering personnel. In that situation we could with relative impunity establish and enforce (though imperfectly) an export control regime. We served as a critically important source of scientific and technological information for the rest of the world; it is an exaggeration to say that others could not substitute for our expertise, but it makes the point.

That is no longer the case. We no longer dominate as once we did. There are signs that in some areas others have caught us and may have surpassed us. In pure science, for example, the Europeans have made the most recent fundamental discoveries in particle physics. The erosion of our position is the result of greatly increased research efforts in other nations, especially in Europe and Japan. In total R&D expenditures as a percentage of GNP, Western European nations and Japan now match us. If military R&D is put aside, at least two other nations now exceed us in research effort so measured. A similar picture emerges when the measure is scientific and engineering personnel.

These increased efforts have paid off for our trading partners. They are no longer so dependent on us for technology; in fact, the opposite is becoming true in some areas. In these changed *scientific* circumstances, the operations of the export control laws must be viewed differently.

First, their effect on our foreign trade is much different; others can now substitute home-grown technology for that embodied in our products. Second, we are increasingly dependent on others for scientific knowledge and opportunities, and damage to our relations with other countries arising from the laws could spill over into these areas as well. Third, the decreasing dependence of other nations on us makes it possible for them to respond to frustrations caused by the laws in a different way; they are no longer so constrained in their possible responses as they once were. Finally, the worldwide change in technological and scientific capabilities means that the actual effect of the control laws on the availability of advanced technology to our adversaries is almost certainly significantly less than before.

The law may still be, taking the changed circumstances into account, of positive net benefit to us. It cannot be evaluated, however, without an understanding of the great changes in science and engineering that have occurred in the past twenty years.

Many other developments have changed the competitive situation facing U.S. firms. Technical information is transmitted internationally through a multitude of channels: licenses, joint ventures with multinational firms, intelligence picked up by foreign visitors, international meetings, and so forth. Information flows at unprecedented rates because of improved means of communication, and there is every reason to expect the flow to increase. It can be put to use in products more rapidly because of the improved R&D facilities available to firms throughout the world. Fundamental discoveries find their way to finished products with a shorter lag than in the past; biotechnology and microelectronics are two well-known examples.

The key implication of these changes for us in the United States is that the world is much more competitive than it used to be. For most of the postwar period, our technological lead was a major source of comparative advantage. That is vanishing fast; it is gone in some areas, and there is no way to retrieve it, as long as others continue or increase their present research efforts. Once again, to understand our situation in the world and to develop policies that can advance our interests effectively, an understanding of the state of science is increasingly necessary.

The Need to Maintain U.S. Scientific Vitality

The world has always been a competitive place, and international trade flows have always been determined by comparative advantage. If other nations are stepping up their research efforts and thereby moving up the technological ladder in relation to us, is this different from changes in any other component that affects comparative advantage? Isn't it to our advantage that other nations exert greater research efforts? After all, research generates external economies; knowledge flows readily from one location to another. Furthermore, American consumers benefit from the advanced technology embodied in goods imported from abroad, where they have been produced as a result, in part, of the R&D efforts of our trading partners. What is the problem? Or, as a noted economist asked rhetorically at a recent conference, what does it matter to us whether any technology is invented here or abroad?

There is, of course, truth in the free trade position. We do benefit from research carried out elsewhere. Certainly in the realm of pure science, when research results are permitted to flow freely through publication, conferences, and the like, our science is enriched. It is also true that the rest of the world benefits from our massive research effort. The Japanese have been very candid about this. In recent statements they have acknowledged that their spectacular technological advances of the past twenty years have been heavily dependent on basic research carried out in the United States.

However attractive this argument is to free traders (among whom I count myself), it goes only so far. Information produced abroad, even if it is "basic" or "fundamental," is not always made public or transmitted without lag to other researchers. As the recent fight over the AIDS virus illustrates, there are powerful incentives to keep such information under wraps and to protect rights to it even after it has become publicly known. The famous book *The Double Helix*, in its description of the activities of the rival teams of scientists seeking the structure of the DNA molecule, reveals this point clearly. Some nations are reluctant to disclose new discoveries, limiting access to their leading laboratories and restricting the publication of results. Sometimes language barriers impede the rapid assimilation even of published results; Japan is the leading example in this respect.

Whether as a nation we continue to maintain our scientific vitality in relation to others is important from another point of view as well. The research done in a particular field produces benefits not only for that field but also for others. Physics produced the laser, but its applications in other fields by now overshadow its importance for physics itself. Developments in microelectronics have transformed virtually every field of research. Indeed, one of the primary driving forces in the rapid pace of science today is the great wave of new instruments of unprecedented power, which owes much of its development to microprocessors. Research itself is becoming increasingly multidisciplinary; many of the most important breakthroughs are taking place at the intersections of the traditional disciplines. In that sense, research progress is increasingly dependent *internally* on spillovers from one field to another.

There are other reasons that it would be dangerous to become reliant on basic research carried out in other countries. Of course, the flow of new results could be cut off by others, just as OPEC cut off a major portion of oil exports to the United States. A less obvious point has to do with the long-run scientific base in the nation. Continuity in research is important; a research enterprise cannot be turned off and on at will. Moreover, adapting the research results of others to local purposes has its limits; some, like the Japanese, seem to be better at it than others.

Adaptation also restricts the experience of domestic researchers with actual, hands-on work, which is in many fields the most important aspect of the research. Several years ago, when a special panel assessed the potential for loss of militarily significant technology to the Soviet Union from university laboratories, one major conclusion was that the most important potential loss lay in precisely that kind of experience.

To all these reasons why it is important that the United States take steps to ensure that its scientific enterprise remains vital must be added the matter of national security. It is frequently argued that military R&D is valuable not only for its contribution to defense but also because it produces knowledge of value to civilian technology— that is, there are positive spillovers. This is no doubt true. But the flow of information also runs in the other direction: fundamental research carried out in the civilian sector has very important spillovers to the military sector. High-energy lasers, supercomputers, directed energy beams, nuclear physics—all ultimately have their roots in the civilian sector. In the system of research that exists in the United States, the health of military technology depends on the health of basic research in the civilian sector.

The Changing Federal Role in R&D

This is a time of great opportunity and challenge in science and engineering. Because of dramatic advances in computational power and instrumentation, unprecedented possibilities for discovery exist. It is now possible to follow chemical reactions in real time as they occur at the molecular level. It is possible to design and fabricate materials almost literally atomic layer by individual atomic layer. It is possible to measure movements of the earth's crust on the order of a centimeter or so by remote sensing from satellites. It is possible to measure variations in the height of the ocean's surface to similar orders of magnitude and to map the distribution of microorganisms in the ocean from space. Everyone is familiar with the advances being made in biology—and of the risks that are thought to be involved. The list of new opportunities goes on and on.

We also face unprecedented challenges from abroad. Our international competitors are keenly aware of the opportunities in science and engineering and are adopting research strategies intended to capitalize on them for their own purposes. Many have initiated very specific plans for R&D to strengthen their competitive positions in the world economy. The best known of these strategies is the Japanese fifth-generation computer project; but that is not the only Japanese project, and the Japanese are not alone in putting such plans and strategies in place. The Japanese have also targeted biotechnology as an area for specific effort and have projects in many other areas as well. The European Community will spend roughly $600 million this year on cooperative research in a number of areas. Our competitors are increasing their investments in R&D, are producing larger numbers of scientists and engineers, and are directing their efforts to areas that are in direct competition with our most advanced industries. Thus the United States today faces a fundamentally different competitive situation. Our rivals have made up much of the gap that once existed between us in science and engineering, the driving forces in today's international economy.

Largely because these opportunities and challenges have been recognized, science has fared well under the Reagan administration. At the same time the administration has followed a policy that is consistent with an overall philosophy of limited government. For R&D, this has meant that the federal role has been to

- support research and development in those areas, such as defense, where the results are needed for other efforts of the government
- support basic or fundamental research in areas with important spillovers, where private incentives would be inadequate to call forth the desired effort
- leave development and most applied research, where these are not connected to government functions, to the private sector

This approach has meant a very substantial shift since 1981 in the distribution of federal support for R&D. In civilian R&D, there have been a dramatic decrease in federal spending for development, a smaller but still significant decrease in the funding of applied research, and a large increase in support for fundamental research. Owing to the increase in the defense budget and the recognition that advanced technology is critical to our national security, the military R&D budget has significantly increased. This increase goes far beyond the funding of the Strategic Defense Initiative, although that is an important element of the increase.

Very significant changes can be seen as a result. Total federal R&D spending has risen from about $29.5 billion in 1980 to an estimated $50 billion in 1986. Civilian R&D has fallen from about half the total in 1979 to less than one-third today. In defense R&D spending, development has increased much faster than applied or basic research; as a result, basic research as a percentage of total federal spending has fallen. For the Department of Defense, basic research now constitutes less than 2 percent of the total, or about half the percentage in 1980. As civilian development expenditures have been cut and basic research spending has increased, the basic research share of civilian spending has risen from about one quarter in 1980 to nearly 40 percent in 1986.

For the National Science Foundation, these shifts meant a very substantial increase in its budget between 1980, when it was about $1 billion, and 1985, when it was just over $1.5 billion, as civilian R&D funding was moved from development to basic research. This increase, together with a smaller increase for the National Institutes of Health and for the Department of Energy's research budget, caused an increase in total federal support (in constant dollars) for universities and colleges during the period. (The increases have come to a jarring stop in this fiscal year, however; NSF's budget is 3 percent less in nominal terms for this year than for fiscal year 1985, after the application of the Gramm-Rudman-Hollings sequestration. The fiscal 1987 budget request contains a significant increase for NSF, but it is highly unlikely that the request will be approved in the present budget climate.)

The increase in the R&D budget shows an understanding of the critical importance of science and technology to the nation, both for our national security and for our international economic competitiveness. The change in its distribution reveals a policy consistent with a commitment to a strong national defense and a free market economic system with limited government. Some will say that the changes have nct gone far enough, but I would argue that the progress has been remarkable in view of the many obstacles to change of any kind.

Conclusions

In the broadest of outlines, these have been the changes in our policies regarding the support of R&D since the Reagan administration has been in office. Are they adequate to take advantage of the opportunities or to meet the international challenges we face? Probably not. I will conclude by leaving you with what I think are some of the critical issues and my own tentative thoughts on them.

First, should we target our basic research, as others are endeavoring to do, by choosing specific areas for R&D? The other day I heard a foreign political leader advocate a policy of choosing an area of technology judged to be important and working backward in the research chain to determine the areas of basic work to support. Should we be taking that approach or something similar to it? My own view on this is that Washington, D.C., does not provide a good vantage point for judging where the most promising areas of research lie or for predicting what areas of basic research will ultimately afford the greatest payoffs. We can and should be thinking about the general kinds of changes that are taking place and should form our programs accordingly. The Engineering Research Centers that NSF has undertaken are a good example; they combine a recognition of the importance of multidisciplinary fundamental research, a realization of the importance of bringing industry and university researchers together, and a view that undergraduate engineering students should be exposed to such research efforts. The supercomputer centers and the associated efforts in computational science and engineering are other such examples. Specific topics for research in these cases are not selected in advance by Washington bureaucrats but are left to working researchers to develop.

Are we investing enough in university-based fundamental research? The United States is almost unique in having combined basic research and education in its universities. For all the problems this causes from time to time, it is also a source of great strength, because the products of the educational system come out already having been immersed in forefront research.

There is no question that problems are looming here. The number of students coming through the pipeline is diminishing, with no sign of a compensating rise in the proportion who are selecting science as their field of concentration. The improvements in instrument capabilities that have afforded such dramatic opportunities in research are not free; instrumentation for forefront research is increasingly costly, and university undergraduate instruction requires increasingly sophisticated and expensive instruments. University research facilities, from general-purpose laboratories to the highly specialized facilities required for advanced fields such as microelectronics and biotechnology, are in bad shape, and the bill for bringing them up to snuff is a big one.

Of course, more could always be spent on anything. There will always be interested parties ready to argue that case, and sometimes there is merit to the arguments they present. In scientific and engineering research, our eroding international position, as much as anything else, makes a legitimate case for additional investment. The hard question is what the role of the federal government should be in each of these areas: increasing the numbers of science and engineering personnel coming through the education system; providing support for university-based research facilities; providing support for instrumentation in university research; and providing support for the research itself. These questions have no conclusive answers; answers emerge from a lengthy and tortuous process of discussion and negotiation, a process centered on annual budgets that is, I have learned, always in progress.

Another issue is that of the distribution of federal R&D effort. I have already pointed out the shifts that have occurred, on the one hand between the defense and civilian sectors and on the other between the basic research and development ends of the R&D spectrum. Now we see the resulting distribution. Is that distribution what it should be? I have argued that basic research is now relatively underfunded, taking all of federal R&D spending into account. Is that a defensible position? Is the division between the defense and civilian sectors what it should be? These questions too have no conclusive answers.

One final issue that is likely to become increasingly important is that of openness in research. Concern is growing about the transmission of research results to others. This discussion generally takes place under the rubric of technology transfer, and it usually refers to the export of militarily significant hardware to our adversaries in the Soviet bloc and, to a lesser degree, to the People's Republic of China. Now, however, attention is shifting to a broader ambit to include information related to commercial development. Furthermore, as the gap between fundamental discovery and commercial application narrows, concern begins to be felt about the communication of basic research results.

What should policy be in these circumstances? That commercially valuable technology can be transferred is undoubtedly true. Similarly, we know that the Soviets obtain militarily useful information by reading our open scientific literature and by attending open scientific meetings. Is it therefore a good policy to impose controls on the transmission of basic scientific results? As I indicated in the related discussion of access by foreign nationals to our supercomputers, the case is not open and shut.

Of course, we must take appropriate steps to prevent undesirable technology transfer. But, at a minimum, policy makers need to understand the difference between technology and basic scientific results and discriminate between them in decision making. One of the great strengths of our scientific system is precisely its openness, and we should be loath to do anything to affect that critical strength adversely. I believe that this issue will attract increasing attention in the years to come.

These few issues are merely illustrations of the great range of concerns with research in science and engineering. Government policy for science has never been as important as it is today, and its importance will only increase in the future. We are living through the technological revolution of the twentieth century, a revolution that has already been as profound as the industrial revolution of the last century. The policies we adopt for science and engineering today are of the greatest importance for our nation's future, and I urge your attention to them.

Spending
and
Deficits

James C. Miller III

October 15, 1986

JAMES C. MILLER III is the director of the Office of Management and Budget. He was chairman of the Federal Trade Commission (1981-1985), and while at the American Enterprise Institute (1977-1980), he was a resident scholar and codirector of the Center for the Study of Government Regulation. He previously taught economics at Georgia State University and Texas A & M University.

Introduction

Robert D. Tollison
Professor of Economics
George Mason University

I have known Jim Miller for twenty years. We were in the Ph.D. program together at the University of Virginia. We marched down the Lawn, side by side, to receive our doctoral degrees on a sweltering summer day laced with a thundershower in June 1969. We, like our colleagues in the Virginia graduate program in economics at the time, were profoundly influenced by our education at the feet of teachers such as James M. Buchanan and G. Warren Nutter.

Many of the students who came out of the Virginia program during those days have done extremely well as scholars, lawyers, corporate executives, government officials, and the like. A small list would include Otto Davis, Charles Plott, Charles Goetz, John Moore, Richard Wagner, John Peterman, Jack Snow, Mark Pauly, Tom Willett, Craig Stubblebine, Jack Albertine, Roger Shields, and many others too numerous to mention. A list of their professional accomplishments would compare favorably with those of the students in any other graduate economics program in the United States at the time. Jim Miller could have chosen any of these routes to success and done well. He chose instead a different route. To use Gordon Tullock's phrase, he chose to do well by doing good.

In a way, Jim is an odd result of his education. Public choice teaches that government is neither perfect nor perfectible and that the idea that people work for the public interest as opposed to their personal private interest is far removed from the reality of day-to-day, election-to-election government. Jim is a glaring exception to such maxims. What Jim Miller took from his economics training was the idea that economics could be used to promote a more rational and effective economy and that, generally, economic freedom within rules, rather than government programs that stifle individual initiative and responsibility, was the key to sound economic policy. As his career evolved, from academia to government, to think tank and back to government, Jim Miller has focused his immense energies on applying this vision of political economy to promote a better world.

In this regard, Jim has been very skillful and very fortunate. His ability as an economic analyst is unquestioned. He has written extensively on the economics of public policy issues ranging from the military draft, to airline regulation and deregulation, to economic regulation generally, to antitrust enforcement, to budgetary policy. He has even made an insightful argument about how to improve the functioning of representative democracy through computer voting.

Jim has also been fortunate. By this I mean that he has lived and worked in government at a time when the relative value of his skills, knowledge, and abilities was high. Who else, after all, had a lifesized poster of Ronald Reagan, posed as a gunslinger from the Old West, prominently displayed on his office wall in 1967? Jim has been at the center of many important policy debates over the past several years. He was a significant analyst and participant in the successful effort to deregulate U.S. airlines. He organized and implemented Executive Order 12291, instituting Office of Management and Budget oversight of the federal rule-making process. He took over the Federal Trade Commission at a time when it was widely viewed as being out of control and, in short order, put the agency back on a saner course. He is now a major player in the "battle of the budget," where his unique background in Virginia political economy has led him to support initiatives by Congress and the president (such as Gramm-Rudman-Hollings) to precommit themselves to a plan for budget balance. Jim understands the difference between behavior with and behavior without constraints. Any one of these accomplishments would be enough for the career of the rest of us. And, remember, Jim is still a young man.

History, then, has been kind to Jim Miller, who will surely go down as one of the most significant public servants of the Reagan era. He is not a creature of the media, nor is he a creature of the Congress where the natural inclination is to make deals. Jim figures out what the best policy for the country is and works to reach that goal. He is that rare individual who has done well by doing good.

I would be remiss in closing if I did not add a personal note about the private Jim Miller. The public success of some people comes at the expense of their private success. The correlation in Jim's case goes in exactly the opposite direction. Over the years, Jim and Demaris Miller have been outstanding examples of what marriage partners and parents should be. My admiration for Jim extends equally to Demaris, and you will not meet three better young people than Katrina, Felix, and Sabrina Miller. Good things do sometimes go together, and in his personal life, Jim Miller has also done well by doing good.

Spending and Deficits

James C. Miller III

Thank you, Bob. It is indeed an honor that you agreed to introduce me. As you mentioned, those of us privileged to be at the University of Virginia in the middle and late 1960s shared a very special time. Of all the students from that heyday, I think you perhaps best represent the hopes and aspirations we all shared. Over the past twenty years some of us have produced a fairly respectable manuscript now and then. You produce reams of them every year. Some of us have been fortunate to have had a few good students. You, as well as Jim Buchanan, have a legion of them—and I count myself fortunate to be a foot solider in both!

Ladies and gentlemen, we are here today to honor the memory of G. Warren Nutter. I dare say he touched the lives of almost everyone in this room; I know he touched mine. A person of commanding intellect, unwavering character, and a self-confidence born of assurance that he knew his facts. Warren did not let go of anything until he mastered it. He knew more about concentration in U.S. industry than anyone else because he conceptualized the issues, read the literature, and did the number-crunching necessary to answer his questions—all the while meeting his standards, not someone else's. When, in the wake of Sputnik, the intellectual elite—or should I say effete?—of this country were praising the Soviet economic system and its potential for overtaking the West, it was Nutter who said, "Hold the presses; has anyone looked at the facts?" And when Nutter

I would like to express my appreciation to Tom Lenard for his advice and suggestions in the preparation of this lecture and to Bob Tollison for his comments on an earlier draft. The usual caveat applies. Portions of this address have been adapted from remarks I made before a seminar sponsored by the Federal Trade Commission. See *The Political Economy of Regulation: Private Interests in the Regulatory Process* (Washington, D.C.: Federal Trade Commission, 1984), p. 293; the National Press Club (November 1, 1985); and the U.S. Chamber of Commerce (July 17, 1986).

published his massive NBER study, a lot of people had a good deal of explaining to do.[1]

But probably no matter occupied Warren more, especially toward the end of his life, than the growth of government in the West. Like Thomas Jefferson, Warren Nutter saw the gradual encroachment of government as the greatest and most pernicious threat to individual liberty. He could understand how authoritarian regimes like Nazi Germany and Communist Russia come to power—through trickery, intimidation, and violence—but he was perplexed why stable, civilized societies, in some cases with democratic institutions stretching back hundreds of years, would succumb to increasing collective domination.

Nutter had only begun his massive work on this issue when a tragic death cut short his efforts. How fortunate might we have been if Nutter had been able to finish his work! We are now left to pick up the pieces, and no doubt most of us in this room, in our own personal writings, are in one way or another groping with the question Nutter articulated for us. And it is to this issue I will turn in my remarks.

BUT first, let me share with you a few personal thoughts about Warren. Beneath that calculating exterior beat a heart of gold. Let me illustrate. Not to be terribly outdone by fellow graduate students Tom Willett, Mark Pauly, and others who had already broken into the big journals, in late 1967 I spotted what I perceived to be a flaw in a piece in the *American Economic Review* and dashed off a note. Wisely, I sought Mr. Nutter's counsel. "You may be right," he said, "but you've got to rewrite it to make the argument much clearer; otherwise, you don't have a chance of getting it accepted." I did rewrite it, but Nutter was not satisfied so he rewrote it himself. And then I worked on it some more, and Nutter rewrote it again. "Mr. Nutter," I said, "this is as much your note as mine, so I insist you share authorship." But Nutter would have none of that. When the note was accepted—to everyone's amazement, including mine—and appeared in the *AER,* it carried the usual footnote reference to Nutter's assistance, as well as appreciation to Roger Sherman and Tom Willett; but that is all the acknowledgment Nutter would accept.[2]

Let me share a second anecdote. In the fall of 1966 I took Nutter's

---

1. G. Warren Nutter, *Growth of Industrial Production in the Soviet Union* (Princeton: Princeton University Press for the National Bureau of Economic Research, 1962).

2. James C. Miller III, "A Paradox on Profits and Factor Prices: Comment," *American Economic Review* (September, 1968), pp. 917–19.

211 Price Theory course and did fairly well. But the next spring I met my match in Nutter's 154, Economic Growth of the Soviet Union. The problem was not economics, but history. I have never been particularly good at memorization, but the large number of history graduate students taking the course most certainly were. Moreover, this was at a time when several of us graduate students were getting under way our book on the volunteer army, and I was somewhat distracted.[3] Anyway, when grades were handed out I got a "B." Not particularly surprised, but somewhat upset over what this might mean for my career, I sought Mr. Nutter's counsel, not really holding out much hope he would change the grade. Nutter was very understanding but explained that my exams simply did not measure up to an "A" or even a "B + ." Before I left, however, he put everything in perspective. "I know how you feel," he said. "Milton Friedman once gave me a 'B'." Somehow this made everything all right.

As I said earlier, Warren Nutter was very concerned about the growth of government and wrote one of his last books on the subject.[4] That book came to mind as I was reading my predecessor's account of his experiences as budget director, shortly after I inherited the job.[5]

Undoubtedly, many of you have read at least excerpts of David Stockman's book and have formed your own opinions of it. In my view, after one gets past the anecdotes, Stockman's message is clear: if the most conservative president in two generations, supported by perhaps the smartest and most zealous budget director ever (my characterization, not his), cannot succeed at trimming government spending, then it simply cannot be done. Politicians—no matter how much in favor of smaller government they profess to be—will reflect their constituents', if not "special," interests and vote for new programs and the continuation of old ones. This inexorably leads to ever-larger government.

Let me say first that I think David Stockman had considerably more success than one would gather from reading his book. But it is also clear that we have a problem—a problem characteristic of virtually all modern democracies.

---

3. James C. Miller III et al., *Why the Draft?: The Case for a Volunteer Army* (New York: Penguin Books, Inc., 1968).

4. G. Warren Nutter, *Growth of Government in the West* (Washington, D.C.: American Enterprise Institute for Public Policy Research, 1978).

5. David A. Stockman, *The Triumph of Politics: Why the Reagan Revolution Failed* (New York: Harper and Row, Publishers, 1986).

The Growth of Government

Let me illustrate the nature of that problem. In 1940, just before the start of World War II, the federal government accounted for 10 percent of gross national product (GNP). This figure grew to 16 percent by 1950, 20 percent by 1970, and reached 24 percent by 1985.[6]

This rising percentage of GNP went primarily to finance an increasingly elaborate array of domestic programs. From the early 1950s, total nondefense spending grew from about 30 percent of the budget to over 70 percent at the present time.[7]

Nutter's review of the data on spending at all levels of government shows an even more dramatic rise in the percentage of national income attributable to government because of greater increases at the state and local levels.[8]

These trends are not unique to the United States.[9] During the twenty-five year period covered by the data Nutter assembled for his book, 1950 through 1974, total government expenditures for the Organization for Economic Cooperation and Development (OECD) countries rose from about 30 percent of national income to about 50 percent—and this as a result of increases in domestic spending. "External" expenditures (mainly defense) were relatively constant, in the 5–6 percent range.

Increased Reliance on Deficit Financing

At the same time that government has been taking an increasing portion of total output, the share of this take financed by debt has also risen. For the first 150 years of our history, the prevailing, indeed unquestioned, belief was that the federal budget should be balanced.[10] While deficits were unavoidable in wartime, all political parties, all presidents, and nearly all members of Congress operated on the assumption that the "norm" would be budgetary balance and even surpluses to repay some of the debt accumulated during wars. We ran surpluses for twenty-eight consecutive years after the War

6. *Historical Tables, Budget of the United States Government, 1987* (Washington, D.C.: U.S. Government Printing Office, 1986), table 1.2.

7. Ibid., table 6.2.

8. Nutter, *Growth of Government*, pp. 13–18.

9. Ibid., pp. 3–13.

10. Richard E. Wagner, Robert D. Tollison, Alvin Rabushka, and John T. Noonan, Jr., *Balanced Budgets, Fiscal Responsibility, and the Constitution* (Washington, D.C.: Cato Institute, 1982).

between the States, and for eleven consecutive years after World War I, amazing as that may seem.

The first erosion of this article of faith came with the emergence of fashionable forms of Keynesian economics, which made deficits not only acceptable but even desirable during recessions.[11] In the period after World War II, however, when this idea gradually became the conventional wisdom, it was also assumed that in times of prosperity the budget would be in surplus—that is, the budget would be balanced over the so-called business cycle. And as we look back, up until the late 1960s this rule was roughly observed. Our deficits, when we had them, were quite small, and we even ran a few surpluses in the 1940s and the 1950s.

Starting with the war in Vietnam, however, and continuing long after the war wound down, even this degree of discipline began slipping away. Deficits gradually ceased to be a respectable countercyclical tool and turned into an escape valve for lack of political will or for political gridlock. We are now in a situation where the deficit is large, chronic, and structural—something that is characteristic of most modern democracies. The deficit was approximately $225 billion, or some 5.4 percent of GNP, in FY 1986, at a time of modest, though respectable, economic growth and reasonably high employment. It is not only that we have had deficits in twenty-five of the past twenty-six years; more important, recently they have become much larger—in excess of 2.5 percent of GNP in all but one of the past ten years.

Nonbudgetary Spending

It is easy to focus on budget figures because they are readily available. The government's claim on the nation's resources, however, is substantially larger than is reflected in those totals. Much of this additional spending bypasses the congressional appropriations process and, therefore, does not receive the scrutiny normally accorded spending programs.[12] Much of it, moreover, represents increased liabilities for future generations, similar to public borrowing. But this

---

11. See James M. Buchanan and Richard E. Wagner, *Democracy in Deficit: The Political Legacy of Lord Keynes* (New York: Academic Press, 1977); and James M. Buchanan, Charles K. Rowley, and Robert D. Tollison, eds., *Toward a Political Economy of the Deficit* (Oxford: Basil Blackwell, forthcoming).

12. See, for example, Herman B. Leonard, *Checks Unbalanced: The Quiet Side of Public Spending* (New York: Basic Books, Inc., 1986).

"borrowing" does not show up in the standard measures of the deficit and public debt.

Let me give you a few examples. The federal role in credit markets is enormous. Credit assistance is extended to a long list of beneficiaries, including farmers, homeowners, exporters, small businesses, and rural utilities, to name a few of the more prominent ones. At the end of FY 1985, the federal government held $257 billion in its loan portfolio and had guaranteed loans totaling $410 billion.[13]

Clearly, the government's credit programs are a way of achieving social goals that otherwise could be achieved by direct spending. The subsidy-equivalent value of these loans and loan guarantees, estimated to be about $16 billion in FY 1985, is not included in the budget totals, however.[14]

Let me give you another example. The federal government operates several major insurance companies. The most important of these supply insurance to depository institutions, namely, banks and savings and loan companies. But others, such as the one that provides pension insurance, are also important. These programs involve immense potential liabilities and payments for future taxpayers. Moreover, they are often structured in a way that induces the insured firms to take risks that further increase taxpayers' exposure. Like credit assistance, none of these future liabilities shows up in our budget totals.

Let me recount one final example, though there are many others. Even as we have been dismantling the antiquated economic regulatory structure, which inhibited competition in a number of important industries for many years, we have erected an elaborate new social regulatory structure that diverts economic resources in the pursuit of a variety of public goals. Most of these goals are worthwhile, but the resources we spend on them, estimated to be between $50 billion and $150 billion annually, for the most part do not show up on our financial ledger.[15]

That government has grown in areas hidden from public view should come as no surprise. It is consistent with the incentive structure faced by our elected representatives, a matter to which I shall

---

13. See *Special Analyses, Budget of the U.S. Government, 1987* (Washington, D.C.: U.S. Government Printing Office, 1986), Special Analysis F; and *Economic Report of the President* (Washington, D.C.: U.S. Government Printing Office, 1986), chapter 6.

14. *Special Analyses*, pp. F-31–38.

15. See *Budget of the United States Government, FY 1987* (Washington, D.C.: U.S. Government Printing Office, 1986), p. 6a–17.

return in a moment. It is, moreover, a problem that might be expected to worsen during an era of budgetary stringency.

No Consensus on What Government Should Do

Part of the problem is that there are no widely accepted criteria, or even a common frame of reference, for determining what government should do and what it should not do. This is not to say that there are no common themes for government's role in this country. Almost everyone agrees that national defense, some forms of welfare, enforcement of contracts, and so forth should be provided—or at least financed—collectively. But within a fairly broad range, public opinion is divided, with "common sense" being perhaps the only underlying identifiable goal.

And lest we economists pat ourselves too firmly on the back for being above all this, with somehow having access to "truth" in matters of public policy, let me ask you, What is the economist's position on the details of national defense, such as the strategic defense initiative, antisatellite testing, chemical warfare, and the proposed missile build-down? Do Gordon Tullock and Kenneth Boulding agree? What about welfare reform? Does Jack Meyer's comprehensive plan mesh with the vision of John Kenneth Galbraith? Or on monetary policy, who is more nearly right: Beryl Sprinkel, Arthur Burns, or Craig Roberts? It may be the case that, unlike most other people, economists can fairly quickly determine the precise nature of their disagreements. But we still do disagree. And, as Paul Samuelson once put it: "If economists cannot agree among themselves, how can the world be expected to agree with them and to respect their recommendations?"[16] Or, as a Mal cartoon published in the *Washington Post* put it recently: "Which economist should we listen to today?"[17]

What is more, economists tend to hold policy views very strongly, though not as strongly as some who come to such views by means of religious conviction. The reason is that we economists pride ourselves on being objective analysts—knowledgeable about human behavior, marshalled with the facts, and sufficiently detached so that our own values will not interfere. I don't say it is true; I just said we think of ourselves in those terms.

I know from personal experience that this propensity on the part of economists to hold policy views firmly makes it difficult for us to

---

16. Joseph E. Stiglitz, ed., *The Collected Scientific Papers of Paul A. Samuelson,* vol. II. (Cambridge: The MIT Press, 1966), p. 1628.

17. *Washington Post,* October 5, 1986.

perform effectively in upper echelons of government, where trades and compromise are the name of the game, and the economist's job, unfortunately, is more that of fashioning a "good deal" than getting his or her way.

I was reminded of this recently when I was watching a TV program on George Washington.[18] The program dealt with the problems Washington faced as the first president and the way he handled them and the conflicts between the factions led by Hamilton and by Jefferson. Hamilton, believing himself to be a failure in government, eventually submitted his resignation to Washington, telling him, "I lack the politician's skill at compromise. Truth is truth and can't be halved."

Despite this difficulty, I do believe that economists' common training provides a methodology for trying to figure out the "right" answer. Frankly, I think it is a great advantage for a public official to have such a framework at his or her disposal, although, as I have mentioned, it does sometimes make it difficult to do jobs that require a lot of compromise. Moreover, such training is not sufficient to yield the "right" action when incentives are overpowering. Let me illustrate.

At one Friday afternoon seminar at the University of Virginia, our speaker was a new congressman who had been a classmate of Warren Nutter and Jim Buchanan at the University of Chicago and who, of course, had learned the lessons of microeconomics from Alfred Marshall and other good price theorists. After this congressman finished his spiel about "life in Washington," one of the bright young graduate students in the audience—who, by the way, is now a very successful Washington-based analyst—asked, "Why in the world would the Congress of the United States enact minimum wage legislation?"

This congressman, who had been in business for many years between graduate school and public service and who probably had not given a lot of thought to the formal analytics of the issue for many years said, "Oh, I understand." And going to the blackboard, he quickly pointed out equilibrium price and employment and showed the effects of a minimum wage, including the adverse effects on employment. He also demonstrated how a minimum wage could be a device to discourage business from moving from high-wage areas to low-wage areas. After thus showing us that his analytical tools were anything but rusty, he said, "I understand all of that very well. But I

---

18. *George Washington: The Forging of a Nation,* CBS Network Television, September 21–22, 1986.

represent a heavily unionized district in the north, and if you think I'm going to vote against minimum wage legislation, you're crazy."

Why Does Government Do What It Does?

In the absence of any generally accepted criteria (whether designed by economists or not) for judging what is an appropriate government function, virtually all areas of activity are fair game. Given the incentives faced by our elected officials, this is a difficult situation.

As is obvious, our federal government has the ability to transfer vast amounts of wealth through its policies. Given this ability, it is natural for groups in society with similar interests to band together and to expend economic resources to try to get some of that wealth moved in their direction.[19] Such groups can be successful because our agents in the political process, our elected representatives, do not feel the full costs and benefits of their actions. This is perhaps the fundamental reason why the political process has great trouble allocating economic resources efficiently.

As is by now a well-known story—thanks to Jim Buchanan, Gordon Tullock, Mancur Olson, and others—politicians have an incentive to transfer wealth to identifiable groups because the benefits are concentrated and the costs, paid by taxpayers in general, are diffuse.[20] Moreover, the beneficiaries are generally well informed about their programs and who supports them, while those who shoulder the burden are generally not so well informed, because it is not worth their while. Politicians have an incentive to search for such issues, where well-organized groups gain and the costs are borne by everyone. Groups with similar objectives have an obvious incentive under these circumstances to organize to obtain the benefits government can provide.

Because the ability of groups to influence the political marketplace depends on the costs of being organized, established groups have a particular advantage. They are able to act quickly when their programs are threatened, and this explains why it is so difficult to eliminate or even reduce existing programs. Unfortunately, our rec-

---

19. For a review of this literature, see Robert D. Tollison, "Rent Seeking: A Review," *Kyklos* (1982), pp. 575–602.

20. See James M. Buchanan and Gordon M. Tullock, *The Calculus of Consent: Logical Foundations of Constitutional Democracy* (Ann Arbor: University of Michigan Press, 1962); and Mancur Olson, Jr., *The Logic of Collective Action: Public Goods and the Theory of Groups* (Cambridge: Harvard University Press, 1965).

ord this year bears this out. Last February, the president's budget proposed eliminating forty-four programs, and it appears we will be successful in terminating only two of them.

Let me recount one incident that demonstrates the ability of organized groups to protect their programs. One of our major budget themes has been privatization, and as part of this we proposed privatizing the five Federal Power Marketing Administrations (PMAs), which account for about 6 percent of the power generated in this country. Of course, the great majority of power is privately generated. Although, in general, private production is less costly than public production, the customers of the federal PMAs get their power at rates substantially below those available in the rest of the country. The reason is that the PMAs are subsidized by the general taxpayer.

Shortly after the PMA privatization proposal appeared in the FY 1987 Budget, the American Public Power Association and the National Rural Electric Cooperative Association (NRECA) mounted a national lobbying campaign, which eventually induced Congress to pass an appropriations rider banning any studies or proposals for transferring the PMAs[21] or the Tennessee Valley Authority out of federal ownership. This prohibition became law as part of the urgent supplemental for 1986.

By the way, the NRECA, which was a part of this lobbying campaign, is the same organization that makes it virtually impossible to cut back subsidized Rural Electrification Administration (REA) loans to "rural" utilities and telephone companies. You will recall that REA was passed back in the 1930s to bring electricity and telephone service to the rural parts of the country, a task that was completed some time ago. The subsidy, however, goes on and on.

Incentives and the Deficit

Given the incentives faced by elected officials, democratic governments will tend to engage not only in too much government spending, but also in excessive deficit financing of public expenditures.

Perhaps the basic difference between resource allocation decisions made in the marketplace and decisions made in a political setting is that market decisions are made with respect to well-defined, transferrable property rights, while political decisions are not.[22] None

---

21. The Alaska PMA was excepted.
22. See, for example, Dwight Lee, "Deficits, Political Myopia and the Asymmetric Dynamics of Taxing and Spending," in Buchanan, Rowley, and Tollison.

of us, as citizens, can sell shares in our government if we feel the wrong decisions are being made. This leads our elected officials to be myopic, that is, to operate with a discount rate that is too high.

In the market, the effect on future profitability of a manager's current decisions is reflected quickly in the price of the company's stock. Shareholders' ability to buy and sell stock provides an immediate test of the wisdom of corporate managers' decisions. In a political setting, there is no comparable indicator of the future effects of officials' decisions. Therefore, they will discount the future excessively, leading them to finance spending in excess of what citizens are willing to pay for out of current taxes.

This political myopia also explains why many of our expenditure programs are structured in a way that the costs of the programs start off modestly and then increase dramatically. Such an arrangement simultaneously benefits the political decision makers, with their excessively high discount rate, and the program beneficiaries, who presumably have a lower, more realistic rate. Rising expenditure patterns for government programs, of course, are also caused by the fact that interest groups find it easier to organize around an existing program. Once organized, they will tend to acquire more influence through time.

Thus, large deficits are the logical outcome of individuals pursuing their self-interest within the existing institutional framework. With the exception of future taxpayers—many of whom are not yet of voting age and many of whom have not yet been born—deficits create many winners and few losers. Politicians can generate support by increasing expenditures or cutting taxes, either of which directly benefits some group. Every legislator is in a position to try to confer such benefits on his or her favorite constituencies, and the incentive for any individual legislator to refrain from such behavior is virtually nonexistent. To do so would involve forgoing specific political support, without materially affecting the deficit.

Running deficits is easy because it makes people feel wealthier. Borrowing by an individual, in this sense, is quite different from borrowing by governments. An individual who borrows to buy a car, for example, does not feel wealthier relative to someone who pays cash, because he knows full well that he will have to reduce consumption in the future in order to pay off the loan. The liability for public debt, however, is dispersed throughout society and is not assigned to anyone in particular. This leads us all to underestimate the costs of deficit-financed spending. And as with any activity where the benefits are personal and the costs are social, deficit financing leads to too much spending. Taxpayers believe public services have become relatively cheaper, so they demand more of them. The true cost of public services has not changed, of course. If we were to pay for public services as we consume them, we would want less of them.

For the same reason that politicians have an incentive to run deficits, they also have an incentive to pursue goals through off-budget or regulatory programs. The costs of our regulatory programs, while substantial, are paid for in the prices of thousands of products purchased by consumers who have little idea that part of the price is going to pay a government-imposed cost. Many of our credit and other programs create future liabilities in the same way borrowing does. But in contrast to direct borrowing, these future liabilities are virtually invisible and are not even part of the political debate.

Gramm-Rudman-Hollings

All of the foregoing suggests that our political institutions, as historically structured, may not be capable of solving the problem of a government that is too big and is financed at the expense of future generations. Rather than give up in despair, we need to modify our institutions and place meaningful constraints on political behavior.

One such change occurred last year with the passage of the Balanced Budget and Emergency Deficit Control Act of 1985, better known as Gramm-Rudman-Hollings (GRH). GRH represents a major innovation on our political landscape and, in my view, has had a very important effect on the budget as well as on the budget process. To most of us who deal with such matters, it comes as no surprise that this scheme was designed by an economist—Phil Gramm.[23]

GRH was passed with great fanfare because elected officials, who find it very easy to vote for any new spending program, find it very difficult to vote against a law that requires balancing the budget. As we all know, GRH mandates that the budget be brought into balance over a five-year period. As originally passed, the most noted feature of the act was its "club in the closet"—its automatic provision that mandated across-the-board cuts in much of the budget if the normal political process did not achieve the specified, declining levels of the deficit. That provision caught all the headlines. The version of the automatic trigger Congress enacted was held to be unconstitutional by the Supreme Court, however, because it required the

---

23. A similar scheme was advanced by another economist, Martin Anderson. See Anderson, "The Budget Amendment—Not So Crazy after All," *New York Times*, August 30, 1985.

comptroller general, an official subservient to the Congress, to perform what was clearly an executive function.

Because the constitutionality of the comptroller general's role in executive functions had been challenged earlier, and because in negotiations on behalf of the administration I insisted, Congress included in the act a fallback procedure under which any automatic cuts that might be necessary to meet the mandated deficit limits would have to be put on a fast track for approval by the House and the Senate in a joint resolution to be presented to the president.

This fallback procedure obviously makes any necessary cuts less automatic, and when the Court made its ruling many people were less confident that any such cuts, in fact, would be made. Well, what has happened?

The first thing Congress did after the Court's decision was to reaffirm the FY 1986 sequester of $11.7 billion, using the fallback procedure. This, however, was not surprising inasmuch as most of the pain of those cuts had already been experienced by beneficiaries.

With respect to the FY 1987 Budget, the process I most wearily hope will be completed soon, Congress appears to have come up with a budget deficit below the GRH trigger level, at least the way the deficit must be measured according to GRH. Thus, there will be no sequester. Moreover, the Senate at least attempted to "fix" the automatic trigger by giving the director of the Office of Management and Budget (OMB)—yours truly—the final say so. So far, the House has not agreed.

This, however, should not cloud the success we are likely to experience this fiscal year with respect to both the deficit and total spending. The FY 1986 deficit was some $221 billion, an all-time record in real, as well as in nominal, terms. For FY 1987—the first full year that GRH is operative—I expect, when all is said and done, the deficit to come in under $170 billion. Although that figure exceeds the $144 billion GRH target by $26 billion, it means that in just one year we will have reduced the deficit by at least $51 billion *without raising taxes*.

As a percentage of GNP, the deficit will decline from 5.3 percent in FY 1986 to a projected 3.8 percent in FY 1987. The reason for this decline is that for the main part spending increases will be held at bay—a remarkable achievement, *especially* during an election year. Over the period FY 1980 through FY 1986, federal spending increased at an average annual rate of 3.6 percent in real terms; this year it will actually *fall* in real terms by approximately 2.4 percent. While a portion of this spending (and deficit) decline for FY 1987 can be traced to lamentable cutbacks in the president's request for defense and international affairs, the message of the figures just cited holds up even for domestic spending: rather than rising at the FY 1980 through FY 1986 average annual rate of 1.4 percent in real terms, this coming year domestic spending will fall by about 3.0 percent in real terms.

In sum, GRH has changed the rules of the game, at least for this year. We now have replaced President Carter's, ill-fated—sounds good in theory; doesn't work in practice—"zero-based budgeting" with what I call "zero-sum" budgeting. Anyone proposing a new spending measure must come up with some way to finance it, either a spending offset somewhere else or an increase in revenues. This coming year not only will the deficit be lower, but also federal spending (in real terms) will actually decline.

One reason Congress complied with the requirements of GRH during its first year is that the political pressures to do so were substantial. It would have been quite embarrassing, only months after passing the law, not to meet its requirements. As time goes on, however, it is reasonable to expect those pressures to weaken. And, as many have noted, what Congress does, it can undo. That is why, in my view, we need to look toward more permanent, constitutional solutions to the problem.

Constitutional Approaches

A permanent solution to the problem of excessive government spending and borrowing requires a constitutional change to restore the discipline we had for most of our history.

In the absence of the type of commitment implied by a constitutional change, individuals have less reason at any particular time to undergo the sacrifice required to reduce spending or balance the budget. Why should we, in 1986, reduce spending, knowing that next year or the year after a new political coalition could make the sacrifice we have undergone virtually meaningless? If, however, individuals could be assured that their current sacrifice would be reflected in permanent increases in future disposable income, they would be much more willing to make such a sacrifice.[24]

Along with President Reagan and 71 percent of the American public, I also support a line-item veto.[25] A line-item veto would enable the chief executive to excise some of the most flagrant special-interest

---

24. See James M. Buchanan, "The Budgetary Bias in Post-Keynesian Politics: The Erosion and Potential Replacement of Fiscal Norms," in Buchanan, Rowley and Tollison.

25. See "Line-Item Veto," *Gallup Report* (October 1985).

spending that all contemporary presidents have been forced to accept in the context of more general spending bills. One possibility might be to provide the president with sufficient line-item veto authority to bring the budget into balance or, in the short run, to meet the GRH deficit targets. This would be a better fix than giving sequester authority to OMB. Another possibility would be to guarantee the president an up-or-down vote on proposed rescissions.

Of course, I am aware that recent evidence from the state level indicates that line-item veto authority does not affect total borrowing (and by implication total spending), suggesting that such authority is used to reorder priorities.[26] But there are differences between the federal and state budgets, and besides, giving the president more authority to reorder priorities is not such a bad idea.

Now that we have settled these global issues, let's think on just a few mundane problems of application. For example, if we are going to require a balanced budget, which budget should be balanced? Our current budgeting methodology has been criticized on a variety of grounds, but one that is made most often is that it is an *operating* budget. Why not institute a capital budget? Proponents of a capital budget point out that investments in long-term assets should be amortized over time, as they are in the private sector and in most state and many local governments. Moreover, since capital assets have a long useful life, borrowing to finance them is justified.

I agree completely. It really does not make a lot of sense to treat capital expenditures the same as operating expenditures, which is what we do now. In many cases, doing so creates a misleading impression of the financial consequences of government decisions and distorts the decision-making process. Accordingly, we in the administration are now in the process of studying these issues and developing proposals to reform our financial accounts and the budget process. I fully expect the president to announce specific changes and legislative proposals in early 1987.

But I must tell you, establishing and maintaining the integrity of a capital budget are not as easy as they sound. First, as New York City experienced, there will be increasing, relentless pressure to transfer expenditures from the operating budget to the capital budget, in order to realize benefits now and postpone costs. Second, aside from incentives, there will be the knotty technical problem of classifying certain programs: which belong to the operating budget, and which belong to the capital budget? What about support for

---

26. See Charles K. Rowley, William F. Shughart II, and Robert D. Tollison, "Interest Groups and the Deficit," in Buchanan, Rowley, and Tollison.

higher education—is it an operating expense, or is it human capital? As a practical matter, how do we amortize nuclear submarines or historic buildings such as the Capitol and the White House?

But the strongest argument against a capital budget, in my opinion, is that given any opportunity to bypass conventional concerns over the deficit, such as posed by a capital budget, our elected officials may simply spend more money and government will grow even more. With the advent of the institutional changes posed by GRH, however, and the possibility of enactment of some form of enhanced rescission authority or line-item veto—and maybe action on a constitutional amendment to control deficits, taxing, or spending—I am more optimistic that establishment of a capital budget would not lead to this adverse consequence. And even if at the margin there were some tendency to increase spending, we must also consider the efficiency gains that a more "businesslike" approach to federal spending and financing decisions could generate.

Concluding Remark

Let me conclude now with an observation and a speculation.

Toward the end of his life, Warren Nutter became increasingly pessimistic about the future of Western institutions. Not only did he see the threat of monolithic Communism, but also he feared that America's leadership was in peril, threatened by a loss of confidence and resolve.

If Warren Nutter were alive today, I think he would be much more hopeful. The repair of our national defense has been nothing short of dramatic. And the restoration of America's self-confidence and its will to lead the free world into the twenty-first century is so self-evident that it is not even contested by what Jeane Kirkpatrick termed the "blame-America-first crowd." Such "revolutions" in thinking and in action are not likely to fade, at least not right away. So, I submit that if Warren Nutter were here among us, he would say, "I'm beginning to believe that everything's going to be all right."

Beyond the
Tower Commission

Melvin R. Laird

May 5, 1987

MELVIN R. LAIRD is senior counsellor for national and international affairs, the Reader's Digest Association. Formerly, he was secretary of defense, 1969–1973; counsellor to the president for domestic affairs, 1973–1974; and U.S. Representative (R-Wis.), 1953–1969.

Introduction

It is my pleasure to introduce the fifteenth and final G. Warren Nutter Lecture in Political Economy sponsored by the Thomas Jefferson Center Foundation and hosted by the American Enterprise Institute. Our speaker today, Melvin R. Laird, offers a unique perspective on issues central to our national security processes, particularly the way the National Security Council should function to serve a president.

It was my privilege to serve with both Melvin Laird, when he was our nation's secretary of defense, and Warren Nutter, during his service as assistant secretary of defense. As a nine-term congressman from Wisconsin's seventh district, secretary of defense from 1969 to 1973, and counsellor to the president of the United States in 1973 and 1974, Melvin Laird played a key role in steering our nation on a steady course through some of its most turbulent times.

The insight Melvin Laird offers us today is particularly timely as the executive and legislative branches are now examining the role of the National Security Council and its relationship with the Oval Office. I am certain that his unrivaled experience in these arenas, particularly in effectively formulating and implementing our nation's security policies, will be of lasting benefit to all of us and to the country he loves so much.

A native of Nebraska and a twice-wounded Navy veteran of World War II, he participated in five battles in the Pacific with Admiral Halsey's Third Fleet and Admiral Marc Mitsacher's Task Force 58. Today Melvin Laird is one of the most respected authorities on national security issues.

JOHN WARNER
U.S. Senator

Beyond the Tower Commission

Melvin R. Laird

Two years ago, in introducing Lawrence Eagleburger as the tenth lecturer in this series, Bill Baroody said, "G. Warren Nutter was one of the great conservative intellectuals of his time." I agree with that.

Warren Nutter was, indeed, a scholar; but he was more than that. Warren understood the power of concepts and ideas. He understood, too, the importance of vision, of taking the longer view. Beyond that, Warren knew that sound ideas and policies rarely came from a single individual. To the contrary, sound ideas and policies were almost always the result of:

• a process that involved an interchange among many people—leaders and subordinates, line and staff
• a process that encouraged and rewarded boldness of thought
• a process that elicited a wide range of views
• a process that addressed and related forthrightly the many aspects of a complex situation
• a process that looked at options and measured objectively the merits and consequences of those options—to include the new problems that most solutions generate

After teaching for a number of years at the University of Virginia, Warren Nutter took a leave of absence in 1969. He joined the Laird–Packard team in the Department of Defense where he served as assistant secretary of defense for international security affairs. For his service he was awarded the highest award of the Defense Department—the Distinguished Public Service Medal.

An Earlier Era

The issues we addressed during that dramatic period from 1969 to 1973 were many and varied. Among the more prominent matters were:

• scaling down the U.S. involvement in Southeast Asia through a program we developed and called Vietnamization

• developing the Total Force Concept for our own regular and reserve military forces

• ending the military manpower draft and developing the all-volunteer force for the Army, Navy, Marine Corps, and Air Force

• focusing on the dominant threat posed by the Soviet Union

• opening dialogues with nations such as the People's Republic of China

• improving the stability of deterrence through arms control agreements such as the antiballistic missile (ABM) treaty

• improving the quality of free-world defense by working closely with our allies in applying the Total Force Concept worldwide

• focusing on appropriate means of sharing in the defense of the borders of our allies

• paying heed to the economic, political, technical, and social realities, as well as to the military aspects of defense

• making realistic trade-offs among the varied and sometimes conflicting goals of national security.

It was not an easy period. It was a period in which the roles of individuals were significant and in which national security processes were tested.

I believe we met many of the tests successfully. In others the record is less striking. Throughout the period, one principle was dramatically clear: a sound governmental process in national security issues leads to sound options and ultimately to effective policy; an unsound national security process spells missed opportunities at best and, at worst, deep trouble.

A More Current View

Recently we have had trouble with the national security process. Our government is sorting out a series of events involving overtures to Iran, hostages, and arms supplies.

This series of events has become a major problem for the administration—and for the country. The problem was serious enough that President Reagan appointed a special review board, the so-called Tower Commission, and gave it a broad charter. It was directed to conduct "a comprehensive study of the future role and procedures of the National Security Council (NSC) staff in the development, coordination, oversight, and conduct of foreign and national security policy."

The Tower Commission has presented its findings. It is, in my judgment, a sound report. It concludes correctly "there is no magic formula which can be applied to the NSC structure and process to produce an optimal system."

The Tower Commission also concluded:

1. The President bears a special responsibility for the effective performance of the NSC system.

2. The tension between the President and the Executive Departments is worked out through the national security process. . . . It is through this process the nation obtains both the best of the creativity of the President and the training and expertise of the national security departments and agencies. (Let me add parenthetically that I felt Henry Kissinger was particularly effective in helping to generate and foster the tension to which the Tower Commission refers. I logged a lot of hours under that tension.)

3. The National Security Advisor should focus on advice and management, not implementation and execution.

4. . . . no substantive change (should) be made in the provisions of the National Security Act dealing with the structure and operation of the NSC system.

I agree with those conclusions. I also believe the arguments that support such conclusions can and should be extended to argue for a more focused national security process.

Allow me first to explain why I agree with the Tower Commission, as far as it goes, and then how I believe the logic can be extended to an improved national security policy process.

The NSC System

The National Security Council was established in 1947 ". . . to advise the President with respect to the integration of domestic, foreign, and military policies relating to the national security so as to enable the military services and the other departments and agencies of the Government to cooperate more effectively in matters relating to the national security."

The key words and concepts are: advise the President; integration of policies; and more effective cooperation in matters relating to national security.

Matters relating to national security? National security itself? What does national security really incorporate?

My good friend Harold Brown, who also served as secretary of defense and who has been in the national security realm throughout his adult life, has defined national security as follows:

> National security . . . is the ability to preserve the nation's physical integrity and territory; to maintain its economic relations with the rest of the world in reasonable terms; to protect its nature, institutions, and governance from disruption from outside; and to control its borders.

That is a broad definition; but it is an accurate definition. Clearly national security involves more than just military forces and a foreign policy apparatus. It involves political and social support at home. It involves preservation of our basic cultural institutions. It also involves such important issues as how much defense the economy can reasonably sustain.

It is important to note, however, that even a broad-gauged definition of national security does not, or should not, violate the precept of the National Security Council system to advise, to help integrate, to assist in cooperation, and to enable others to operate more effectively. The broad-gauged definition of national security, moreover, places a high premium on the NSC staff's responsibilities: to be clear about U.S. goals and objectives; to be analytical and imaginative in facilitating policy discussions; to be objective and clear in laying out alternatives; to be precise in describing the pros and cons and the implications of alternative courses; and to be even-handed, especially avoiding an advocacy role, in working with the many departments and agencies involved.

All of these principles bear close attention. The first, being clear about U.S. goals and objectives, is a precept I shall come back to in a few moments.

People. In the meantime, it is worth emphasizing that despite a broad national security charter, there is no need for a large NSC staff. The 1947 National Security Act specified as statutory members the president, the vice president, the secretary of state, and the secretary of defense. While others may serve as ad hoc members or advisers, the structure was meant to be lean. There is strength in a lean structure. From such a structure can come a focus on the truly important national security issues. A lean structure helps to obviate the temptations to become involved in tangential and operational matters. The truly important matters to be addressed by a quality staff that is small in number include, again, national security objectives and goals, alternative policies to attain those goals, and analyses that outline the full implications of each alternative.

Dean Acheson, in writing about the NSC staff nearly three decades ago, specified: "A few recordkeepers, agenda makers, prodders, or gadflies, yes. But a separate staff cannot add knowledge, which remains in the departments; or responsible advice to the President, which is the duty and right of his Cabinet Secretaries. More bodies only clutter up a meeting and strain a flow of communication."

I believe Dean Acheson went too far; but the logic behind a small, high quality NSC staff is contained in his remarks. The logic is sound.

Process and Organization. Beyond the number and quality of people there is organization. The Tower Commission, in one of its most important statements, said: "We recommend that no substantive change be made in the provisions of the National Security Act dealing with the structure and operation of the NSC system." The Tower Commission, in my judgment, is correct in that view.

From time to time, notable individuals have suggested major modifications to the NSC organization. Allow me to mention two such suggestions.

In 1984 General Albert Wedemeyer outlined the idea of a National Security Council that would operate much like the NSC specified in the 1947 act, except, as General Wedemeyer specified: "It would encourage the integration of matters (for example, economic and military programs) which too often have been treated in isolation, and thus unrealistically or unwisely."

The general's charge that integration has not occurred among key areas does not indict the original NSC organizational structure. It simply suggests that a better job could be done within the context of the 1947 act.

General Wedemeyer departs from the 1947 act most prominently in suggesting a relatively small, continuing council of perhaps eleven distinguished citizens who would devote their full time and talents to studying national strategy in its broadest aspects. The body would possess advisory functions only. It would have semiautonomous status comparable to that of the Federal Reserve Board. Members of the council would be appointed for life by the president with the advice and consent of the Senate.

The Wedemeyer plan is unique. It carries the suggestion that broad-gauged advice would get to the president on major objectives, policies, and alternatives.

The existing NSC structure, however, could accomplish the same ends. It should not be necessary to restructure the NSC to cause it to function properly. Qualified people, working cooperatively, do not need another organizational arrangement. Saying it another way, misguided procedures and inadequate quality of staff, could subvert the Wedemeyer National Strategy Council just as well as they have the currently authorized NSC system.

Another major departure from the 1947 NSC approach was the late General Maxwell D. Taylor's proposal for a National Policy Council (NPC). In General Taylor's well-written book *Precarious Security*, he outlined a council not unlike the current NSC. The major difference was that of bringing into NSC/NPC membership other Cabinet members and advisers, for a total NPC membership of seven. The NPC would contain representatives from what General Taylor called, "the four principal sectors of national policy: (1) foreign, military, and intelligence; (2) economic; (3) fiscal and monetary; and (4) domestic welfare."

Although General Taylor is correct in recognizing that national security and national policy involve a wide range of disciplines, he offers no proof that the existing NSC establishment is faulty in design. The fault, even by General Taylor's reasoning, lies in the implementation of the NSC system.

The point is that simply modifying the organizational structure of the NSC delivers no promise of success—or even of improvement. In fact, the opposite may be true. By modifying the organization or by adopting a new organization, one may create grossly misguided expectations and hopes without really addressing underlying problems of personnel, procedure, and supervision.

Process at Work—The Nixon Period

In fact, the NSC structure outlined by President Nixon in his 1970–1973 annual foreign policy reports to Congress still looks solid. The philosophy was articulated clearly. President Nixon wrote:

> The NSC system is designed to marshal all the resources and expertise of the departments and agencies of the Government. The National Security Council is the apex of the system. It's here that the final refinement of studies conducted at lower levels provides a common framework for thorough

deliberation. The Council's discussions assist me by illuminating the issues and focusing the range of realistic advice before I make my decision.

President Nixon supplemented this philosophy with a brief review of the various committees and groups that are central to the NSC system. The names of the committees and groups are not important. What is important is that a structure was available to formulate policies and alternatives and to integrate ideas. The NSC structure was the facilitating mechanism through which the major departments and agencies could function more effectively. It was quite consistent with the 1947 National Security Act.

That is not to suggest that the Nixon NSC system worked to perfection. Some would contend it failed in major ways. But the failures had more to do with implementation than with organizational design. The design seemed most appropriate. The breakdowns in implementation included the following:

Failure to use the structure as it was intended to be used. The Defense Program Review Committee (DPRC) was a case in point. The DPRC was created upon our recommendation in the Defense Department to address more systematically the relationships between defense spending and the economy. It was clear that changes in defense spending patterns substantially affected economic growth, employment, price stability, the balance of payments, and our ability to fund nondefense programs. To help advise the president on alternative military and economic programs, the national security adviser was to chair a group that included not only the usual NSC participants, but also the Department of the Treasury, the Office of Management and Budget, the Council of Economic Advisers, and, as appropriate, the Federal Reserve. We wanted to address national security in its broadest context.

The DPRC aborted. The DPRC, rather than being used for its original purposes, was manipulated by NSC staff members and other DPRC participants to nonproductive ends. Some tried to affect the design of individual defense program systems. Some tried to interject pet theories in force design. Some claimed inadequate staff help and declined to participate in the DPRC. Others just simply were not interested in the economics of national security. As DPRC members violated the advertised DPRC charter, they killed the idea. I believe the idea is one that still has validity.

Failure by the NSC adviser and staff to communicate freely with the departments and agencies. An example of this second breakdown of the Nixon NSC system was the Washington Special Action Group (WSAG). The WSAG was to be the group that handled special and currently hot issues, especially after the initial crisis stage had passed. It was a good idea to have a WSAG structure. The problem was that repeatedly WSAG meetings would be called with no agenda specified. Therefore, the secretary of defense could not provide guidance to the deputy secretary of defense or to the chairman of the joint chiefs of staff—both of whom attended WSAG meetings for the Defense Department. By controlling the agenda and meetings so exclusively, the NSC adviser lessened significantly the utility of the group.

Failure to coordinate outside explicit NSC boundaries, for example, with congressional officials. This third failure may seem a curiosity. There is no explicit call for the NSC to consult with or to integrate congressional views. There is, however, clear merit in doing so. Congress is a separate and equal branch of government. There are many exceptionally capable and thoughtful people in Congress who know the national security field well. We need their contributions.

Involving the NSC staff in operations. Yes, it has happened before. Air operations in Southeast Asia were sometimes a contentious issue. The temptations at the NSC to become involved were not always controlled. The implications of NSC involvement in operations during the Southeast Asia conflict were no more favorable then than during the more recent operational excursions.

The point in citing breakdowns or limitations of the Nixon NSC system is not that the basic NSC organizational blueprint is flawed. To the contrary. The advertised NSC organization and process was and is sound. It is, however, subject to misuse and to abuse. With proper leadership and motivation, the national security process works and works well.

People, as we have seen, are a key ingredient—maybe *the* key ingredient to sound national security policy. Process—or organization, if you will—is another key element. A third and final necessary factor is perspective.

Perspective—The Need for Strategy

By perspective I mean the longer or the broader view. Indeed, with perspective we soon get to strategy.

It is important to our national security that we have not only the right people, keenly motivated, and working within a positive organizational process; it is important also that we have at least our best people working on more than single issues. They must be working on national strategy.

The late Senator Henry Jackson was wise in many ways, but especially on national security matters. He observed as long ago as 1959 that "Our governmental processes do not produce clearly defined and purposeful strategy for the cold war." Senator Jackson continued: "What seems most to be missing is a coherent and purposeful national program that sets forth in simple terms what we have to do to survive, and why." And finally, Senator Jackson asked this question: "Can a free society successfully organize itself to plan and carry out a national strategy for victory in the cold war?"

My response to Senator Jackson's question is a resounding yes. Moreover, I believe the National Security Council system can be the vehicle to get the national strategy process started.

My good friend Henry Kissinger made a cogent observation last December. Henry said:

> The failure at Reykjavik was not the predominance of the NSC staff but the administration's inability to develop a strategy that related diplomacy, military policy, and arms control policy to a coherent national purpose.

Henry was correct. But the national strategy of which I speak has still other dimensions. We might recall Harold Brown's definition of national security. The national security dimensions are economic, social, and cultural, as well.

There are a number of ways to get a true strategy process started. One approach would be that suggested by Richard Halloran in his recent book *To Arm a Nation*. Halloran suggests, in essence, gaining a strategic oversight by appointing a presidential commission, which was successful, at least in part, in issues such as social security, Central America, and the MX missile.

The commission I suggest would be responsible to the administration and to Congress and would be a one-time body comprising former secretaries of state and defense, retired military officers, former members of Congress, industrial and labor leaders, scholars, and prominent persons not beholden to special interests. It would be a blue-ribbon panel with a mission to produce a new strategic charter, perhaps modeled after the famous NSC-68 document of 1950. The strategic charter would define national objectives and illuminate a national strategy to achieve them.

Perhaps Halloran's method is appropriate. I believe, however, that the National Security Council can and should do the job. The NSC can and should turn to a longer view and initiate a national security strategy. It is imperative for our nation that we turn from a system of individual, ad hoc decisions and programs to an integrated, long-term view. It is an opportunity for the NSC. That organization can and should lead the way. It would be a major mistake not to.

The Tower Commission, after looking at people and processes, concluded that "modest improvements" within the national security apparatus "may yield surprising gains." Indeed, I am in total agreement, as I hope my remarks have indicated.

But beyond people and process is perspective—the broader view, national security objectives, and a long-range strategy. Therein lies not just a modest, but a major, opportunity for the NSC. It should and can get started to that end. I submit it is a good idea and a timely idea.

Senator Henry Jackson said:

> We fail to act on good ideas available. We fritter away our strength on secondary matters. We fiddle trifling tunes while the world burns. But back of all that . . . is a central conviction: The world *can* be made a decent place to live in—a world of peace, material well-being, justice, and freedom . . ."

I say, let's go to work now on a strategy to turn conviction into conclusion.

DATE DUE